IGNATIUS OF LOYOLA,

FOUNDER OF THE JESUITS

This book is

No. 6 in Series II: Modern Scholarly Studies
about the Jesuits
in English Translations

On the cover: an authentic portrait of Ignatius, painted shortly
after his death by Jacopino del Conte. (See
page 297 below.)

Cándido de Dalmases, S. J.

IGNATIUS OF LOYOLA,
FOUNDER OF THE JESUITS

His Life and Work

Translated by Jerome Aixalá, S. J.

THE INSTITUTE OF JESUIT SOURCES
St. Louis, 1985

in cooperation with
Gujarat Sahitya Prakash
Anand, India

This book is an authorized translation of

El Padre Maestro Ignacio: Breve biografía Ignaciana, by
Cándido de Dalmases, S.J., and published by Biblioteca
de Autores Cristianos, de la Editorial Católica, S.A.,
Mateo Inurria, 15, Madrid, Spain, 2nd edition, 1982.

IMPRIMI POTEST: Very Reverend David L. Fleming, S. J.
Provincial of the Missouri Province
June 22, 1983

IMPRIMATUR: Reverend John R. Gaydos, Chancellor
Archdiocese of St. Louis
October 11, 1983

This is the
First Edition, for the Americas, Western Europe,
Australia, and New Zealand

Note: There is a *Second Edition,* authorized for
sale ONLY IN ASIA AND AFRICA which
can be ordered from Gujarat Sahitya Prakash,
Anand 388 001, India

© 1985   The Institute of Jesuit Sources
Fusz Memorial, St. Louis University
3700 West Pine Boulevard
St. Louis, Missouri 63108

Printed in the United States of America
Library of Congress Catalog Card Number: 83-80349
ISBN 0-912422-58-0 Smyth sewn paperback
ISBN 0-912422-59-9 cloth bound

CONTENTS

Contents

Contents

EDITOR'S FOREWORD

The Place of This Biography among Others of Ignatius

Accuracy, reliability, and the comprehensive perspective which springs from expertise ought surely to be mentioned among the salient features of this compact and authoritative life of St. Ignatius of Loyola.

The author, Father Cándido de Dalmases, S.J., a member of the Jesuit Historical Institute in Rome, has spent more than forty years in editing the primary sources about the life, writings, and times of the founder of the Jesuits. He composed the Spanish original of the present biography in a plain, straightforward, and gently warm style which echoes the clear thought, terminology, and nuances of much of Ignatius' own style but avoids its occasional complexities. Into these updating pages, however, he has unobtrusively incorporated the findings of the unusually extensive research from which this book has sprung. To do anything else, in fact, would have been for him difficult and unlikely. Features such as those mentioned above have won abundant praise in the reviews of the Spanish original which have appeared in scholarly and popular periodicals.[1]

This original, *El Padre Maestro Ignacio: Breve biografía ignaciana*, has a pre-history and a history which will aid English-speaking readers to see the significance, and even the unique place, which this new biography has among the many lives of St. Ignatius which have appeared during some four centuries.

---

1 Some important reviews are: by M. Colpo, *Ai nostri amici*, 50 (1980), 86-97; *La Civiltà cattolica*, 132 (1981), 310-311; L. González, *Archivum Historicum Societatis Iesu*, 49 (1980), 526-527; F. Guerrero, *YA* (Madrid), March 27, 1980; J. Iturrioz, *Manresa*, 52 (1980), 264-274; V. Ramallo, *Razón y Fe*, 201(1980) 558-559; Ruiz Jurado, *Gregorianum*, 62 (1981), 414-415.

The very amplitude of the materials available to a modern scientific biographer of this saint is at once encouraging and disconcerting. Previous lives in earlier centuries slowly added fiction to facts and worked from sources incomplete by modern standards. The first comprehensive life was a masterpiece, published in 1572 by Pedro Ribadeneira largely from notes he had written during his nearly sixteen years of intimate association with Ignatius. But in the many later lives during some two centuries, through embellishments aimed at satisfying the literary or hagiographical tastes of successive generations, exaggerations and imaginative inventions were added and many important facts were lost. More and more Ignatius was portrayed as a rather colossal figure but in many ways not human or winning. Efforts began in the eighteenth and nineteenth centuries toward producing lives which were more scholarly and scientifically based on primary sources. But most of these sources for deeper knowledge about Ignatius, including many of his own writings, were still existent only in handwritten manuscripts in the archives in Rome and inaccessible to biographers. For example, the fragment of his *Spiritual Diary*, the chief source for study of his infused contemplation, was first published (but somewhat incompletely) by Juan José de la Torre only in 1892, and in its complete text by Arturo Codina in 1934. An immense task of sifting the wheat from the chaff in the earlier lives and then updating them remained ahead.[2]

That task of sifting and the greater work of publishing the primary sources of and about Ignatius in modern critical editions has been under way in earnest especially since 1894, through the patient labor of the competent Jesuit scholars who in Madrid and after 1929 in Rome have published the now 124 thick volumes of the Historical Sources of the Society of Jesus (*Monumenta Historica Societatis Iesu*) in critically edited

2 An authoritative history of the biographies of St. Ignatius and an appraisal of the more important ones is furnished by Ignacio Iparraguirre in pages 3-38 of *Obras completas de san Ignacio de Loyola*, 4th edition, (Madrid; Biblioteca de autores cristianos, 1982).

This history of the biographies is competently compressed in English by Mary Purcell in her revised edition, *The First Jesuit: St. Ignatius Loyola* (Chicago: Loyola University Press, 1981), pp. 273-278.

texts. In one division of this collection, the Ignatian Sources (*Monumenta Ignatiana*) now numbering 26 volumes, all the primary source materials pertaining to the life of Ignatius which are preserved in the Archives of the Jesuit Curia and in other archives of various countries have now been edited and published, in four series: Series I, Ignatius' Letters and Instructions (12 volumes); Series II, the Spiritual Exercises (3 volumes); Series III, the Constitutions and Rules (4 volumes); Series IV, Narrative Sources, that is, writings about St. Ignatius by his contemporaries, especially by those who knew him personally (7 volumes).

As these volumes gradually appeared from 1894 until now, the quality of scholarship in them naturally grew progressively better, because later editors could draw from the constantly increasing materials previously existent only in handwritten manuscripts, and also from the scholarly articles, introductions, footnotes, and bibliographies of their predecessors. In the 1900s, lives of Ignatius became better informed and based. All this brought about a need for a revision of the Narrative Sources, in which the earlier two volumes of *Scripta de Sancto Ignatio* (1904 and 1918) were expanded into five: *Fontes Narrativi*, (Volume I [1943], II [1951], III [1960], IV [1965], and *Fontes Documentales* [1977]). Of these five volumes of revisions, Father Dalmases was a coeditor of the first and the editor of the remaining four. For the Monumenta he also edited the revised critical edition of the ancient texts of the *Spiritual Exercises* (1969).

By 1977, therefore, Father Dalmases had devoted some thirty-nine years of his mature scholarship chiefly to preparing these critically edited volumes of all the narrative primary sources for our knowledge of the life, works, and thought of St. Ignatius as seen against the background of his times.

Shortly later, the directors of the extensive series *Biblioteca de autores cristianos* ("*BAC*") decided to include St. Ignatius in their series or "collection" of popular lives of important saints, *BAC popular*. Each life in this series was to be authentic and scholarly, yet addressed to the general public in about 275 pages which were to be without footnotes or scholarly apparatus. It is not surprising that the directors invited Father Dalmases to write this life of St. Ignatius, or that he accepted the task, for him a labor of love.

His acceptance turned out to be a challenge forcing him to select from his vast knowledge the most important facts known about St. Ignatius and to synthesize them into a well-rounded whole within one brief volume. As he stated in a letter to the present writer, he aimed to present all the important things which a cultivated reader could reasonably expect to find in a book of this kind and size; and although he omitted amplifications, discussions, and technical details inharmonious with the series *BAC popular*, the adjective *popular* when applied to his biography of Ignatius is only partially true. Reviews in learned periodicals have already stressed its value also to scholars.

The final result of these circumstances and procedures was a biography warmly received both by the general public and by those with scholarly interests. At the time of the present writing, a second printing of the original Spanish edition has appeared in 1982, with slight revisions by Father Dalmases himself, which, along with a few additions also by him, are incorporated into the present English version.

When the details of producing an English translation of this *Breve biografía ignaciana* were being discussed with Father Dalmases by the present writer and the translator, it was pointed out to him that this new book in English would not be subject to the limitations of space or format which the nature of the Spanish original imposed; further, that references to the chief documents for citations and to reliable sources for further reading on important items would be of great help to many readers who have interests moderately or even intensively scholarly; and further still, that since such references can be so easily skipped in reading, their presence would not diminish the utility of the book for the general readers. Many reviewers and friends in conversation, too, had expressed to the author this desire for the documentation. Hence he consented to supply the footnote references and a bibliography of selected titles which are included in this English volume. In granting the rights of translation, the original publisher, Biblioteca de autores cristianos, graciously permitted these additions. Deep gratitude for this cooperation is hereby expressed to this *Editorial*, and to many others who have helped in making this book possible.

Through unusual God-given qualities of nature and favors of grace, St. Ignatius had a personality of enormous richness. Not very many persons in history have been more written about during the last four hundred years than he, and especially during the last five decades. Writer after writer has become fascinated by one or another facet of his character and composed an article, or a monograph, or a book about his achievements, or his organizing ability, or his skill in winning and forming men and women, or his spiritual principles, or his Spiritual Exercises, or his teachings on prayer, or his mystical contemplation, or what not else. Because of the constantly changing circumstances of history, men and women of each succeeding generation approach Ignatius with new viewpoints, problems, and questions; and from and about him they draw satisfying suggestions or answers, helpful insights, and encouraging inspiration which make their lives happier for time and eternity. It is obviously an immense benefit to have a brief, reliable, comprehensive, updated, and authoritative life of Ignatius from one so expert as Father Dalmases. Such a biography can serve well as a foundation for better understanding of the many specialized treatises focusing on various aspects of his character; and in it, too, one can learn what this experienced researcher thinks about many details of Ignatius which have been treated differently by other authors or are perhaps controverted. Hence the Institute of Jesuit Sources feels privileged to offer this compact biography to its readers.

George E. Ganss, S.J.
Director and General Editor
The Institute of Jesuit Sources
St. Louis, Missouri
September 27, 1983

TRANSLATOR'S FOREWORD

Aims and Procedures in Preparing This Version

A pressing request made to me during a meeting in Rome in September, 1980, by Fathers Cándido de Dalmases, the author, as well as by Fathers George E. Ganss and Xavier Diaz del Rio, the publishers respectively for the First and Third Worlds, is what led me to undertake the translation of *El Padre Maestro Ignacio: Breve biografía ignaciana.*

This book, although composed with an eye to the needs and tastes of the general public, is in reality a masterpiece of scientific scholarship by a highly trained historian who has spent almost half a century in research on the sixteenth-century sources of the life, writings, and thought of the Jesuit founder. Beneath the author's simple and terse style is a treatment which is objective and scientific but not cold, apologetic, or distant.

Every effort has been made, therefore, to preserve these characteristics of the original, by means of an intercontinental cooperation of the translator, the editor, and the author. The basic aim agreed upon was accuracy, an effort to communicate the author's message faithfully, with no idea added or subtracted. The present writer produced the first draft in Bombay and sent it to Father Ganss in St. Louis, who edited it word by word, scrutinized it for fidelity to the Spanish text, and wrote queries about his doubts, to such an extent that he could be considered a co-translator of the book. He then sent it to Father Dalmases in Rome, who in turn examined this text minutely and made further corrections or decisions. In work such as this, suggestions about addition or omission of details naturally arose. Some few such additions have been made, but never without approval by the author, Father Dalmases.

Jerome Aixalá, S.J.
Editor of IGNIS[1]
St. Xavier's High School, Bombay
March 12, 1982

1 IGNIS (Ignatian Information Service) is a periodical published ten times a year from St. Xavier's High School, Bombay 400 001, India.

"Father Master Ignatius" (*El Padre Maestro Ignacio*) was the phrase which the earliest Jesuits ordinarily used when they referred to the founder of the Society of Jesus. For this reason, *El Padre Maestro Ignacio: Breve biografía ignaciana* was chosen as the title of the original Spanish edition of this brief biography of St. Ignatius, which was first published in the series BAC Popular, Madrid, in 1979.

Ignatius had obtained his degree of Master of Arts from the University of Paris on March 14, 1535. Hence it is clear that when his contemporaries designated him by this academic title, they were following the habits of their era.

But when they called Ignatius "Father" or "our Father," these words had for them a significance which went beyond that of a mere formula. Without any doubt all of them considered him their father in the spirit. This became manifest on a solemn occasion, when the first companions elected the first general of the Society. The unanimous vote of the founding fathers fell upon Ignatius. Francis Xavier, echoing the sentiments of the entire group, specified that he was casting his vote for "our old leader and true father, Don Ignacio, who, since he brought us together with no little effort, will also with similar effort know how to preserve, govern, and make us advance from good to better, since he knows each one of us best."[1]

The subtitle of the Spanish original, *Breve biografía ignaciana*, indicates that what is being offered to the readers is a brief

1 *EppXav*, I, 26.

biography of St. Ignatius. It is a biography, because it has no other aim than to narrate the life of the saint in a plain and unadorned style. It is a brief life, because the character of the series (or *colección*) for which it was originally composed "BAC popular," made it necessary to keep the presentation within a limited number of pages and to exclude all erudite and critical apparatus.

There is no dearth of lives of St. Ignatius. But even so, all those competent to judge agree that the true life of this saint remains still to be written. It will be an arduous task, one almost unattainable in spite of the abundance of the material. All the known documentation pertaining to Ignatius which has been preserved in the archives has now been published. It fills twenty-six thick volumes in the series of Historical Sources of the Society of Jesus (Monumenta Historica Societatis Iesu). Hence the difficulty comes not only from the enormous spiritual and human dimensions of Ignatius, but also from the very richness of the materials available to a modern writer. Still further, the bibliography of studies about Ignatius grows continually richer, with dozens of new titles every year.

In order to get closer to that elusive goal we find two roads open to us: first, to devote specialized monographs to the various periods of his life or to some aspects of his personality, achievements, or teaching; or second, to repeat the attempts at a comprehensive biography.

This latter road is the one chosen in this book, by which St. Ignatius of Loyola is included in the gallery of "Great Witnesses of God," which the series "Biblioteca de Autores Cristianos Popular" (BAC Popular) offers to its readers.

Cándido de Dalmases, S. J.
Jesuit Historical Institute
Rome
December 3, 1979

A FURTHER NOTE

In this English translation of his book the author, complying with suggestions made by many readers, has deemed it wise to add footnote references and a bibliography of selected titles. To keep this biography a brief one, however, these notes are largely limited to the citation of the documentary sources of the texts which are transcribed. An index of names and topics has also been added.

C. D.
J. A.

CHRONOLOGICAL TABLE

IGNATIUS		GENERAL HISTORY
Iñigo is born (most probable date)	1491	
	1492	Conquest of Granada, Jan 2 Alexander VI, pope, Aug 11 America is discovered, Oct 12
	1496	Juan Pérez, Iñigo's eldest brother, dies in Naples
	1498	Savonarola dies, May 23
	1503	Julius II, pope, Oct. 31 Erasmus' *Enchiridion* first published
	1504	Queen Isabella dies, Nov 26
Iñigo at Arévalo, as a page of Juan Velázquez de Cuéllar	1506	Bramante begins the new Basilica of St. Peter's
Iñigo's father, Beltrán Ibáñez de Oñaz, dies	1507	
	1509	Henry VIII, king of England, Apr 23 Calvin born, July 10
	1513	Leo X, pope, Mar 9
Iñigo is **accused** of "enormous transgressions"at Azpeitia	1515	St. Theresa is born, Mar 28, and St. Philip Neri, July 21
	1516	King Ferdinand dies, Jan 23. Charles I, king
Iñigo is *gentilhombre* of Antonio Manrique, Viceroy of Navarre	1517	Luther publishes his 95 theses, Oct 31
	1519	Charles V, Emperor, June 28
Iñigo wounded at Pamplona, May 20	1521	Luther excommunicated, Jan 3. Diet of Worms

Iñigo a pilgrim at Montserrat and Manresa. Begins his *Exercises*	**1522**	Adrian VI, pope, Jan 9
Pilgrimage to the Holy Land	**1523**	Clement VII, pope, Nov 19
Student in Barcelona	**1524**	
	1525	Battle of Pavia, Feb 24. Francis I a prisoner
Student at Alcalá	**1526**	
Student at Salamanca	**1527**	Philip II born, May 21 Sack of Rome, May 6
Iñigo arrives in Paris, Feb 2. Studies at Montaigu	**1528**	
	1530	Charles V crowned at Bologna, Feb 24. The Confession of Augsburg, June 25
	1531	Ferdinand I, king of the Romans, Jan 5 Henry VIII, head of the Anglican Church
Bachelor of Arts	**1532**	
Licentiate in Arts	**1533**	
Master of Arts, (with his diploma dated Mar 14, 1535) Vow of Montmartre, Aug 15	**1534**	Paul III, pope, Oct 13 Affair of the placards in Paris
At Azpeitia, May-July	**1535**	John Fisher, June 22, and Thomas More, July 6, martyrs
Mayorazgo of Loyola founded, Mar 15	**1536**	Calvin publishes his *Institutio Religionis Christianae* Erasmus dies at Basle, July 11 or 12
Iñigo is ordained a priest, June 24 Vision at La Storta, Nov	**1537**	

In Rome. Judicial process. First Mass, Dec 25	**1538**	St. Charles Borromeo born, Oct 2
Deliberations about founding the Society	**1539**	Paul III approves the Society orally, Sept 3
Xavier departs for Portugal and India, Mar 16	**1540**	
Bull *Regimini* of Paul III approves the Society, Sept 27		
Ignatius elected general, April	**1541**	Presentation of Michelangelo's Last Judgment, Oct. 31
Profession, April 22		
	1545	Council of Trent opens, Dec. 13
Pierre Favre dies, Aug 1	**1546**	Luther dies, Feb 18
	1547	Henry VIII dies, Jan 28
Paul III approves the book of the *Spiritual Exercises*, July 31	**1548**	The Interim of Augsburg, May 15
Bull of Julius III, *Exposcit*, confirms the Society anew, July 21	**1550**	Julius III, pope, Feb 7
Ignatius completes text A of the *Constitutions of the Society*		
	1554	Marriage of Philip II and Mary Tudor, July 25
	1555	Marcellus II, pope, Apr 9
		Paul IV, pope, May 23
Ignatius dies, July 31	**1556**	Charles V abdicates, Jan 16
He is beatified, July 27	**1609**	
He is canonized, Mar 12	**1622**	

IGNATIUS OF LOYOLA,

FOUNDER OF THE JESUITS

ABBREVIATIONS

used in the footnotes

AHSJ   —*Archivum historicum Societatis Iesu (periodical, Rome)*

Autobiog   —*The Autobiography of St. Ignatius* (his *Acta* dictated to Gonçalves da Câmara)

Cons   —*The Constitutions of the Society of Jesus,* in any edition

*Cons*MHSJ —*Constitutiones Societatis Iesu,* 4 volumes, the critically edited texts in the Monumenta historica Societatis Iesu.

ConsSJComm —*The Constitutions of the Society of Jesus. Translated, with an Introduction and a Commentary,* by G. E. Ganss, S.J.

EppIgn   —*S. Ignatii Epistolae,* 12 volumes in MHSJ

EppMixt   —*Epistolae Mixtae,* 5 volumes in MHSJ

EppXav   —*Epistolae S. Francisci Xaverii,* 2 volumes in MHSJ

FD   —*Fontes documentales de S. Ignatio de Loyola,* MHSJ

FN   —*Fontes narrativi de Sancto Ignatio,* 4 volumes in MHSJ

LettersIgn   —*Letters of St. Ignatius,* translated by W. J. Young.

LittQuad   —*Litterae Quadrimestres,* 7 volumes in MHSJ

Memoriale —Luis Gonçalves da Câmara's *Memoriale* or Memoirs about St. Ignatius, critically edited in *FN,* I, 527-752

MHSJ   —Monumenta Historica Societatis Iesu, 124 volumes of critically edited primary sources of Jesuit History

MI   —Monumenta Ignatiana, a 26-volume section of the MHSJ

MonLain   —*Lainii Monumenta,* 8 volumes in MHSJ

MonNad   —*Epistolae et Monumenta P. Hieronymi Nadal,* 6 volumes in MHSJ

PolSum   —Polanco's *Sumario de las cosas...a la institución y progreso de la Compañia...,* in *FN,* I, 151-256

RibVita   —Ribadeneira's *Vita Ignatii Loyolae,* the critically edited texts of his Life of Ignatius in Latin and Spanish, in *FN,* IV, 1-931.

SdeSI   —*Scripta de Sancto Ignatio,* 2 volumes in MHSJ

SpDiar   —The *Spiritual Diary* of St. Ignatius (1544-1545)

SpEx   —The *Spiritual Exercises* of St. Ignatius

Chapter 1

THE SON OF THE LORD OF LOYOLA

1. The History of a Name

The original name of the saint usually known as Ignatius of Loyola was Iñigo López de Loyola. He received the name of Iñigo when he was christened at the baptismal font, still preserved in the parish church of Azpcitia, by the rector Juan de Zabala, who gave him as patron saint the eleventh-century abbot of the Benedictine monastery of Oña near Burgos.

Iñigo is a Pre-Roman language name which took the Latin form of Enneco. In modern Basque it would be spelled Eneko. In the course of time, Iñigo changed his name to Ignatius, which has no connection with Iñigo. He never gave the reason for this change. Ribadeneira, his earliest biographer, tells us that "he took the name of Ignatius because it was more widespread" or "more common to other nations."[1] Probably he was moved by his devotion, which he did profess, to St. Ignatius the martyr bishop of Antioch. The fact is that in the official registers of the University of Paris for the year 1535, the new Master of Arts appears already as 'Dominus Ignatius de Loyola, dioecesis Pampilonensis.'[2]

---

1 *FN*, II, 393; Ribadeneira, *Vida del B. P. Ignacio de Loyola*, Book I, ch. 1, in *FN*, IV, 81.

2 *FD*, p. 395. The name Iñigo came down from Enneco, an indigenous name of pre-Roman Spain; and it is not related in any way with the Latin Egnatius or its Spanish form Ignacio. The Latin word is Enneco, Enneconis, belonging to the third declension. As the centuries passed it took on various forms in the Romance languages in Spain, for example, in Castile, León, Aragón, or Navarre. In Spanish the transformation went through the stages Eñeco to Yeñego to Iñego to Iñigo or Yñigo. In modern Basque it would be written Eneko. The *n* in Iñigo was always pronounced as a palatal nasal (ñ), even though it was sometimes written without the tilde (ñ).

The change from Iñigo to Ignacio, insofar as it has reference to him, was not

3

López was one of the common family names in the Basque country which, with the passage of time, had lost its character as a patronymic. In the Loyola family the names Pérez, López, and Ibáñez occur frequently. This, however, does not necessarily mean that those who bore the surname were sons or descendants of Pedro, Lope, or Juan.

Loyola was the name of the manor-house and farmland (*casa y solar*) of his ancestors. For the surnames of the Basques derived from the house or estate to which they belonged. If we have a look at the genealogical tree of Iñigo's family, we shall see that the surnames of Oñaz and Loyola alternate in its branches. This is explained by the fact that these were the two manor-houses or estates of this Guipuzcoan family, made one by the marriage of Lope García de Oñaz and Inés de Loyola about the year 1261.

The more ancient house, considered as the cradle of the family, was that of Oñaz, situated on a hill not far from the town of Azpeitia. The house no longer stands there; but there does remain today the country shrine or *ermita*, dedicated to St. John the Baptist. In 1536, when Ignatius' eldest brother, Martín García de Oñaz, set up the primogeniture (*mayorazgo*) —whereby the property rights in a family became vested in the eldest child—he ordered that "whoever inherits this family estate of mine (*mayorazgo*) must be named after my surname and lineage or clan (*abolengo*) of Oñaz."[3] As it was, his first-born son and successor, Beltrán, took the surname of Oñaz to which he ordinarily added that of Loyola.

2. The Oñaz-Loyola Family

"Lope de Oñaz, lord of the manor-house and estate (*casa y solar*) of Oñaz, flourished about the year 1218, which is 1180

made in any one uniform manner or at one determined time. It can be said that until 1545, the form Iñigo was predominant in letters and familiar conversation, while Ignacio or the Latin Ignatius predominated in official documents. After 1545 Ignacio and Ignatius were the forms most frequently used. On this, see G. M. Verd, S.J., *AHSJ*, XLV (1976), 95-128; Hugo Rahner, S.J., *Ignatius von Loyola als Mensch und Theologe* (Freiburg, 1964), pp. 31-42.
3 *FD*, p. 498.

of the Christian era."[4] With this historic information Father Antonio Arana—a Castilian Jesuit who in the middle of the seventeenth century explored the family's archives—opens his *Account of the Ancestors and Descendants of the House and Estate of Loyola (Relación de la ascendencia y descendencia de la casa y solar de Loyola)*. He adduces no documentary source; in view of the fact, however, that he handled documents no longer available to us, he deserves our trust. Therefore, all those who attempted to reconstruct the genealogy of the Loyolas follow him, and start with the name of Lope de Oñaz, thence going back to the twelfth century. Lope was followed by García López de Oñaz around the year 1221. The third lord of the house of Oñaz of whom we have knowledge was Lope García de Oñaz. He married Inés de Loyola, lady of the house of this name and, according to the said Arana, "this matrimonial union joined into one the two houses and estates of Oñaz, which was the more ancient, and that of Loyola, which was only a little less old but had greater holdings and revenues."[5] The union must have been effected, as mentioned above, about the year 1261.

A daughter of this marriage was Inés de Loyola, lady of the house of this name, who married her kinsman Juan Pérez. They lived around the year 1300, and had seven children, the eldest of whom was *jaun (señor)* Juan Pérez de Loyola. Along with one of his brothers and another five men, whose names are unknown, he participated on September 19, 1321, in the battle of Beotíbar, in which a handful of Guipuzcoans routed the troops of the Navarrese and the Gascons, commanded by the captain Ponce de Morentain, governor of Navarre. As a reward, tradition has it, King Alfonso XI of Castile granted them the seven red bars on a field of gold that constitute the coat of arms of the Oñaz family. According to the same tradition, one of the seven brothers founded a branch of the house of the Loyolas in Placencia.

Whereas the information we have of this earlier period may

4 *FD*, p. 750. The Spanish era, used in medieval Spain, began with the year 38 B.C. It was also called the era of Caesar, although it is not known with certainty what historical event is referred to.
5 Ibid.

sound somewhat legendary, the documentary history of the
Oñaz-Loyola family begins with Beltrán Ibáñez de Loyola,
son of *jaun* Juan Pérez. This is where the ancient Biscayan
historian Lope García de Salazar started, in his history
entitled *Book of Luck and Happy Chances* (*Las Bienandanzas e
Fortunas*). Two documents of the years 1377 and 1378, the
oldest we possess, inform us about this Beltrán Ibáñez. By a
royal charter (*albalá*), dated March 15, 1377, King Juan I
of Castile granted to Beltrán de Loyola "the hereditary right
to the sum of two thousand *maravedís*, to be paid from the tax
on iron foundries and forges, payable in the port of Zumaya."[6]
The workshops or smithies in question were those of Barrenola
and Aranaz, situated within the town limits of Azpeitia. In
1378 the district judge (*merino mayor*) of Guipúzcoa, Ruy
Díaz de Rojas, at the request of several towns, summoned to
Mondragón "the chieftains of the bands of Gamboa and
Oñaz" to demand that they hand over to him a list of knight-
errants and felons (*escuderos andariegos e malfechores*) under their
pay, and to have them put a stop to their harassing and plun-
dering of neighboring towns. Among those assembled were
Beltrán Ibáñez de Loyola, "one of the knights of the Oñaz
band," and Juan López de Balda, "a knight of the Gamboa
band." Those summoned answered that they would obey
"for the service of the aforementioned lord and king and for
the defense and improvement of the aforementioned land of
the said lord and king."[7]

The first-born son of Beltrán Ibáñez, Juan Pérez de Loyola,
"died when still young in Castile, of herbs given him by a
woman of ill repute in the house of Diego López de Stúñiga,"[8]
according to the above mentioned Lope García de Salazar.
He was succeeded in the house of Loyola by his eldest sister,
Sancha Ibáñez, who in 1413 married Lope García de Lazcano,
a descendant of Martín López de Murúa. This marriage united
two leading families of the Oñaz clan. Thus Lope García de
Lazcano became the lord of Loyola. In 1419 he purchased
from the brothers Iñigo and López de Berrasoeta, citizens of
Guetaria, all the lands, apple orchards, and chestnut groves

6 *FD*, pp. 1-2, fn. 2; 73.
7 *FD*, pp. 762-763.
8 *FD*, p. 764.

(*manzanales y nogales*) they owned near the house of Loyola, between the Urola river and the Sistiaga torrent. By Lope's will, made in 1441, and that of his wife Sancha, made in 1464, we come to know the goods that constituted the patrimony of the Loyola family. There also are given the names of their two sons, Juan Pérez and Beltrán; and of the five daughters: Ochanda, María Beraiza, Inés, Teresa, and María López.

The eldest son and heir, Juan Pérez, was the grandfather of St. Ignatius. He married Sancha Pérez of Iraeta, "an ancient house near Cestona," belonging to the band of Gamboa.

The grandfather of the future saint soon appears implicated in the fight that disturbed the peace between the clan chiefs (*parientes mayores*, the heads of the twenty-four leading noble families, or clans) and the towns of Guipúzcoa. The event most talked about was the provocative poster which Juan Pérez and other chieftains of his band nailed to the gates of Azcoitia on July 31, 1456, challenging eight Guipuzcoan towns, among which were Azpeitia and Azcoitia. The reasons were "many and great." Chief among them was that the towns "had established a brotherhood (*hermandad*) and alliances and detachments against them and had made them demolish their castle-homes (*casas-fuertes*), slaughtered their kinsmen, spoiled them of their possessions and placed them in the king's bad books."[9]

The *hermandad* referred to in this challenge was an organization mainly of a defensive character, created by the towns, still too weak to withstand the powerful influence of the clan chiefs (*parientes mayores*). This armed force enjoyed the king's favor and protection.

The statement that the *hermandad* had caused the strongholds of the lords to be razed to the ground makes one suspect that the towns themselves may have effected the demolition, partial at least, of their fortified houses; and even today we see vestiges of this in the castle of Loyola. The house of Oñaz must have been razed at about the same time. Being strongly fortified

9 *FD*, p. 57.

and strategically situated, it commanded the valleys of Loyola, Landeta, and Aratzerreka, and thus it constituted a greater hazard.

It is not clear whether this demolition or dismantlement was the work of the brotherhood (*hermandad*) or of King Enrique IV, as punishment for the misdemeanors of the lords. What is certain is that the king personally visited the lands of Guipuzcoa and passed sentence on April 21, 1457 against the defiant lords and their allies. The sentence was exile in the towns of Estepona and Jimena, in far away Andalucía, in the frontier zone of the territory still dominated by the Moors. Juan Pérez de Loyola was banished for four years to Jimena de la Frontera, in what is today the province of Cádiz. The king's clemency cut short the term of exile by an amnesty granted on July 26, 1460. By a decree of the same time King Enrique permitted the lords to restore their manor-houses, but he insisted on two conditions: That they be not rebuilt on their former sites, and "that they be flat without towers or fortifications of any kind." As far as Loyola is concerned, we see that only the second condition was complied with. Ignatius' grandfather rebuilt the house of Loyola just as it appears to the visitor today, with the two upper stories of arabesque brickwork and without fortifications. These stories are standing on the original massive stone walls.

From the marriage of Juan Pérez de Loyola and Sancha Pérez de Iraeta, the grandparents of Ignatius, were born a son, Beltrán, and two daughters, María López and Catalina. María was married to Pedro de Olózaga; and Catalina, to Juan Pérez de Emparan, of the noble house of this name at Azpeitia. Of this marriage was born María López de Emparan, who was a sister (*serora*) taking care of the shrine of San Pedro de Elormendi. In 1496, this cousin of Ignatius, together with another Guipuzcoan young lady, Ana de Uranga, embraced the rule of the Third Order of St. Francis, thus giving rise to what was to become the convent of the Immaculate Conception which exists to this day. We know that Iñigo's grandfather died suddenly at Tolosa on an unspecified date, and without leaving a will.[10]

10 *FD*, p. 121-122.

In 1467 Beltrán Ibáñez de Oñaz (ca. 1439-1507), father of St. Ignatius, married Marina Sánchez de Licona, a daughter of Martín García de Licona. Of Beltrán we know that he fought on the side of Ferdinand and Isabella, the "Catholic Kings" (*Reyes Católicos*). In the war of succession to the throne of Castile after the death of Enrique IV, Alfonso V, king of Portugal, took sides with Juana la Beltraneja and, penetrating into Castile, occupied the town of Toro and besieged Burgos. Beltrán took part in the counter-offensive that culminated in the reconquest of Toro and the liberation of Burgos in 1476. A little later, too, he took part in the defense of Fuenterrabía against the assault of the French.

The Catholic Kings were mindful of all these deeds of valor in their charter of privileges, dated June 10, 1484, in Córduba. In it they confirmed in favor of the lord of Loyola the right of patronage of the church of Azpeitia: "In consideration of the loyal service which you rendered to us during our siege of the city of Toro when the king of Portugal had seized it, and likewise in the siege of the castle of Burgos, as well as in the defense of Fuenterrabía at the time when the French had surrounded it, where you remained in person for a long time with your kinsmen, shut in at your personal risk and exposing your person to danger and adventure, and for many other services which you have rendered and which we hope you will render in future..."[11]

In 1490 Beltrán, as patron of the parish church of Azpeitia and in agreement with the rector and the seven beneficiaries, arranged the manner in which the tithes paid by the parish were to be distributed. In 1499 he ordered that the constitutions of the synod of Pamplona, held that same year, should be applied to the church of Azpeitia. In 1506 we see him elaborating, in agreement with the clergy, an ordinance on the procedures to be followed in the ordination of new ministers of the altar. Perhaps the most important norm was one that prescribed that no candidate should be admitted to sacred orders before he had completed a course of studies for four continuous years in a university or private college "in such

11 *FD*, p. 126.

a way that the would-be cleric would be good at grammar and singing."[12] These ordinances were submitted to the vicar-general of Pamplona. He declared them null and void, "as having been made by persons who were and are devoid of any power and jurisdiction for that matter."[13] Nevertheless, the vicar-general made the ordinances his own, and with a few modifications he confirmed them on February 20, 1507.

We are indebted to the father of St. Ignatius for the preservation of important documents about his family. On September 10, 1472 he appeared before the mayor of Azpeitia, Juan Pérez de Eizaguirre, asking him to order the notary Iñigo Sánchez de Goyaz to draw up a copy of seven documents, written between the years 1431 and 1440, which throw light on some interesting aspects of the Loyola family.[14] In particular, we see the lord of Loyola admit into his alliances (*treguas*) other citizens of Azpeitia, who bound themselves "with all their goods to make war or peace with the lord or lords of Loyola and never to abandon the alliance."[15] In doing this the lord of Loyola acted like a typical head of a band. He leagued together with other citizens to get their support in his enterprises. Measures directed against the king were excluded.

It is on record that Beltrán made his last will and testament in the presence of the notary Juan Martínez de Egurza, on October 23, 1507. He seems to have died that very day. Iñigo, his youngest son, was then sixteen years old.

3. *The Mother's Family*

If we possess clear and precise data in what pertains to the family of the father of St. Ignatius, not a few doubts and lacunae remain to obscure the mother's ancestry. His maternal grandfather was Martín García de Licona, known as "Doctor Ondárroa" from the Biscayan town of this name, whither his family moved in 1414 from their native Lequeitio. At

12 *FD*, p. 180, no. 2.
13 *FD*, p. 183, no. 8.
14 *FD*, pp. 90-109.
15 *FD*, p. 107; see also p. 102.

10

Ondárroa stands to this day the *casa-torre* of the Liconas. Martín was the son of Juan García de Licona and María Yáñez de Azterrica. Given to legal pursuits, he became "a member of the council of our king and lord, and an auditor in his high court of justice, lord of Valda,"[16] as we read in the marriage contract of his daughter Marina, the mother of Iñigo.

His title as Señor de Balda was acquired by the purchase, in 1459, of this Azcoitian house from Pedro, illegitimate son of Ladrón de Balda. The latter had died as an exile in Andalucía, where he had been banished by decree of Enrique IV in 1457. In 1460, the same king had granted to Martín the patronage of the Church of Azcoitia. In 1462, Martín secured the post of auditor of theo yal chancery (*cancillería*) of Valladolid, with a salary of 30,000 *maravedis* and eight *escudos*. It may be supposed that, after the purchase of the house of Balda, he moved his residence to Azcoitia, though for official purposes he must have spent long spells in the court at Valladolid. Azcoitians considered him always a stranger and nicknamed him "el Vizcaíno." He died around the year 1470, leaving as successor his son Juan García de Balda, who married María Ortiz de Gamboa.

We are not absolutely certain as to who was the wife of Martín García de Licona and the maternal grandmother of St. Ignatius. She had certainly died by 1467, when her daughter Marina married Beltrán de Oñaz, lord of Loyola. The most common opinion, founded on such competent authors as Lope García de Salazar, Esteban de Garibay, and Gabriel de Henao, is that Marina belonged to the Balda family and was a daughter of Fortuno de Balda. Her name was, according to some, Marquesa (the feminine form of Marcos); according to others, Gracia. But this opinion contrasts with the explicit declaration of four witnesses who, in 1561 deposed that the wife of Martín García de Licona was María de Zarauz. According to this, the maternal grandmother of Iñigo would be not a Balda but a Zarauz. We must admit that there are reasons in favor of either opinion, and that therefore the question cannot be considered a closed one.

16 *FD*, p. 80.

About Iñigo's mother we know little beyond the date of her marriage, 1467, and the names of her many children. We may calculate that at the time of her wedding, she was about twenty years of age; certainly more than ten. If then Doctor Ondárroa, her father, did not buy the house of Balda before the year 1459, we shall have to agree that the mother of Iñigo was not born in this Azcoitian house. This is another question that must remain unanswered. Regarding the lady's moral qualities we must be content with the eulogies, somewhat vague, pronounced by witnesses summoned to depose in the process for the beatification of her son in 1595. They present her to us as firm in the faith and obedient to Holy Church. We must suppose that it was in these sentiments that she brought up her numerous progeny. We do not know when she died; certainly before 1508.

4. The Brothers

The number and the name of Iñigo's brothers have been endlessly debated but, unfortunately, no definite conclusions have ever been reached. We lack their father's will which would, no doubt, have dissipated all doubts. In the process of beatification mentioned above it is stated that Ignatius "was the last and youngest of the thirteen children which this honorable couple, Beltrán and Marina, had."[17]

This precise number had earlier been given by the first biographer of St. Ignatius, Pedro de Ribadeneira, who specified that Iñigo's parents had eight sons and five daughters. From unquestionable documents the following list of names emerges: among the male children, Juan Pérez, Martín García, Beltrán, Ochoa Pérez, Hernando, Pero López, and Iñigo López; among the daughters were Juana, Magdalena, Petronila, and Sancha Ibáñez. We do not know whether this last one was legitimate or not. Certainly illegitimate were Juan Beltrán, called "the bastard" (*el borte*) by one of his brothers, and María Beltrán. Some would count a certain Francisco Alonso de Oñaz y Loyola among Iñigo's brothers; but the reasons adduced are not very convincing. The order of birth

17 *SdeSI*, II, 249.

is not certain in respect to all, nor do we know if Iñigo was the last of the children or only of the boys.

On the whole it can be said that, following the example of their ancestors, all the brothers were in the service of the kings of Castile, either bearing arms or participating in the conquest of the Americas. Exception must be made of Pero López, who embraced the clerical state and was rector of Azpeitia. The first-born, Juan Pérez, took part, in a ship of his own, in the war against the French for the possession of the kingdom of Naples; and he died in this city in 1496, after the first military campaign was brought to a close by the *Gran Capitán* Gonzalo Fernández de Córdoba in the battle of Atella. We say that he died at Naples, for it was there that he drew up his will in the house of the Spanish tailor Juan de Segura, on June 21, 1496;[18] and afterwards he is no longer heard of. He left two sons, Andrés and Beltrán, of whom the former succeeded his uncle Pero López as rector of Azpeitia.

Thus the second son, Martín García de Oñaz, remained as heir of the ancestral house of Loyola. He took part in the wars of Navarre. In 1512, he fought for the annexation of this kingdom to Castile in the battle of Belate. In 1521, he rushed with fifty or sixty of his men to the defense of Pamplona, in which his brother Iñigo was wounded; but seeing the squabble of the leaders regarding the way to conduct the campaign, he abandoned the field. After the reconquest of Pamplona, we see him fight in the defense of Fuenterrabía, where he was one of the staunchest opponents of the surrender of the stronghold to the French, decided on October 28, 1521, by the captain Diego de Vera.

In the inventory of the goods of Martín García, drawn up in 1539 soon after his death,[19] are enumerated his arms and other military outfit. Yet most of his life was devoted, not to warfare, but to the administration of the patrimony of the house of Loyola and to his patronage of the church of Azpeitia. In 1518, he married Magdalena de Araoz, daughter of Pedro

18 *FD*, pp. 139-146.
19 *FD*, pp. 599-622.

de Araoz, provost of San Sebastián, a native of Vergara. With a view to preserving his family possessions whole and undivided, in 1536 he established that the right of primogeniture (*mayorazgo*) should devolve upon his first-born son, Beltrán.[20] As patron of the church of Azpeitia he defended its interests and worked for the improvement of the divine services. In 1526, in agreement with the clergy, he prepared statutes for the better management of the parish, which were submitted to the approval of the king and of the bishop of Pamplona. He died in his ancestral house of Loyola on November 29, 1538, after having made his will and testament accompanied by five codicils within that same month.[21]

Among the other brothers of Ignatius, Beltrán was a knight bachelor, and he seems, like the eldest brother Juan Pérez, to have fought and died in the war for the possession of the kingdom of Naples. Ochoa Pérez, as he tells us in his will of 1508,[22] took up arms in the service of queen Juana in the Low Countries and in Spain. Hernando, after renouncing the rights he might have to the parental inheritance, set sail for America in 1510 and died on land in Darien. As to Pero López, we have already seen that he embraced a church career. From 1518 onward he was rector of the parish church of Azpeitia. He journeyed to Rome three times to safeguard his family interests. On his last return journey in 1529 he died as he passed through Barcelona.

All the sisters of Iñigo made good marriages. The eldest, Juaneiza, married Juan Martínez de Alzaga, the notary of Azpeitia. Magdalena's husband was Juan López de Gallaiztegui, notary of Anzuola, lord of the houses of Gallaiztegui y Echeandía. Petronila married Pedro Ochoa de Arriola, a native of Elgóibar. The illegitimate daughter María Beltrán was a sister (*serora* or *freila*) taking care of the shrine of San Miguel; but abandoning her commitment not to marry, she contracted marriage with Domingo de Arrayo. Though belonging to this well-to-do family, some of these ladies could neither

---

20 *FD*, pp. 472-506.
21 *FD*, pp. 563-599.
22 *FD*, pp. 185-194.

read nor write, not even enough to write their signatures on legal documents.

5. Azpeitia, a Town in the Heart of Guipúzcoa

Azpeitia is a town nestling in the valley of Iraurgui, which is crossed from south to north by the Urola, the central river of Guipúzcoa. This river follows its course across the narrow defile formed by the Elosua and Pagotxeta mountains. Half way along its course, the river valley opens up rapidly when it reaches Azcoitia, whence the stream flows towards Azpeitia. Between these two towns stands the house of Loyola, dominated by the mountain range of Izarraitz. After passing by Azpeitia the river enters again a narrow pass along which it runs through Cestona and Iraeta, until it finds the sea at Zumaya.

Father Pedro de Tablares, who visited Loyola in the year 1550, in the lifetime of St. Ignatius, was particularly struck by the valley's "fresh verdure which only doubtfully can be surpassed for refreshing the eyes." Loyola appeared to him as "surrounded by woods and orchards with all kinds of fruit trees, so dense that one can hardly see the house until one comes to the very gateway."[23] He does not mention the kind of trees that covered the landscape; but we know that these were, in the main, apple and chestnut trees.

Azpeitia received the charter of foundation (*carta-puebla de fundación*) from the hands of King Ferdinand IV on February 20, 1310. All those who wished to inhabit Garmendia, "which is in Iraurgui," would be permitted to preserve "the voting rights and freedom which they enjoy in the places in which they now dwell." In another document the town is called Salvatierra de Iraurgui, a name it preserved till the sixteenth century, when it was gradually replaced by that of Azpeitia. The king granted to the inhabitants of Salvatierra the patronage of the church of San Sebastián de Soreasu, with the right of presentation of the rector and beneficiaries to the bishop of Pamplona on whom it depended in church matters. We shall

23 *FN*, III, 745.

have occasion to see the lawsuits with the house of Loyola to which the granting of this patronage gave rise.

In the Basque region the institution of the farmhouse (*caserío*) is of the utmost importance. Together with the surrounding lands, the *caserío* constitutes the house and estate (*casa y solar*) of the lord. It is the house that imparts the name to its owner and his children. In the family of St. Ignatius the two names of Oñaz and Loyola alternate, because the heads of their ancestral lines were lords of these two houses.

Oñaz, set on a hill, and Loyola, nestling in a valley, were manor-houses of the clan chiefs (*parientes mayores*). The Basque social structure was patterned around the various ancestral stocks that composed it. These lines of ancestors, in their turn, constitute a whole effected by the bonds of blood relationship. The clan chiefs (*aide nagusiak* in Basque) wielded a real power in their territories; this they often used against the towns which, being of more recent foundation, still lacked a strong and well-knit organization. In addition, the clan chiefs were themselves divided into two bands or parties, called the *oñacinos* and the *gamboínos* after the two original families of Oñaz and Gamboa. The Oñaz family belonged of course to the band of *oñacinos*, among which it was the most powerful except for the family of Lazcaño.

To increase their power, the heads of the leading families tried to strike alliances with others of the same band by means of matrimonial unions. Likewise they sought the support of other neighbors who "entered into alliances" (*entraban en treguas*) with them, that is to say, they undertook to stand by them in their fight against their rivals. Throughout the fifteenth century several citizens of Azpeitia, among them the lord of the leading house of Emparan, made alliances with the lord of Loyola. This strengthened the union between two of the most important court houses of Azpeitia, sealed with the marriage of Inigo's aunt Catalina with Juan Martínez de Emparan, lord of the house of this name. Rival of these two houses was the family of Anchieta, rooted in Urrestilla. The houses of Loyola and Emparan pledged never to enter in alliance with that of Anchieta.

On the feuds between the two parties and disastrous results of their rivalries we are amply informed by local historians, among them Lope García de Salazar who wrote his *Book of Luck and Happy Chances* (*Las Bienandanzas e Fortunas*) between 1471 and 1476, the year of his death. The readers of those chronicles get the impression that the life of the Basque people was dominated by these rival factions. The reality perhaps was not as tragic as one might think. In the course of the fifteenth and sixteenth centuries, the struggle subsided and the tensions eased. We see that neither the father nor the eldest brother of St. Ignatius were implicated in these party struggles. However, Martín García considered and called himself a *pariente mayor*.[24]

The gap separating the *parientes mayores* and the towns continued to be felt for yet some time. An inkling of it may be discerned in the disposition, coming in 1518 from the civil and judicial magistrate (*corregidor*) of Guipúzcoa, Pedro de Nava, whereby *parientes mayores* were excluded from participation in the meetings and deliberations of the city council of Azpeitia. The same happened with the Baldas at Azcoitia. When this arrangement was applied to Iñigo's brother in 1519, the measure was softened, at least in part. Martín and his successors could "attend such councils if they so wished..., provided the said Martín García and his descendants, lords of the said *casa e solar* [of Loyola], would have no voice or vote in such general assemblies any more than other citizens of the land."[25] The lord of Loyola was thus placed on the same footing as any townsman of Azpeitia.

6. Social, Economic, and Religious Situation of the Oñaz-Loyola Family

We have seen that the family of St. Ignatius was one of a score of families called clan chiefs (*parientes mayores*) which, divided into the two bands of *oñacinos* and *gamboínos*, dominated the Guipuzcoan scene. In the political field, the Loyolas were always loyal servants of the crown of Castile. When offering

24 *FD*, pp. 570, 782.
25 *FD*, p. 257.

a sketchy portrait of some principal members of the family
we have had occasion to recall some deeds that prove this.

And how did the kings on their part correspond to the fealty
of these noble vassals? The Castilian kings of the house of
Trastámara, from Juan I to Isabella the Catholic and her
husband Ferdinand, showed their grateful recognition to the
lords of Loyola for their services and loyalty. Two principal
concessions were made and repeatedly confirmed. The first
was the granting of an annual allowance, by hereditary and
perpetual right passing from father to son, of 2,000 *maravedís*
"based on the rights of the royal charters (*albalaes*) and ancient
tithes of the irons wrought in the foundries and forges of
Barrenola and Aranaz." This concession was made in the
first instance by king Juan I to Beltrán Yañez de Loyola on
March 15, 1377.[26] The two iron workshops were within the
town limits of Azpeitia. The farmhouse (*caserío*) of Barrenola
still stands on the road between Régil and Azpeitia. A few feet
beneath the surface there remain vestiges of the old smithy.

A more important privilege was the right of patronage over
the church of Azpeitia, bearing the title of royal monastery
of San Sebastián de Soreasu. This church, considered as royal
patrimony, passed to the lord of Loyola who held it as his own
and included it among his possessions. More than patron,
the lord of Loyola was, one might say, also the lord of the
church. Father Pedro de Tablares wrote in 1550 that the
lord of Loyola was "like a bishop who sees to the benefices
and all that appertains to the church."[27] Besides occupying
a seat of honor in the church and choosing there the place
for his tomb, he enjoyed the right to present the nominees for
the office of rector and the seven beneficiaries and to appoint
the two chaplains. He was the recipient of three fourths of
the tithes offered by the faithful to the parish and of one
fourth of the other offerings, called stole fees (*de pie de altar*).

The history of the patronage of Azpeitia is long and involved.
We have seen how King Fernando IV had granted this right

26 *FD*, pp. 1-2, 73.
27 *FN*, III, 745.

to the town in 1311. But it happened that when the office of rector fell vacant by the death of a certain Juan Pérez, the bishop of Pamplona appointed as successor Pelegrín Gómez, vicar forane (*oficial foráneo*) of San Sebastián, a member of the important family of Mans or Engómez in that city. At first the people opposed such an appointment as infringing on their rights. The affair came up to Pope Clement VII at Avignon, to whom the diocese of Pamplona and the whole kingdom of Navarre offered allegiance. The pope — who counted the bishop of Pamplona, Martín de Zalba, among his staunchest defenders — ordered that the case be investigated and he finally approved the appointment of Pelegrín Gómez. This was in 1388.[28] But the people did not submit to the decision. The result was the decree of excommunication issued in 1394 against the recalcitrant townsmen and the interdict imposed on the church. This violent situation lasted for full twenty years. But at last the Azpeitians yielded. This annoyed King Enrique III, who considered that church a property of the Crown and decided to transfer the right of patronage to Beltrán Ibáñez de Loyola and his successors, the lords of Loyola. This happened on April 28, 1394.[29]

An agreement was reached in 1414 between the administrator of the diocese of Pamplona, Lanciloto de Navarra, and the lords of Loyola. Sancha Ibáñez de Loyola and her husband Lope García de Lazcano accepted the rector nominated by the bishop, Martín de Erquicia, and the diocesan administrator recognized the right of patronage in the lords of Loyola. The agreement was sanctioned by Pope Benedict XIII (Luna) on September 20, 1415.[30]

The fight then shifted to the people who did not acknowledge the legitimacy of the transfer of patronage to the lord of Loyola. A lawsuit was filed in the court but the lords of the house of Loyola continued to enjoy their rights for a long time.

Among the confirmations of the two privileges we have mentioned may be singled out those granted by Ferdinand

28 *FD*, pp. 4-12.
29 *FD*, pp. 2-3.
30 *FD*, pp. 30-43.

and Isabella to the father of St. Ignatius, Beltrán Ibáñez de Loyola in the year 1484.[31]

The dealings of kings with the house of Loyola were not limited to these two concessions. Queen Juana and her son Emperor Charles V granted to the eldest brother of St. Ignatius, Martín García de Oñaz, the power to institute the primogeniture (*mayorazgo*) "in recognition of the good and loyal services that you, the said Martín García de Oñaz and the said Beltrán de Oñaz, your son, have rendered to us, and we hope will henceforward render, and with a mind that there be a lasting memory of your persons and services. . ."[32] This concession was made on March 18, 1518.

In a letter addressed to the same Martín García on March 16, 1537, Charles V announced the dispatch of his palace guard (*contino*) Juan de Acuña "for what you will understand from him to pertain to my service and to the welfare and defense of that province, that the matter may be executed with all possible speed. . ."[33] We have no inkling as to what "the matter" might have been.

Again on September 25, 1542, Charles V in person wrote to the nephew of St. Ignatius, Beltrán, requesting him to execute the order which he would receive by letter or word of mouth from the constable of Castile, Pedro Fernández de Velasco, or Sancho de Leiva, captain general of Guipúzcoa.[34] Here again we do not know what matter the emperor might refer to. But the significant fact conveyed by these references is that the emperor could rely upon the brother and the nephew of St. Ignatius and did entrust affairs of some importance to them.

Were the Loyolas wealthy? An authoritative answer comes, in the middle of the fifteenth century, from the historian Lope García de Salazar: "This lord of Loyola is the most powerful

31 *FD*, pp. 125-128.
32 *FD*, p. 477.
33 *FD*, p. 525.
34 *FD*, p. 653.

among the lineage of Oñaz, both in revenues and wealth and relations, except for the lord of Lescano."[35]

For the times nearer to St. Ignatius, we have more concrete information, chiefly from three documentary sources: the primogeniture (*mayorazgo*), instituted in 1536; the will of Ignatius' elder brother, Martín García de Oñaz, made in 1538; and the inventory of his possessions made by the executors of his will soon after his death. Throughout these documents we see that the lord of Loyola was the possessor of a considerable patrimony, consisting of the houses and estates of Oñaz and Loyola, four houses in Azpeitia including that known as "*Insula*" at the entrance to the town, a certain number of *caseríos* or country homesteads, two blacksmith shops, numerous *seles* or meadows, orchards of fruit trees, and one water mill. Francisco Pérez de Yarza, in his *Memorial* composed in 1569, says that in the days of the niece of Martín García, Lorenza, the *caseríos* numbered twenty-one[36] The sources list also among the patrimony of the Loyolas the church of Azpeitia with its possessions.

A concrete detail toward calculating the sum of the patrimony of the house of Loyola is afforded by Father Antonio de Araoz in a letter addressed to St. Ignatius on November 25, 1552. Araoz, wishing to squash the rumors that had spread regarding the marriage of Lorenza de Oñaz, the grandniece of Ignatius, with Juan de Borgia, son of the saintly duke of Gandía, says that the party that stood to gain by that matrimonial alliance was the bridegroom, who had only the rank of knighthood (*encomienda*) of the Order of Santiago, while the bride was already the lady of Loyola because of the death of her father Beltrán de Oñaz. On this occasion Araoz says that the property of the house of Loyola was estimated to be more than 80,000 ducats:

For, besides the antiquity and quality of the house of Loyola

---

35 L. García de Salazar, *Las Bienandanzas e Fortunas*, lib. XXI. Edition of Rodríguez Herrero, IV (Bilbao, 1967), p. 74. Regarding the properties and revenues of the lords of the house of Loyola, see C. Dalmases, "El patrimonio de los señores de Loyola," *AHSJ*, XLIX (1980), 113-134.

36 *FD*, p. 740, no. 4.

and the prestige of its perpetual patronage [of the church of Azpeitia], its properties are estimated at more than 80,000 ducats; and the duke [of Gandía, Don Carlos, Juan's brother] and his agents have shown so much interest that, as I know, he offered to advance 300 ducats as an earnest [*de albricias*] that the [marriage] contract should be settled.[37]

The duke of Nájera Juan Esteban Manrique de Lara had wished that Lorenza should marry one of his own kinsmen, and to secure this he had approached St. Ignatius. As it is known, Ignatius excused himself from intervening in this affair "of such a nature and alien to my humble profession."[38]

Regarding the revenues, the above mentioned Pérez de Yarza informs us that the church of Azpeitia yielded to its patron a yearly income of 1,000 ducats. The other properties brought him 700 ducats; and half a scrivener's office (*escribanía*) which he had purchased yielded another 200. In all, according to these data, we may conjecture that the lord of Loyola was receiving annually a sum of about 1,900 ducats. To this other amounts are to be added, in particular the 2,000 *maravedís* from the hereditary rights granted by the kings.

From these data we may deduce that the revenues of the lord of Loyola, while not so large as those of some others, which amounted in some cases to 10,000 and even 20,000 ducats, could be considered satisfactory for a lord in the middle of the sixteenth century. Probably they were not inferior to the revenues of other clan chiefs in Guipúzcoa. More details can be got from the dowries which these chiefs gave to their daughters at the time of marriage, the quality of their bridal trousseaus and jewelry, and the furniture of their houses. About all this we gather information in the documents mentioned, in particular in the inventory of Martín García. We may make still another observation. Writing to his brother in 1532, Iñigo told him that "since God blessed you with an abundance of temporal goods," you should try with them to gain the eternal.[39]

---

37 *EppMixt*, II, 849.
38 *EpppIgn*, IV, 386.
39 *EppIgn* I, 81.

As to what concerns the religious life of the Loyolas, we may say that it was, more or less, that of the people of Spain at that time. A profound and sincere faith and a substantial fidelity to religious practices was accompanied by moral lapses, which they themselves found no difficulty in admitting. Of all this we have concrete proofs in the wills, all of which invariably begin with a fervent profession of faith, the request for abundant spiritual suffrages for the "enormous sins" committed, and the legacies for various pious works. Some indications lead us to think that the Loyola family did not lack persons decidedly virtuous, as Ignatius' sister-in-law Magdalena de Araoz and his nephew Beltrán, both of whom Ignatius praised.

Religious matters played an important role in the life of the lords of Loyola, above all because their condition as patrons of the church gave them the right and the obligation of intervening in the church affairs of Azpeitia. When speaking of the father and the brother of Ignatius, we have had occasion to refer to such actions. Speaking in general terms, one can say that the religious life of the family was closely bound with that of the parish.

A vexing controversy disturbed the minds of the patron and of the parish clergy for many years. It was a conflict which confronted them with the *beatas*, or devout women, of the convent of the Immaculate Conception. There are many documents that re-echo to this struggle which was maintained for reasons that might appear rather trifling today, but were not so at the time. The proximity of the convent, then situated in Emparan street, just a few yards from the parish church, created problems of competition in what referred to schedule of Masses, ministers of worship, funerals, and the like. The matter reached Rome, whence came dispositions which on the whole favored the viewpoint of the patron and clergy. But the situation was not settled until an agreement was signed in 1535.[40] The first to append his signature was Iñigo, who no doubt had a preeminent role in securing the accord between the two parties. This was one of the matters he tried

40 *FD*, pp. 397-439.

to leave settled when he passed through Azpeitia, for he could not bear having his brother still implicated in an affair that troubled the religious peace of the town. The text of the agreement (*acordio*) is highly interesting for our gaining knowledge of some of the most characteristic aspects of religious practice in the Azpeitia of the sixteenth century. As on other occasions, Ignatius gave proof of his skill as a negotiator.

As was natural, Ignatius, who showed such detachment regarding the temporal matters of his relatives and fellow townsmen, did all in his power to promote their spiritual good. Of this he gave abundant proof, especially during his stay of three months at Azpeitia in 1535. But even from Rome he continued to occupy himself with what for him was of paramount importance.

7. The Last Son of the Lord of Loyola

Iñigo was born, in all probability, in the year 1491. In the absence of the baptismal records of the parish of Azpeitia, which begin in 1537, we are forced to have recourse to conjectures, as he himself was neither explicit nor coherent on this point. There is no need to resuscitate here a question on which all that could be said has been said.[41] When Iñigo died, the fathers of the Society gathered in Rome found themselves forced to make a decision when the time came to record this historical event in the epitaph to be placed on his tomb. After some deliberation they wrote that the Saint died at the age of 65 years, which, given that he died in 1556, was equivalent to saying that he was born in 1491. This opinion coin-

---

41 The ancient and the modern biographers alike have lacked uniformity in their efforts to determine the year of Ignatius' birth. Some of them, such as Polanco and Ribadeneira, have changed their own opinions more than once. Polanco oscillated among the dates 1491, 1493, and 1495 (see *FN*, II, 512). Ribadeneira too opted for 1495; but in his *Vita Patris Ignatii*, first published in 1572, he gave the date as 1491 (see *FN*, IV, 78, fn. 2). Among modern authors, Dudon showed an inclination for 1593, but with a doubt (see *Saint Ignace de Loyola* [Paris, 1934], "La date de la naissance de Saint Ignace," pp. 613-614; English translation by Young, p. 448). On all this, see the long scholarly study of Pedro de Leturia, "De anno quo Ignatius natus est disceptatio critica," in *FN*, I, 14*-24*; also, *Obras completas de San Ignacio* (4th ed. [Madrid, 1982], pp. 75-76).

cided with that of Iñigo's wet-nurse María Garín, who had suckled the child in the farmhouse of Eguíbar, near the house of Loyola, an opinion corroborated by other valid arguments, which need not be repeated here.

If Iñigo left his ancestral home a little before or a little after his father's death, that is around the year 1507, we must conclude that by then he was about sixteen years of age. What is the picture of the local surroundings and family atmosphere which could have been impressed on his memory at that early age? Granted that grace does not destroy nature, we must conclude that Ignatius remained a Basque and a Loyola throughout his life. Psychology attributes the greatest importance to the hereditary factors and environmental circumstances of the early years in the psychological make-up of an individual. I leave to experts the study of somatic features, such as are presented by the death masks taken soon after he passed away and some faithful portraits, such as those of Jacopino del Conte and Sánchez Coello.

The biographical sources offer us abundant evidence to prove that Iñigo preserved to his dying day the characteristic traits of the people of his land. Here are two details, small but very significant. Toward the end of his life, because of both his abstinence and his physical infirmities, he showed himself indifferent to any kind of food, as though he had lost all sense of taste. This notwithstanding, if his companions wished on some festive occasion to give him a treat, they would offer him three or four roasted chestnuts, which they knew he liked "because it was a fruit of his country and one on which he had been brought up."[42] On another occasion, unable to dispel the gloom of a melancholic person who approached him for spiritual comfort, Ignatius asked him if there was anything he could do to give him pleasure. The disconsolate visitor conceived the bizarre notion of saying that he would be highly delighted if Iñigo would there in his presence break into a folk song and dance of his Basque country. Iñigo did not consider it a loss of his dignity to grant this request, and he complied. But afterwards he told his visitor not to ask that again.[43]

42 *Memoriale*, no. 189, in *FN*, I, 642.
43 *FN*, IV, 761.

Leturia attributes to Iñigo's Basque origins his personal concentration, his reflective spirit, his speech which was slow but courageous, as confident of itself as it was poor in colorful expression, and as a result of all this, his unshakable firmness of will. To this trait the Portuguese Simão Rodrigues alluded when he remarked to Gonçalves da Câmara in 1553: "You must realize that Father Ignatius is a kindly man and of much virtue, but he is a Basque, and once he has taken something to heart..."[44] Rodrigues left his sentence unfinished but it was easy to guess what he meant. It is the same trait which Cardinal Rodolfo Pio de Carpi, protector of the Society, observed when he remarked about some decisions of Ignatius: "He has already driven in the nail."[45] It was an allusion to Ignatius' firmness in adhering to his decisions.

From the people of his country he imbibed the purity and integrity of his faith. At Alcalá, when the vicar-general Figueroa asked him if he kept the Sabbath, Ignatius replied drily: "There are no Jews in my country."[46] And Nadal, writing in defense of the *Exercises* in 1554, could say: "Ignatius is a Spaniard from the highest nobility in the province of Guipúzcoa, in Cantabria, where the Catholic faith is kept incorrupt. Its inhabitants' zeal and constancy have been so great from time immemorial that they do not allow any 'New Christian' to live there. From the very beginning of Christianity there is no record of anyone who was censured for or in any slight way suspected of heresy. This should have been enough to ward off any suspicion from him."[47]

His Basque stock appears clearly through his language and style, which is far from fluent. Most probably, in his home he spoke Basque, the common language of the people of the region. In his letters to Ignatius Araoz would sometimes fall back into Basque expressions when the matter was confidential. And throughout his writings, Ignatius' continual fondness for elliptic constructions, his long strings of infinitives and gerunds, and his omission of the articles are some of the

44 *EppMixt*, III, 34.
45 *Memoriale*, no. 20, in *FN*, I, 539.
46 *FN*, II, no. 44; see also *FN*, I, 174.
47 *FN*, I, 318.

traits that betray an early education received in a non-Castilian atmosphere. These are vestiges which neither long years in Castilian lands nor familiarity with writings in this language could ever obliterate.

As a youth of sixteen, Ignatius was conscious and proud of belonging to an important family of Guipúzcoa that had distinguished itself in the service of the kings of Castile. His father and eldest brother never ceased to tell him of the exploits of their ancestors and the rewards their monarch had heaped on them. Later on as general of the Society he did not hesitate to employ this "human means" for his apostolic purposes. The matter in question in 1551 was the founding of a college of the Society in Louvain. Through his secretary he recommended to Father Claude Jay that he speak on the subject to the king of Spain "mentioning the services rendered to the Crown by Father Ignatius and his kinsmen."[48] Again, in a letter to his nephew Beltrán, at the time already lord of Loyola, he told him: ". . . and just as our ancestors endeavored to signalize themselves in other things—and would to God it may not have been in vain—you wish to signalize yourself in things imperishable."[49] We may note here that phrase "signalize themselves" (*señalarse*). It is no less characteristic of Ignatius than his "more" (*magis*). He uses this expression, among other places, in his crucial meditation on the Kingdom of Christ when he exhorts "those who will want to be more devoted and *signalize* themselves in all service of their King Eternal and universal Lord" to offer themselves and "make offerings of greater value and importance."[50] We cannot doubt that already in those early years he was forging that temperament "strong and valiant, and even more, ardent to undertake great enterprises,"[51] of which Polanco speaks.

48 *EppIgn*, III, 333.
49 *EppIgn*, I, 148.
50 *SpEx*, [97].
51 *PolSum*, no. 4, in *FN*, I, 154.

Chapter 2

IN THE SERVICE OF THE TEMPORAL KING

1. In the House of the Chief Treasurer, Juan Velázquez de Cuéllar

What course was Iñigo's life going to take? Were we certain that he had received the tonsure, we could suppose that the first intention of his parents, or his own, was that of entering the ecclesiastical career. But events showed that such was not for the time being his true calling. We soon see the teenager take the road to the town of Arévalo. A distinguished Castilian *hidalgo*, Juan Velázquez de Cuéllar, chief treasurer (*contador mayor*) of Castile, had written to the lord of Loyola suggesting that he might like to send one of his younger sons to Arévalo to be brought up as one of his own in his household. The choice fell upon the last son of Beltrán de Oñaz, Iñigo.[1]

An invitation of this kind cannot be explained unless bonds of at least closest friendship existed between Velázquez de Cuéllar or María de Velasco, his wife, and the lords of Loyola. In fact, there was a blood relationship. María de Velasco was a daughter of María de Guevara, who was related to the family of Iñigo's mother, Marina Sánchez de Licona. This is what has been repeatedly said by Iñigo's biographers, following the illustrious genealogist Father Gabriel de Henao, who wrote that María de Guevara was Iñigo's aunt. According to this historian, María de Guevara foretold Iñigo's future, when, seeing his boyish pranks, she told him: "Iñigo, you'll never learn sense until someone breaks one of your legs."[2]

---

1 On Iñigo's youth, and particularly his stay at Arévalo, see Pedro de Leturia, S.J., *El gentilhombre Iñigo de Loyola* (Barcelona: Labor, 1949); English translation by A. J. Owen, S.J., *Iñigo de Loyola* (Syracuse, 1949 and Chicago, 1965); Luis Fernández Martín, "El hogar donde Iñigo de Loyola se hizo hombre," *AHSJ*, XLIX (1980), 21-94.
2 Gabriel de Henao, S.J., *Averiguaciones de las antigüedades de Cantabria* (nueva edición, Tolosa, 1894-1895), VII, 182.

28

If we try to specify, as far as it is possible, this degree of kinship between the Guevara and the Balda families, we find that a certain Ladrón de Guevara was the great grandfather of Marquesa (or Gracia) de Balda, Iñigo's grandmother. We have this on the authority of the Basque historian Lope García de Salazar. It is probable that the relationship was still closer, for the same historian states that "these lords of Guevara had other sons and daughters, legitimate and illegitimate, from whom came many descendants, though here we mention only the chief ones."[3] One of these descendants was María de Guevara, the mother of María de Velasco and mother-in-law of the chief royal treasurer, Don Juan Velázquez.

We therefore have Iñigo settled at Arévalo, a town situated in the heart of Castile, between Valladolid and Avila, on the banks of the Adaja river. New horizons were opening before the eyes of the son of the lord of Loyola. His future would not be that of warfare in Naples or Flanders; nor that of a conquistador in the New World, as two or three of his brothers had been; nor that of a churchman, as had been the case of another brother, Pero López. His would be the life of a courtier in the service of high officials , who would set him on a career of public administration, political intricacies, and eventually the profession of arms.

We cannot say with certainty when Iñigo set out from Loyola to Arévalo. According to Fita, it was in 1496, when the boy was only five years old.[4] This would seem to be too early a date. The other extreme would be 1507, the year when Beltrán, the boy's father, died. The invitation of Don Juan Velázquez must have been sent in Beltrán's lifetime. We may conjecture that most probably it was within the years 1504 to 1507. And since Iñigo remained at Arévalo till the death of the royal treasurer in 1517, we find that his stay there extended over a period of more than ten years. Those

---

3 Lope García de Salazar, *Las Bienandanzas e Fortunas*. Códice del siglo XV. (Edición de Angel Rodríguez Herrero), IV, 31.

4 F. Fita, "San Ignacio de Loyola en la corte de los Reyes Católicos," *Boletín de la Real Academia de la Historia,* (Madrid), XVII (1890), 498.

were momentous and decisive years for Iñigo, involving his passage from adolescence to manhood.

Who was Don Juan Velázquez de Cuéllar? We have a character description of him from the historian of Emperor Charles V, Prudencio de Sandoval:

> "This gentleman was the chief treasurer of Castile, son of the licentiate Gutierre Velázquez, who had charge of Queen Juana [*sic*, for Isabel de Avís], mother of Queen Doña Isabel, at Arévalo. A native of the town of Cuéllar, Juan Velázquez was on very familiar terms with the Prince Don Juan and Queen Doña Isabel, so much so that he was made the executor of their wills. He was a prudent and upright man, exceedingly generous and a good Christian, of fine appearance and very conscientious. He held the fortresses of Arévalo and Madrigal with all their lands under his domain and administration, and he was the lord of all as though it were his own property."[5]

Velázquez de Cuéllar was appointed treasurer-general of the kingdom of Castile in 1495 with Prince Don Juan, the son of Ferdinand and Isabella, and he held this office for the rest of his life. From 1497 he was member of the Royal Council. Though his habitual residence was at the royal palace of Arévalo, his official duties required him to follow the kings in their itinerant court.

His wife, María de Velasco, was an intimate friend and first favorite of the second wife of Ferdinand the Catholic, Germaine de Foix, "even more than what was proper," as the contemporary Carvajal remarked. The queen could not bear to be a single day without her and Doña María would spend all her time attending on her and expensively entertaining her with banquets. The hint of impropriety is confirmed by the saying of Pedro Mártir de Anghiera, who in his *Epistles* referred to the young queen as being "fat and not always sober" (*pinguis et bene pota*).[6] When Juan Velázquez fell into disgrace, María, leaving her house at Arévalo, took refuge under the protection of the marquesa of Denia. Seven years later, in

---

5 P. de Sandoval, *Historia de la vida y los hechos del emperador Carlos V*, lib. II, cap. XXI (edición de la Biblioteca de Autores españoles, Madrid, 1955), p. 93.
6 Leturia, *El gentilhombre*, p. 72.

1524, she accompanied Princess Catalina, Charles V's sister, when the latter set out for Portugal to marry King John III. There she remained as the queen's chief lady-in-waiting till she died in 1540.

Nothing so clearly reveals the standing of Juan Velázquez in the court of Ferdinand and Isabella as the fact that they chose him to be one of the executors of their will. He was one of those who "gave me great and very loyal service,"[7] says Isabella in her will. Events soon after the queen's death on November 26, 1504, clearly show, as the marquis of Lozoya wrote, that Juan Velázquez "must have been the man in whom Ferdinand the Catholic had the highest trust."[8] By the king's orders, the queen's chamberlains, Sancho de Paredes and Violante d' Alvión, among others, took up the task of transporting to the chief treasurer's residence cases and cases containing countless objects that had belonged to the late sovereign. Among them priceless jewelry, rich reliquaries, precious garments, reredos and tapestry, sets of cutlery, and stacks of books kept passing through the hands of the faithful majordomo who made an exact inventory of them. Many of these valuable objects were sold by public auction, and in more than a few cases Don Juan Velázquez with his wife were successful bidders. This we know from the execution of the queen's will (*testamentaría*), which contains an impressive catalogue of her belongings.

For us the books are of particular interest. Prominent among them were many works on religious subjects, with no lack of the classical authors and chronicles of the reigns of earlier kings. Present was the much-thumbed copy of the grammar which the author himself, Antonio de Nebrija, had presented to the queen. Skimming over the inventory of the queen's possessions, we see that María de Velasco purchased, among other objects, "a little book in print on the order of reciting the Psalter"; "another tiny little book, written by hand in Romance, which begins with the prayer of St. Augustine"; another book in quarto of St. John Chrysostom"; "a book of

7 A. de la Torre y del Cerro, *Testamentaría de Isabel la Católica* (Barcelona, 1974), p. 51*.
8 Ibid., p. 51.

Hours, written by hand on parchment, which begins with the martyrology and the history of King David"; "another book of the Little Hours, written on printing paper, which begins with the words On the Imitation of Christ."

All these books were a significant addition to the library which Juan Velázquez had in his Arévalo mansion. Iñigo, no doubt, took not a few of these books from their shelves to satisfy his curiosity and to acquire some culture. It is evident that if he asked, during his convalescence at Loyola, to be given "worldly books of fiction and knight errantry" (*libros mundanos y falsos que suelen llamar de caballerías*),[9] it was because he had been very fond of reading them at Arévalo. And if, after his conversion, he thought of entering the Carthusian monastery of Santa María de las Cuevas in Seville, it was, probably, because he had had an occasion at Arévalo to read the classic works of " the Carthusian" (*el Cartujano*) Juan de Padilla: *A Reredos of the Life of Christ* (*Retablo de la vida de Cristo*), and *The Twelve Triumphs of the Twelve Apostles* (*Los doce triunfos de los doce apóstoles*).

It was at Arévalo that the personality of Iñigo was forged. Ribadeneira, his first biographer, describes him as "a lively and trim young man, very fond of court dress and good living" (*mozo lozano y polido y muy amigo de galas y de traerse bien*).[10] As Iñigo himself confesses at the beginning of his *Autobiography*, we know that "up to the age of twenty-six he was a man given over to the vanities of the world, and took special delight in the exercise of arms, with a great and vain desire of winning fame".[11] Polanco tells us that "Iñigo's education was more in keeping with the spirit of the world than of God; for from his early years, without entering into other training in letters beyond that of reading and writing, he began to follow the court as a page; then he served as a gentleman of the Duke of Nájera and as a soldier till the age of twenty-six when he made a change of life.'[12]

9 *Autobiog*, no. 5, in *FN*, I, 370.
10 *RibVita*, lib. I, c. ii (hereafter I, ii), in *FN*, IV, 85.
11 *Autobiog*, no. 1.
12 *PolSum*, no. 3, in *FN*, I, 154.

Worldly vanities and, above all, the craving for renown filled his aspirations during this period. At Arévalo he improved "his already fine handwriting, for he was an excellent penman," as Ribadeneira declares.[13] The poem which, according to Polanco, he composed in honor of St. Peter,[14] to whom he was especially devout, belongs to this period. We should remember that to him were dedicated the shrine of St. Peter of Eguimendía just a few yards from the house of Loyola, and the parish church of Arévalo. During his years at Arévalo he cultivated his love for music, a fondness which remained with him throughout his life and which he had to sacrifice for the sake of the apostolate. We should also recall that there resided in the court, since the days when he was appointed music master of the royal chapel to Prince Don Juan, the celebrated musician from Urrestilla, Juan de Anchieta, who since 1504 was rector of the church of Azpeitia—though never a great friend of the Loyolas. There Iñigo acquired the traits of that fine distinction and courtesy, which in his years at Rome brought him the reputation of being "the most courteous and polite of men."[15] He gave indications of this manner of bearing himself even at his frugal table, at which a certain indefinable courtly atmosphere could be noticed, as Palmio wrote.[16] There too he was schooled in the art of dealing with the grandees of the land, an experience which stood him in good stead when he had to deal with princes, cardinals, and popes. It was also at Arévalo, and in a later period of life when he was in the service of the Duke of Nájera, that he fell into the faults of morality to which he alluded in the words we have quoted from his *Autobiography*, and which Polanco depicts in more concrete expressions: "Up to this time [of his conversion], although very much attached to the faith, he did not live in keeping with his belief or guard himself from sins; he was particularly careless about gambling, affairs with women, brawls, and the use of arms; this, however, was through force of habit. But all this made it possible also to perceive many natural virtues in him."[17]

13 *RibVita*, I, ii, in *FN*, IV, 95.
14 *FN*, II, 517.
15 *Memoriale*, no. 290, in *FN*, I, 697.
16 *FN*, III, 164.
17 *PolSum*, no. 4, in *FN*, I, 154.

Some more details about this period of Iñigo's life are available in an account by Father Antonio Lárez, the founder of the college opened by the Society at Arévalo in 1588.[18] This Jesuit priest had gone with a companion to preach a mission in that town in 1577. Touched by his sermons, a leading citizen, called Hernando Tello, conceived the idea of founding a Jesuit college. Lárez had then the occasion to gather some testimonies still fresh about Iñigo's sojourn in that Castilian town. Of particular interest to him were, above all, the declarations of a very wealthy and noble gentleman, named Alonso de Montalvo (d. 1578), who in his youth had himself been a page of Don Juan Velázquez, together with Iñigo whose intimate friend he was. When Montalvo came to know that his friend had been wounded in the siege of Pamplona, he visited him at Loyola and found him wounded in one leg and already healing from the wound. The same Father Lárez heard also from the priest Alonso Esteban, among other things, that Iñigo when, already general of the Society, "was wont to write at times" to Catalina, one of the daughters of the chief treasurer. None of these letters have reached us but we do know that throughout his life Iñigo cherished fond memories of his Arévalo friends. In 1548 he wrote a reply to the lawyer Mercado of Valladolid, who had written to him that "Juan Velázquez, the governor of this town and the son of Gutierre de Velázquez [the son of the now deceased chief treasurer] kisses your Reverence's hand and commends himself to your prayers."[19] Iñigo wrote:

> I have received great comfort in our Lord from the remembrance of Don Juan Velázquez. You will give me great pleasure if you convey to him my humble regards, as from one formerly inferior to him, and still so, and to his father, grandfather, and entire household; about all this I am still happy and I shall always be happy in our Lord.[20]

Was Iñigo a page of King Ferdinand the Catholic? This was stated by Father Giovanni Pietro Maffei, the elegant Italian Latinist in his *Life of St. Ignatius,* in 1585, and repeated

18 *FN*, III, 462-466.
19 *EppMixt*, V, 653.
20 *EppIgn*, I, 705.

34

by Father Francisco García in his biography printed in 1722. But already Ribadeneira corrected that statement in a critical review of the *Life* by Maffei, stating that "he was not a page of the Catholic King but of Hernán [*sic*] Velázquez, his chief royal treasurer."[21] What we can say is that, since Iñigo was in the service of Juan Velázquez, it would be natural for him to accompany Velázquez and his sons in some of his trips to the royal court. That Iñigo was at least occasionally at the court is evidenced by an event that took place in 1524. Back from his pilgrimage to Jerusalem, he was at Genoa waiting for a chance to set sail for Barcelona. There "he was recognized by a Basque named Portundo, who had spoken to him on several occasions when he was serving at the court of the Catholic King."[22] This we are told by Ignatius himself in his *Autobiography*. Rodrigo Portuondo, for this was his real name, was in the port of Genoa during that year of 1524 with the commission of watching over the movements of the imperial fleet in Mediterranean waters. If he had met Iñigo "on several occasions," we may deduce that Iñigo frequented the court, but we have no proof that he held any office there, not even that of a page.

The death of Ferdinand the Catholic on January 23, 1516, had as an indirect consequence the downfall of Don Juan Velázquez. The new monarch Charles I ordered from Flanders that the widowed Queen Germaine de Foix be given as pension the estates of the Castilian towns of Arévalo, Madrigal, Olmedo, and Santa María de Nieva. The first two, as we have said, had till now been entrusted to Juan Velázquez who had them in fief. The young king ordered that "Juan Velázquez should exercise power over them on behalf of her [Germaine] and pay homage to the queen."[23] Apparently this disposition was not to entail any financial loss for the treasurer-general, but it did carry a diminution of prestige and a substantial alteration in the status of the said towns, which thus became dismem-

---

21 *FN*, III, 217.
22 *Autobiog*, no. 53.
23 Fita, op. cit, (in fn. 4 above), p. 513; Leturia, *El gentilhombre*, p. 97; trans. of Owen, p. 50.

bered from the royal patrimony and alienated from the Crown of Castile. This went counter to the laws of the kingdom and the privileges of the towns, as the king himself admitted four years later. The regent, Cardinal Ximénez de Cisneros, counseled the young monarch not to carry out his decision. But as Charles did not revoke his order, Cisneros had no other alternative but to accept it and require its execution from Velázquez. But the chief treasurer did not yield. In November, 1516, he withdrew to Madrid and placed Arévalo and its fortress on a war footing. In the end he had no choice but surrender. Charged with a debt of sixteen million *maravedís* and saddened by the death of his first-born son, Gutierre, he passed away in Madrid on August 12, 1517. Queen Germaine had turned against him and against her former favorite friend María de Velasco.

Young Iñigo de Loyola had been a witness, step by step, of the gradual moral and economic crumbling of his noble protector. That fall was for him the first major experience and disillusionment which could not fail to have a lasting influence on his future career. The twenty-six-year-old courtier was then entering upon a new period of his life.

2. The Gentleman of the Viceroy of Navarre

Juan Velázquez's fall into royal disfavor and his death on August 12, 1517, left Iñigo an unemployed youth. But the generosity of María de Velasco, the late treasurer's widow, found a solution for this problem. She gave him 500 coins and two horses that he might go to visit Don Antonio Manrique de Lara, duke of Nájera, who in May, 1516 had become viceroy of Navarre. The duke took Iñigo into his service as a gentleman (*gentilhombre*). Thus, after some ten years spent in the court of Castile under the orders and patronage of a high official, he passed into dependence upon another important personage of the realm.

To avoid the danger of exaggerations, it is appropriate to mention here the fact that Iñigo was never a professional soldier; nor was his father or his eldest brother Martín García. He was simply a gentleman (*gentilhombre*) who served the viceroy of Navarre, carrying out errands or executing requests; and when occasion required he took up arms and participated in military expeditions. This does not contradict his own statement that "he delighted especially in the exercise of arms,"[24] for — as he himself mentions in specifying his objective — what moved him to this was "a great and vain desire of winning fame." His aim, above all, was to secure for himself a brilliant future in the world; and in the society of his day he could not attain this without the use and experience of arms.

It is probable that Iñigo was in the company of his new lord when this official attended the cortes in Valladolid in February, 1518, for the ceremony of the official recognition of Charles I as king of Castile. Also present there was his brother Martín García, lord of Loyola, to whom on that occasion the king granted the permission to establish the primogeniture (*mayorazgo*) of Loyola, a favor which he secured at the request precisely of the duke of Nájera.

It did not take long for Iñigo to make himself useful to his master. When, in the course of riots that disturbed the towns and cities of Castile, the city of Nájera rose in rebellion against its lord, Iñigo took part in the expedition that quelled the rebellious citizens on September 18, 1520. On this occasion, as Polanco remarks, he showed himself "magnanimous, noble-minded, and liberal,"[25] for while some members of the expedition gave themselves to sacking and looting the town, Iñigo took nothing for himself, deeming it "unworthy."[26]

In 1521 the viceroy of Navarre availed himself of the assistance of his *gentilhombre* for a delicate mission: the appeasing of the towns of Guipúzcoa. They were at loggerheads with one another about the acceptance of Cristóbal Vázquez de Acuña for the office of chief magistrate (*corregidor*) of the province. Some towns, including Azpeitia and Azcoitia, maintained that the office had been conferred on him without

24 *Autobiog*, no. 1.
25 *PolSum*, no. 5, in *FN*, I, 155.
26 *FN*, I, 156.

account being taken of the privileges of Guipúzcoa. Other municipalities, led by San Sebastián, recognized the new chief magistrate. The disputes grew into a confrontation which much resembled a civil war. Either side took to burning down the other's houses and felling their forests. The case was all the more alarming because it coincided with the war of the Communities of Castile, (the party that upheld Spanish rights against the encroachments of Charles V), and also with the French threat of invading the kingdom of Navarre in order to replace the family of Albret on its throne.

In the absence of Emperor Charles V from Spain, the solution which the Council of Castile chose was recourse to negotiation with the contending Guipuzcoan towns. The person chosen to act as negotiator was Fortún García de Ercilla, who had among his sons Alonso de Ercilla, the renowned author of the epic *La Araucana*. The duke of Nájera was entrusted with the task of being in readiness to intervene with an armed force, in case Ercilla's mission of negotiation should end in failure.

The outcome was that the towns decided to submit to the mediation of the duke of Nájera. He wrote in a letter of January 17, 1521: "I set myself to meeting their differences by sending them persons of my household for that purpose." He does not state who these persons were; but if we are to believe Juan de Polanco, we must agree that one of them was the *gentilhombre* Iñigo López de Loyola. As a native of that region who knew its traditions and customs, he was an obvious choice for this undertaking. We need not think that Iñigo had the role of chief negotiator, but he certainly was one of those who took part in the negotiations. Polanco informs us that in this affair he gave indications of being "a man of great ingenuity and prudence in worldly affairs and very skillful in the handling of men, especially in composing differences and discord."[27] Through this finding of an arbitrator the matter was brought to a happy conclusion, according to the conditions specified by the duke of Nájera in a document of April 12, 1521.

27 *PolSum*, no. 6, in *FN*, I, 156.

3. The Wound of Pamplona

Soon after the happy conclusion of that conflict, Iñigo took part in an enterprise of military type, on which was to hinge the future of his life. Taking advantage of the coincidence of the absence of Charles V and the revolt of the *comuneros*, the uprisings in the towns which in those first months of 1521 absorbed the Castilian army, the king of France, Francis I, decided to support the claims of Henri d'Albret to the throne of Navarre, relying on the support of the local party of Agramont. Barely nine years had passed since Navarre had been incorporated into the kingdom of Castile. This explains why the Navarrese people did not yet feel fully accustomed to the new situation. Notwithstanding the instant and repeated requests of the viceroy of Navarre, the reinforcements of troops necessary for the defense of the kingdom did not come. Meanwhile the French troops, composed of 12,000 infantry, 800 lances, and 29 artillery pieces, crossed the frontier on May 12, 1521, under the command of André de Foix, lord of Asparrós. Four days later he was encamped about a mile from the city walls of Pamplona. The following day the viceroy took the road to Segovia, where the three governors had assembled: the admiral of Castile, the high constable, and the cardinal-bishop of Tortosa, Adrian of Utrecht, in order to ask in person for the urgently required reinforcements. Before his departure he entrusted the defense of Pamplona to Francés de Beaumont with a body of 1,000 soldiers and ordered Iñigo to place himself under his command. On May 18, a revolt broke out in the city. The townsmen with their council claimed that in the absence of the viceroy the command belonged to them. This was denied resolutely by Don Frances and his men. As the situation could not be brought under control, Don Francés and his soldiers decided to quit. As the duke of Nájera said, "strong winds against the defense of the city were blowing."

Meanwhile, probably on May 18, Martín de Oñaz arrived with his brother Iñigo and a group of soldiers whom they had rallied to their side in Guipúzcoa. Finding themselves faced with all that confusion, Martín García and his band turned back without even setting foot in the city. Iñigo refused to follow him. Polanco relates that "Don Francés wished to depart from the city because he despaired of being able to resist the French forces and mistrusted the loyalty of the populace in the city; but Iñigo refused to follow, feeling shame that departure might seem to be flight. Instead, he entered the fortress at the head of those who were going to its defense."[28] Nadal's additional detail is that Iñigo made for the fortress "at full gallop" (*incitato equo*).[29] The following day, Pentecost Sunday, May 19, the governor (*alcaide*), Don Miguel de Herrera, also took his stand in the citadel. That very day, the deputies of Pamplona took at Villava the oath of fealty to Henri d'Albert. Once the city was occupied, the French troops began to assault the fortress whose fortifications, still unfinished, offered little resistance. It was only through Iñigo's stubborn determination that the thought of surrender was not accepted.

The events of that day are well known. A cannon ball of a culverin or falconet passed between the young soldier's legs, shattering the right one and damaging the other. The disabled Iñigo was out of the fight, and his fall meant the end of all resistance. A tradition passed on by Nicolas Orlandini dates the wounding of Iñigo on Pentecost Monday, May 20.[30] This may have been true; but the latest research has shown that the castle did not surrender before May 23 or 24.[31]

Iñigo's wound was serious. This became clear in the course of his illness at Loyola, and we know it from the testimony of the governor of the castle, Miguel de Herrera. In the judicial process instituted against him after the surrender of the castle, Herrera asked his judges to hear, among other eyewitnesses present, the brother of the lord of Loyola; and he insisted on the urgency of the case, for Iñigo was seriously wounded, and he did not know whether he would arrive in

---

28 *PolSum*, no. 4, in *FN*, I, 155.

29 *FN*, II, 63.

30 Orlandini, *Historiae Societatis Iesu prima pars*, Lib. I, no. 10.

31 On the battle of Pamplona and the wound of Ignatius, see L. Fernández Martín, *Iñigo de Loyola y el proceso contra Miguel de Herrera, Alcaide de la fortaleza de Pamplona*. Príncipe de Viana, números 140 y 141 (Pamplona, 1975), pp. 471-534, especially p. 486.

time to give his testimony.[32] Other witnesses summoned by
the governor of the castle, all Iñigo's fellow soldiers, were
Pedro de Malpaso, superintendent of the castle, who died at
the end of June as a result of wounds he had received; Master
Pedro, master of works; Alonso de San Pedro, majordomo of
the artillery, and a soldier named Santos. We do not know
whether the questioning of Iñigo himself ever occurred. One
thing we know, Miguel de Herrera came out from the trial
with an acquittal.

In the meantime Iñigo, who had received the first medical
attention from the French, was carried by his fellow country-
men in a litter to the house of Esteban de Zuasti, and from
there to his house of Loyola. There he must have been welcomed by his sister-in-law Magdalena de Araoz.

The healing of the patient was a matter of urgency. Physicians and surgeons were summoned from various quarters.
They soon realized that the first attempts had not been
effective, as it was done in great haste and probably by un-
skilled hands. Ignatius himself relates the facts for us in his
Autobiography. The bones, "either because they had been badly
set or because the jogging of the journey had displaced them,
would not heal. Again he went through this butchery (*carni-
cería*) in which, as in all the others that he suffered before or
after, he uttered not a word nor showed any sign of pain
other than the tight clenching of his fists."[33]

In spite of all the care, he continued to get worse and fears
were entertained for his life. On St. John's day the physicians
advised him to make his confession and receive the sacrament
of the sick. June 28, the vigil of Saints Peter and Paul, was
the most critical day. The doctors agreed that if his condition
did not improve by midnight, he could be given up as dead.
"As the sick man always cherished a special devotion to St.
Peter, it pleased God that by midnight he should take a turn
for the better. So rapid was his initial recovery that within
a few days he was declared to be out of danger of death."[34]

32 Ibid., pp. 527, 529.
33 *Autobiog*, no. 2.
34 *Autobiog*, no. 3.

A later tradition, popularized by some paintings of the wounded soldier, has it that on that night St. Peter appeared to him and restored him to health. This is stated by Ribadeneira in his Life: "And thus it is understood that this glorious apostle appeared to him on that same night of his greatest necessity."[35]

But the road to full recovery had not ended. The bones began to knit, but under Iñigo's knee one bone had become superimposed upon another, which made the right leg shorter than the other and also caused a lump to protrude. Ribadeneira says that the protuberances would have prevented him from putting on "his smart and close-fitting boots," which he liked to wear. This he would never tolerate, for — adds his biographer — "he was a lively and trim young man who liked court dress and good living."[36] Here he gave us a glimpse of his character. "He inquired of the surgeons whether they could cut away the bony projection. They replied that undoubtedly they could, but that the suffering entailed would be greater than any he had hitherto borne, because the bone had already set and a long time would be necessary to shorten it. He determined, nevertheless, to have his way and make himself a martyr to his own pleasure. His elder brother was amazed and declared that he himself would never have the courage to go through this torture. But the wounded man bore it with his usual composure. Having cut into the flesh and sawed off the projecting bone, the surgeons set themselves to applying remedies to prevent the leg from remaining so short. Many ointments were applied and stretching devices employed, which for many days caused him a martyrdom. But our Lord at last cured him."[37] It could be said that he was cured but had to remain immobile for a long period. That enforced rest was providential for him.

Although Ignatius in his *Autobiography* speaks of physicians and surgeons in the plural, we have the name of the chief surgeon who attended him, Martín de Iztiola from Azpeitia. For his professional services he claimed from the family

35 *RibVita*, I, i, in *FN*, IV, 85.
36 Ibid.
37 *Autobiog*, no. 5.

thirteen ducats of which he was paid ten. Martín de Iztiola himself declared this to the executors of the will of Iñigo's eldest brother, when he submitted his account of services rendered to the house of the lord of Loyola "in the afore-mentioned service of surgery." Adding up all that was owing to him, including the three unpaid ducats for Iñigo's cure, he rounded off the amount to another 10 ducats.[38] A curious coincidence: Alonso de San Pedro, one of Iñigo's comrades in the defense of the citadel of Pamplona, received from the authorities twelve ducats "as aid toward curing the wound he received in the defense of the fortress of this city of Pamplona."[39]

4. The Convert of Loyola

To while away the long hours of enforced inactivity the patient thought of resorting to the reading of books of chivalry, with which he had become familiar in the household of Juan Velázquez. Surprisingly enough, in the house of Loyola such literature was not to be found. The only books then available were the four volumes in folio of the *Vita Christi* by the Carthusian Ludolph of Saxony, translated into Spanish by the Franciscan Ambrosio Montesino and printed in Alcalá in the years 1502 and 1503. There was also another volume, *Flos sanctorum*, a selection from the lives of the saints by Jacopo da Varazze, in the Spanish version with a prologue by the Cistercian monk Gauberto María Vagad. As there was no other reading matter to be had, the invalid took up the reading of these spiritual books. That reading transformed him. During the intervals in his reading, his thought went at times to worldly things and at other times concentrated on what he had read.

Among other thoughts there was one that absorbed him to such a point that he turned it over in his imagination three or four hours without a break. He kept on turning over in his imagination "what he would have to do in the service of a certain lady, the means he would have to take to enable him to go to the land where she was, the well-turned phrases

38 *FD*, pp. 625-626.
39 L. Fernández Martín, op. cit., p. 487, note 60.

and words which he would address to her, and the deeds of arms which he would do in her service." These were dreams all the more difficult to realize because the lady in question "was not of the lower nobility, neither a countess nor a duchess, but her station was higher than any of these."[40] Many conjectures have been ventured as to who the idol of ailing Inigo's dream might have been. It is probable that the lady was not some existing person but some imaginary creature. If the person was truly existent, the probabilities are greater that she was the sister of Charles V, Catalina, whom Iñigo could have seen in Valladolid or Tordesillas, where the young princess provided company for her unfortunate demented mother, Queen Juana la Loca. Catalina married John of Portugal in 1525.

In this alternation of pious thoughts and vain dreams a factor intervened which was decisive not only for the patient's own transformation but also for the later composition of the *Spiritual Exercises*. What is meant is the discernment of spirits. Reflecting on what was taking place in his interior, Iñigo noticed "that while he was thinking about what pertained to the world, he had great pleasure; but when later on from fatigue he dropped it, he found himself dry and discontented; and that while he was thinking about going unshod to Jerusalem, and eating nothing but herbs, and performing all the other rigors which he saw that the saints had practiced, he not only kept on finding consolation while he had such thoughts in mind, but he also remained contented and joyful after he let them pass from his mind." At first he did not reflect on this difference but little by little his eyes were opened and he recognized that what was happening in his interior was a struggle between two contrary spirits, one good and one evil. "And this was the first reflection he made on the things of God; later on, when he was drawing up the *Exercises*, it was from this experience within him that he began to draw light on what pertained to the diversity of spirits."[41]

The good thoughts that came to him insistently were: "What would happen if I should do the things that Saint

40 *Autobiog*, no. 6, as in *FN*, I, 372, 374.
41 *Autobiog*, no. 8.

Francis and Saint Dominic did?" He thus let his thought run over many things difficult and great which he could accomplish, and his will inclined toward putting them into practice. And his whole reflection consisted in saying to himself: "St. Francis did this? Then I must do it. St. Dominic did that? Then I must do it."[42]

The continued effort of reflection and the light of grace finally prevailed in the mind of the convalescent soldier. From day to day he saw more clearly that he had to make a complete break with his past and enter upon a radically different way of life. At last the decision was taken. All that was left was to determine the manner and the time of carrying it out. Two points occurred to him as having the highest priority. As soon as he felt sufficiently recovered to leave his house, he would undertake a pilgrimage to Jerusalem. Second, to imitate the example of the saints, he would start a life of rigorous penance. As is the case with many other converts, he measured sanctity by the severity of corporal austerities. The power of these convictions was so great that the fanciful dreams of a worldly life gradually faded away from his mind.

As a confirmation of his resolutions came what Ignatius called a "visitation" and described in these terms: "Lying awake one night, he saw clearly the likeness of our Lady with the Holy Child Jesus, and from this sight he drew for a considerable time very great consolation. Forthwith he felt so great a loathing for the whole of his past life, especially for the things of the flesh, that he seemed to be delivered there and then from all the imagery which had formerly occupied his mind." And from that hour until August, 1553, when he narrated this, "he never gave the slightest consent to the things of the flesh."[43]

The external indications of the interior change effected in Iñigo were so obvious that his eldest brother and the other members of the household could not fail to see them. Meanwhile he was maturing his plans for the future. He was soon

42 *Autobiog,* no. 7.
43 *Autobiog,* no. 10.

able to leave his bed a little and, consequently, to jot down some notes. The thought came to him to transcribe some passages from the books he was reading. In a copybook of some 300 leaves of polished and lined paper, he set himself with great diligence to copying his excerpts. He copied the words of Christ in red ink, our Lady's in blue, all in a good hand "for he was a very good penman."[44]

While the convalescent was fully immersed in his deep reflections, the world outside was following its wonted course. Martín García, in his capacity of patron, took an active interest in the welfare and good administration of the parish church of Azpeitia. We see him with the rector and the seven beneficiaries discussing the religious services that were to be celebrated, about appointed days and exact hours, and the distribution of the various tithes offered by the faithful. He had also to deal with the nuns of the convent of the Immaculate Conception, who were planning to build a church next to their convent. Martín García offered to cede to them a site he possessed in the vicinity, with an eye to being named patron of the new chuich as he was of the parish church. In October of the same year, Martín García rushed to the defense of Fuenterrabía, then under attack from the French. He sided with the party that favored the defense of the besieged fortress at all costs, even at the sacrifice of their lives, and stoutly advised against surrender. This, however, was decided by captain Diego de Vera on the 28th of the same month.

Iñigo's thoughts were now extending into the future. What would he do on his return from Jerusalem? An idea struck him, that of shutting himself up in the Carthusian monastery of Nuestra Señora de las Cuevas, near Seville, without disclosing his identity so that he would be held in less esteem. So he directed a servant of the house, who was leaving for Burgos, to make inquiries in the monastery of Miraflores concerning the Carthusian rule. The information thus received on the subjects pleased him, but he did not follow up the idea, partly because he considered this a still distant

44 *Autobiog*, no. 11.

goal, and partly because it seemed to him that, if he should live under a rule, he would not be free, as he wanted, to lead a life of penance.

The moment arrived for Iñigo to take the great step. Talking to his brother Martín he told him he had to go to Navarrete, where he was to meet the duke of Nájera. We shall see later that this was not a mere pretext, for he was keen to pay his respects to his former master. Martín García and others in the house of Loyola suspected that Iñigo "desired to make a great change."[45] Restless and disturbed by Iñigo's designs, Martín took him aside and led him around the ancestral house, from room to room, and earnestly begged him not to throw himself away, and to consider what high hopes the people had placed in him, how influential he could be."[46] These were, it is true, honest and affectionate words dictated by brotherly love, but they also reveal to us the opinions and the high expectations which people entertained of young Iñigo. But he was adamant in his resolve "and stole away from his brother."[47] It was probably in late February, 1522 when, crossing the Gothic doorway and arch of the Loyola house, he set out on his long pilgrim route.

Before we tell the story of his pilgrimage, it will be helpful to survey the external situation of his country at the beginning of that year 1522. The occupation of Navarre by the French lasted barely a month. It came to an end in the battle of Noáin on June 30, 1521. But the French troops attempted a fresh assault, this time against the fortified town of Fuenterrabía, which surrendered, as we have seen, on October 28. This danger had caused the three governors, who administered the realm during the absence of Charles V, to move to Vitoria. On January 24, 1522, there reached this capital of the Alava province the first announcement of the elevation to the supreme pontificate of one of the three governors, Cardinal Adrian of Utrecht, to be known as Adrian VI. The official communication followed on February 9, and the following day the acceptance by the man who had been elected.

45 *Autobiog*, no. 12.
46 Ibid.
47 Ibid.

Present also at Vitoria at the time, as governor, was the Constable of Castile, Iñigo Fernández de Velasco. He maintained a long-standing sworn enmity against the duke of Nájera, Iñigo's protector. The duke, after his downfall in prestige and fortune, retired to Nájera and Navarrete in his domains of La Rioja. For some twenty months he received no salary and, as a result of the disturbances of the year 1521, "he had lost and spent whatever he had and had seen his house looted."[48] The unkindest cut of all came on August 27, 1521, when he was suddenly relieved of the office of viceroy of Navarre, which was entrusted to the count of Miranda.

Iñigo was aware that the duke was at Navarrete, as the latter had more than once despatched messengers to inquire about the condition of his wounded *gentilhombre*.

The announcement of the election of the new pope must have reached Loyola before Iñigo's departure. At any rate the route the pilgrim had intended to take on his way to Montserrat and Barcelona coincided with the one which the new pope and cortège would have to follow in the triumphal procession, through La Rioja and the southern border of Navarre, to Zaragoza, Lérida, and Barcelona. Iñigo took all the precautions not to cross or follow the papal route at any point, lest he should find in the papal retinue acquaintances who might recognize him. He wished his plans to remain secret, at any cost. His tactics consisted in forestalling the arrival of the papal cortège which left Vitoria on March 12 and halted at Nájera on March 15.

48 Leturia, *El gentilhombre*, p. 233.

Chapter 3

THE PILGRIM AT MONTSERRAT

1. *The Road to the Holy Mountain*

Iñigo set out from Loyola at the end of February, 1522, mounted on his mule. One of his brothers, whom he does not mention by name, chose to accompany him as far as Oñate. This must have been the rector of the church of Azpeitia, Pero López de Oñaz. Iñigo persuaded him to make a stop at Aránzazu, where he intended to make a prayer vigil before the venerated image of the Virgin. Years later, in a letter to Francis Borgia, Ignatius would recollect the graces received in the memorable vigil. It is probable that he pronounced a vow of perpetual chastity on this occasion. All he said is that he had made it on his way to Montserrat, and that he had offered it to the Blessed Virgin, unaware — as already Laínez remarked — that vows are made directly to God. This circumstance does add credibility to the hypothesis that the vow was made at a Marian shrine, and he seems to have visited no other than Aránzazu before he reached Montserrat. The one thing certain is that our Lady took him under her special protection, for — as the same Laínez points out — "whereas he had hitherto been attacked and overcome by the vice of the flesh, henceforth from then till now God has given him the gift of chastity and, as I think, in the highest degree."[1]

At Anzuola, where he bade farewell to his sister Magdalena, or at Oñate he took leave of his brother, and alone he made for Navarrete in La Rioja. He wished to say goodbye to his protector, the duke of Nájera, and also to recover "a few ducats owed to him in the duke's household." For this he wrote out a statement of his claim for the duke's steward; but that official replied that he had no money on hand. That this was not an evasion can be understood from what has

[1] *Epistola P. Lainii*, no. 5, in FN, I, 76.

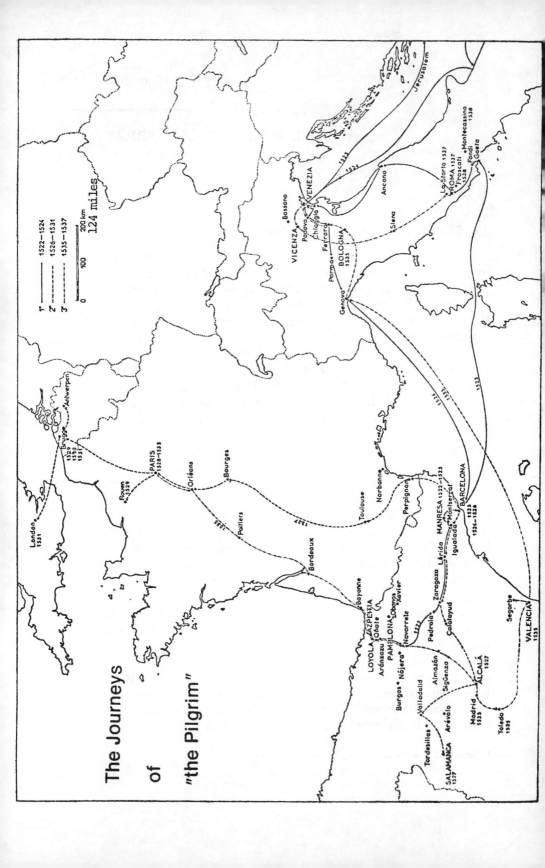

The Journeys

of

"the Pilgrim"

1* 1522—1524
2 1526—1531
3 1535—1537

0 100 200 km
124 miles

been said about the financial straits of the duke of Nájera at the time. The duke, hearing of this, said that "money might indeed be wanting to pay all others, but there is no lack of it for a Loyola, to whom he desired to give a good lieutenancy in consideration of his past services, if he cared to accept it." On receiving the money, Iñigo directed that part of it should be shared out "among some people to whom he felt an obligation, and the rest spent on the repair and decoration of an image of our Lady which had been long neglected."[2] From Navarrete he rode on towards Montserrat, anticipating by eight days the retinue of the pope.

From the region of La Rioja the road went through Tudela, Pedrola, Zaragoza, Lérida, Cervera, and Igualada. During the long hours of his peregrination, his thought went up constantly to God and the deeds he fancied he would achieve in his service. As he had little understanding of humility, charity, patience, or of the discretion necessary for the exercise of these virtues, all his attention concentrated on the great penances he had in mind to perform, thus using them as a measure of sanctity. There was, however, a special circumstance, that although he deeply detested his sins, in undertaking corporal penances he did not think so much of his sins as of performing great external austerities, since in this way the saints had acted for the glory of God.

An episode interrupted the tranquillity of his journey. On the road he was overtaken by a Moor, mounted like himself on a mule. The two wayfarers entered into conversation and fell to discussing our Lady's virginity. The Moor readily agreed that Mary could have been a virgin before Christ's birth, but he could not believe that she could have remained a virgin in giving birth. In spite of the many arguments to the contrary which the pilgrim urged, the Moor remained unconvinced, and suddenly leaving his fellow traveler, he went his own way so quickly that he was soon out of sight. Upon finding himself alone, Iñigo was struck by this doubt: Had he done everything in his power to defend Mary's virginity? Here there came into play, as he himself states,

2 *Autobiog*, no. 13.

"some motions which were producing discontentment in his soul, as it seemed to him that he had not done his duty." Thus "desires came upon him to go in search of the Moor and give him a few stabs of his dagger because of what he had said."[3] For a long time he remained in doubt about what he ought to do. The solution he found was to give free rein to the mule up to a fork where one road led to a neighboring village, probably Pedrola, where the Moor was going, and the other was the highway. It pleased God that, although the road to the neighboring village was broad and in better condition, the animal kept to the highway, and Iñigo saw no more of the Moor. With this the pilgrim's conscience remained at ease.

On arriving at a large town before Montserrat — the place seems to be Igualada — he bought a length of hemp-linen, such as is used in the making of sacks, and had a pilgrim's tunic tailored from it; he also bought a pair of *esparteñas* or rope-soled sandals. Of these he put on only the one for the right foot, which was the one that had remained more sensitive from the wound he received. This leg was still completely bandaged, and in spite of this and though he was riding, he found it swollen every night.

2. His Vigil of New Arms at the Shrine of the Black Virgin

Finally he reached the goal of his Marian pilgrimage, Montserrat. The exact day we do not know. The only date of which we are certain is that of the night vigil before the altar of the Virgin, carried out between March 24 and 25. The vigil was preceded by his confession, which took three days. Accordingly, the arrival must have occurred, at the latest, on March 21. Probably it was a day or so earlier.

Pilgrimages to the mountain of Montserrat were very popular in those days. Hence Iñigo had conceived the idea of undertaking it, all the more so because the celebrated sanctuary lay on the route he had to follow on his way to Barcelona,

3 *Autobiog,* no. 15.

the port of embarkation for Rome, where he had to request the pope's permission to proceed on his pilgrimage to Jerusalem. Besides placing his plans and uncertain future in the hands of the Blessed Virgin, as he had already done at Aránzazu, he intended to clothe himself there with the arms of his new spiritual warfare, in the fashion of young knights who entered upon the service of earthly warfare. This investiture ceremony was always preceded by a night vigil, during which the would-be knight stood watch over his arms. This was prescribed in the Seven Laws (*Siete partidas*) of King Alfonso X the Wise, and Iñigo had seen it practiced in the books of chivalry.

Before keeping the vigil he wanted to purify his soul by a general confession of his entire life. His confessor was a French monk of the Benedictine monastery who was at the disposal of the pilgrims. His name was Jean Chanon. This monk was the first person to whom Iñigo revealed his plans, which he had kept secret till then. The confessor must have put in Iñigo's hands one of the confession manuals in use at the time for the benefit of penitents. It is probable that, either then or on subsequent occasions, Chanon initiated Iñigo in the methods of prayer, having him read the *Exercises for the Spiritual Life (Ejercitatorio de la vida espiritual)*, composed by the reformer of that monastery, García Jiménez de Cisneros (the famous cardinal's cousin), and printed in the same monastery in the year 1500. To make sure that the confession was more complete, he put it down in writing and took three days over it.

On the eve of the feast of the Annunciation of our Lady, March 25, he went in search of a ragged tramp, and divesting himself of his rich garments, he handed them over to the astonished but delighted man. He put on the pilgrim tunic he had bought. Thus attired, he observed his vigil of arms at the feet of the Black Virgin, now standing, now on his knees, spending the whole night in prayer.

Chapter 4

MANRESA, IÑIGO'S PRIMITIVE CHURCH

In his *Autobiography* Iñigo tells us that "he left Montserrat at daybreak in order that he might not be recognized and took, not the direct road to Barcelona, on which he might encounter people acquainted with him and prepared to honor him, but a side road leading to a town named Manresa. For he desired to stay for a few days in a hospital of that town and also to write some things in his book, which he carefully carried with him and from which he derived much consolation."[1]

This explicit statement removes all possible doubt about the date when he walked down from the holy mountain and the destination to which he directed his steps. Less clear are the reasons for his diversion to Manresa and, above all, for his prolonged stay in the town by the river Cardoner. He speaks of his fear of meeting persons who might recognize him. As far as we know, he had no friends in Catalonia. Clearly, therefore, he was alluding to persons who formed part of the retinue of the new Pope, Adrian VI, among whom there must have been officials of the court of Castile known to Iñigo. In fact, this danger was rather remote. For, as we have seen, he reached Manresa on March 25, whereas the papal cortège was still at Zaragoza on the 29th of the same month.

1. Why Did Iñigo Prolong His Stay in Manresa?

His immediate plan was to withdraw to Manresa for a few days "in order to note some things in his book." Without doubt, he was referring to the lights he had received at Montserrat. He intended to remain "a few days," but these became some eleven months. Why? As he has left us no clear statement on

1 *Autobiog,* no. 18.

this point, we must have recourse to conjectures. One reason may have been the plague, cases of which were then recorded in the principality of Catalonia and which led the authorities of Barcelona to ban the entry of foreigners into the city. We know of some such proclamations, one of them on May 2, 1522, that is, a little more than a month after Iñigo's arrival at Manresa. At the end of the few days he had intended to stay in this city, he may have encountered difficulties in entering Barcelona to board a ship.

There is another probable reason. If we remember that the pilgrimage to Jerusalem could be realized only within a limited period of the year, we may think that Ignatius missed the opportunity of undertaking it during that year 1522. For intending pilgrims required the permission of the pope. He granted this to them at Easter, which that year fell on April 20. A few days of delay at Manresa, added to the longer wait at Barcelona before he could arrange his sea passage to Rome, may have made it impossible for him to reach the Eternal City in time. This consideration may have moved him to remain at Manresa. We know, besides, that the new pope did not reach Rome before August. Another influencing factor may have been the infirmities that afflicted Iñigo at Manresa, or simply the fact that he found there the conditions favorable for his life of prayer and penance. He had no need of haste now in pursuing his plans and could put off the pilgrimage for a later occasion.

In any case, and this is what matters most, Iñigo's stay at Manresa should be considered as providential. In the midst of interior trials and divine illuminations, Iñigo gradually went through a spiritual transformation, which culminated in the practice of the Exercises. In a felicitous expression, he spoke of Manresa as his "primitive church,"[2] alluding to the extraordinary fervor of that initial period, and possibly also to his first apostolic endeavors with the group of persons near him.

2. His Exterior Life

Iñigo's exterior manner of life was the one proper to a poor

---

2 A statement of Laínez, in *FN*, I, 140.

pilgrim. He was clad in his tunic of rough cloth (*paño burdo*), which won for him the nickname of "the sackcloth man" (*l'home del sac*), soon to be changed into one more meaningful, "the holy man" (*l'home sant*). At first he found lodging in the hospital of Santa Lucía, where the poor and the sick were brought. His habitual residence, however, was the Dominican friary. Here lived Galcerán Perelló, whom the Pilgrim chose as his confessor, though on occasion he treated matters of conscience with other priests too. When afflicted with severe illness (*enfermedades* "*muy recias*") he was charitably welcomed in the home of some benefactors. He himself tells us of the house of a certain Ferrer, whose son was later a servant of Baltasar de Faria, who was charged to carry on the affairs of the king of Portugal in Rome. The processes for Ignatius' beatification speak also of the houses of Amigant and Canyelles. From the same processes we learn that for his prayer he was wont to withdraw to one of the rocky caves carved out from the hillside sloping down to the river Cardoner.

Apart from his devotional practices, he employed himself in works of charity with the poor and the sick. His chief apostolate was that of conversation, which won for him the goodwill of the people of Manresa. He was keen on finding persons with whom he might converse on spiritual topics. But he did not find them either at Manresa or Barcelona. There was only a devout old woman, known as a servant of God throughout the region, who after conversing with the Pilgrim of Manresa, said to him: "May it please our Lord Jesus Christ to appear to you some day."[3] And he, taking the expression literally, was very much puzzled.

It is very likely that the Pilgrim went at times up to the monastery of Montserrat to confer on the things of the spirit with Jean Chanon, the monk to whom he had made his general confession. And one may well suppose that, in the course of these conversations, the devout Benedictine monk initiated him into the practice of methodical prayer. In any case, Montserrat was certainly the only religious center of methodical prayer with which Iñigo could have any contact

3 *Autobiog*, no. 21.

during this period. Ignatius did not mention the *Ejercitatorio* of Abbot García Jiménez de Cisneros among the books he read; but he did mention, and with the highest praise, the book of *The Imitation of Christ,* which many at the time attributed to Jean Gerson, the chancellor of the University of Paris, wherefore it was known in Spain as "el Gersoncito," just as we now call it "a Kempis." He liked the little book so much that from the day it came to his hands he did not look for any other spiritual book. He assimilated its teachings to such an extent that this could be said of him: In his words and actions he seemed to be "a Gerson carried into practice."[4] Even when he was general of the Society, on his desk he had only two books, the New Testament and *The Imitation of Christ,* which he used to call "the partridge among spiritual books."[5]

But God, more than men and books, was guiding him. He himself tells us that God "dealt with him as a schoolmaster deals with a child whom he is instructing."[6] In fact, he was so convinced of this that he thought he would offend God if he entertained any doubt about it.

3. The Three Periods of His Interior Development

The process of Iñigo's interior evolution during the eleven months of his stay in Manresa can be divided into three periods. The first was one of tranquillity, in which he maintained "one same interior state of great equanimity coupled with joy, without, however, any clear knowledge of interior spiritual things."[7] The second was characterized by a severe interior struggle with doubts and scruples. In the third period he received marvelous divine illuminations and composed the *Spiritual Exercises.*

During the first period there is only a little to point out. He lived on alms. He ate no meat and drank no wine even though they were offered to him, except on Sundays, when he interrupted his fast. His hair, which was abundant and

4 *Memoriale,* no. 226, in *FN,* I, 659; see also no. 97, in *FN,* I, 584.
5 *FN,* III, 431.
6 *Autobiog,* no. 27.
7 *Autobiog,* no. 20.

which until then he had arranged according to the fashion of those days, he now let grow as it would. He did not pare his fingernails or toenails, a matter in which he had previously been extremely fastidious. He heard Mass daily and attended the chanting of Vespers in the cathedral church (*la Seo*) or in the Dominican church, by which he was deeply consoled. During the Mass it was his custom to read the gospel story of the Passion. His principal occupation was prayer, to which he devoted seven hours each day, some of them during the night. In his conversations with others whom he met he tried to speak of spiritual things. The rest of the day he spent in things of God, reflecting on what he had meditated or read.

The even tenor of those first months was transformed, more or less suddenly, into a fearful interior battle. This doubt assailed him persistently, "What new type of life is this which you are now undertaking?"[8] It seemed to him, when compared with his earlier life, to have no meaning. Another violent thought worried him: "How can you bear this life for the remaining seventy years of your life?" But Iñigo recognized that this came from the enemy and he answered interiorly also with great strength: "Wretched being, can you promise me a single hour of life?"[9] And with that he overcame the temptation and remained in peace.

More anguishing and prolonged was his combat with scruples. His doubts were concerned with past confessions. Although he had with great diligence made a general confession at Montserrat and repeated his confessions at Manresa, he was besieged by doubts of having omitted some sin or of not having sufficiently explained those he had confessed. He made further confessions but did not recover his peace. A doctor of the cathedral advised him to write down all he could remember. This he did but to no avail. He states that after confession "the scruples still returned, each time in more detail, so that he became quite upset."[10] One day it occurred to him that the one efficacious remedy would be a prohibition

8 *Autobiog*, no. 21.
9 *Autobiog*, no. 22.
10 *Autobiog*, no. 22.

by his confessor against further confession of past matters. But he did not propose it, thinking that this remedy could not be valid, since it came from himself. One day, however, his confessor, of his own accord, bade him not to return to past matters, unless there was question of something very clear. This last exception rendered the whole remedy useless, since all those things seemed very clear to him.

In the midst of this anguishing situation he did not abandon his seven hours of prayer or the spiritual practices which he had adopted. One day, in a moment of great tribulation, he exclaimed in a loud voice: "Help me, O Lord, who find no help among men or in any creature. If I thought I could find it, no hardship would seem too great for me. Show me, Lord, where to find help; and if it be necessary for me to follow a puppy dog (*perrillo*) to get the remedy from it, I shall do so."[11]

His disturbance mounted at times to torturing anxiety, with impetuous temptations to commit suicide by throwing himself out through a large hole in his room. But realizing that to kill oneself was sinful, he cried aloud, "Lord, I will not do anything that offends you,"[12] and he repeated those words, as on the other occasion, many times.

One day he recalled his having read that a saint went without eating until he obtained a favor which he eagerly desired from God. A similar story is told about St. Andrew the Apostle and about St. Paul the Hermit. Iñigo may have had one of these examples in mind. He decided to follow their example and one Sunday after Communion he began his fast. He passed that whole week without taking a mouthful, but nevertheless continued his seven hours of prayer and other spiritual practices. But the following Sunday his confessor, informed by his penitent, ordered him to break his excessive fast.

What all his human efforts could not achieve, divine grace did. Suddenly he was delivered from these agonies of conscience. "In this way the Lord wished to awaken him as if from a dream.

11 *Autobiog*, no. 23.
12 *Autobiog*, no. 24.

As he already had, from the lessons which God had given him, some experience of the diversity of spirits, he began to look for the means through which that spirit had come. And in this way he made up his mind with great clarity not to confess anything from the past anymore. From that day forward he remained free of those scruples and held for certain that our Lord through his mercy had wished to deliver him."[13]

The cure from the scruples was, therefore, a fruit of the discernment of spirits which, already during his convalescence at Loyola, had been the foundation of Iñigo's conversion. That terrible ordeal had served to complete the work of his purification and to transform Iñigo into a master experienced in the art of curing scruples. For there is no doubt that the "Rules toward Perceiving and Understanding Scruples and Persuasions of Our Enemy" of the *Exercises*,[14] which have returned peace of soul to so many, owe their origin to the personal experience of Iñigo himself.

The third period of his stay at Manresa was characterized by spiritual consolations and divine illuminations. The object on which these focused varied considerably. He used to pray daily to the Blessed Trinity. One day, as he was reciting the Hours of our Lady on the steps of the Dominican church, "his understanding began to be elevated so that, as it were, he saw the Most Holy Trinity under the figure of three organ keys (*en figura de tres teclas*), and that with so many tears and sobs that he could not control himself. He took part that same morning in a procession which set out from that church, and throughout the whole time he was unable to restrain his tears until the dinner hour; and even after the repast he could not stop talking about the Most Holy Trinity, and that with many and various comparisons."[15] For the rest of his life he experienced a great devotion to the mystery of the Trinity, of which he has left us moving testimonies in his *Spiritual Diary*.

"On one occasion, there was represented in his understanding, with great spiritual joy, the manner in which God had

13 *Autobiog*, no. 25.
14 *SpEx*, [345-351].
15 *Autobiog*, no. 28.

created the world.''[16] Another intellectual vision consisted in his seeing clearly how Jesus Christ was present in the Most Holy Sacrament. On many occasions he saw with his interior eyes the humanity of Christ and his figure, which appeared to him as a white body, without the members appearing distinctly. He saw this at Manresa many times, and again on his pilgrimage to Jerusalem, and once more on a journey near Padua. Many times too he saw our Lady, under a similar form, without members appearing distinctly.

All those divine illuminations confirmed him in his faith so strongly that "he often thought to himself: Even if there were no Scripture which teaches us these truths, he would be ready to die for them solely on the strength of what he had seen."[17]

4. The Illumination beside the Cardoner

Among Iñigo's experiences there was one which had a special repercussion in his soul and enormously transformed his whole future. This is what has come to be known as his "outstanding illumination" (*eximia ilustración*). He himself gives us this account:

"One day, he was going out of devotion to a church which stood just over a mile from Manresa and which, I believe, is called St. Paul's. The road ran next to the river. On his way, occupied with his devotions, he sat down for a little while with his face toward the river, which there ran deep. As he sat there, the eyes of his understanding began to open. It was not that he saw some vision, but he understood and knew many things, spiritual things as well as things about faith and learning. This was accompanied by an enlightenment so great that all of them appeared to him to be new. It is impossible to explain the details which he understood then, although they were many, except that he received a great clarity in his understanding. This was such that in the whole course of his life, through sixty-two years, if he gathered together all the helps he had received from God and all the things he had known,

16 *Autobiog*, no. 29, "Second."
17 *Autobiog*, no. 29, "Fourth."

and added them together, he does not think that he received as much as he did on that one occasion." In a marginal note his trustworthy secretary, Gonçalves da Câmara, added this clarification, which he had heard from Ignatius' own lips: "This experience was so profound that his understanding remained illuminated, so that he seemed to himself to be another person and had an intellect other than he had before."[18] Ignatius' last words are sufficiently clear to reveal to us all the magnitude of the grace he received.

In regard to the precise place where this outstanding illumination took place, Iñigo tells us only that it was on the road leading to the church of St. Paul. This church could be reached either by the left bank of the river or by a road following the ridge of the hill. It seems more likely that the road in question here was the second one, from which it can be truly said that the river runs deep below for anyone stopping to gaze at it. By the side of this road stood the Cross of Tort, to which Ignatius refers after relating the illumination, when he says "and after this had lasted for a good while, he went to kneel before a nearby cross to give thanks to God."[19] From here one has a beautiful and inspiring view of the region, with the serrated silhouette of Montserrat on the horizon.

As he himself explicitly states, there is question, not of a vision, but of an intellectual illumination. Its object was not any particular mystery of the faith. Rather, it was an opening of the eyes of the understanding, so that "he understood and knew many things, spiritual things as well as things about faith and learning." The enlightenment was such "that all these things appeared to him to be altogether new." That is to say, he emerged from the experience completely transformed in his interior self. Striking indeed is his emphatic affirmation that when all the graces he had received in his life up to that moment are taken together, at a time when he calculated that he was more than sixty-two years old, he had not received from God as much as he did on that one occasion alone.[20]

18 *Autobiog*, no. 30, "Fifth," in *FN*, I, 404.
19 *Autobiog*, no. 31.
20 *Autobiog*, no. 30, "Fifth."

Since we know the mystical graces he received from the Lord in the course of his life, we can describe that grace received in Manresa as truly extraordinary.

It was indeed particularly unusual—and perhaps Ignatius was alluding to this—because of the transcending effect it had for the future not only of his own interior life but also for that of the Society. Beyond any doubt, he was alluding to this illumination when, in reply to questions about his new Institute, he said that he could respond "because of something which happened to me at Manresa."[21] With good reason, therefore, did Câmara—to whom Ignatius expressed his confidences—comment on this statement by saying that at Manresa the Lord showed to him many of the things which he later ordained in the Society. On this some have based an attirmation that on that occasion Ignatius was given a foreknowledge (*prenoción*) of the Institute of the Society. Later events do not confirm this opinion, for many years after Manresa we see Ignatius uncertain of his distant future. As Nadal tells us, "he was being led gently towards something he himself did not know,"[22]—the foundation of a new religious order. It was only when he saw his plans for the pilgrimage to Jerusalem with his Paris companions thwarted by circumstances, and after protracted deliberations within this whole group, that he decided to undertake the new foundation.

What can be said is that in his Cardoner enlightenment Iñigo saw the new course his life was to take. He was no longer to be the solitary pilgrim who in prayer and penance endeavored to imitate the example of the saints, but from now onward he would devote himself to laboring for the good of the neighbor, to seeking companions who would join him in this enterprise and with whom he would form an apostolic body. Therefore without having a precise vision of what he had to do with the passing of the years, he gradually oriented himself toward the realization of what was to be his life's mission. In this sense it is correct to relate the foundation of the Society of Jesus with the great illumination of Manresa. This vision of

21 *Memoriale,* no. 137, in *FN,* I, 610.
22 *FN,* II, 252, no. 17.

the future will also have to be related with the meditations on the Kingdom of Christ and the Two Standards. Their origin must be placed within the period of Manresa, and witnesses as authorative as Jerónimo Nadal have asserted their relationship to the founding of the Society of Jesus.[23]

5. The Spiritual Exercises

One fruit of Iñigo's prolonged experiences in meditation on spiritual things and of the special illumination of the Holy Spirit was the book of the *Spiritual Exercises*. According to the unanimous account of witnesses, he wrote these Exercises at Manresa after he had experienced them in his own self. However, he did not write them all at one time just as they have come down to us. Rather, he kept on correcting and completing them, in accordance with his experiences, up to his days in Paris and Rome.

It is surprising that Ignatius, who in his *Autobiography* related some episodes of his life at Manresa in so much detail, such as that about his scruples, said nothing about the composition of the *Exercises*. Only at the end of his autobiographical account, and at the request of his confidant Gonçalves da Câmara, did he make a brief but compact declaration on this point: "After he had recounted these things to me," writes Câmara, on October 20, [1555], I asked the Pilgrim about the *Exercises* and the *Constitutions*, as I wished to know how he had drawn them up. He answered that he had not composed the *Exercises* all at one time, but that he put into writing some things that he had observed in his soul and found useful and thought they might be helpful also to others; for example, the method of examination of conscience with the form of the lines and the like. He spoke to me especially about the elections, that he had drawn them from that variety of spirits and thoughts which he had had at Loyola, while he was still convalescing from his leg. He told me he would speak about the *Constitutions* that evening.[24]

23 *FN*, I, 307.
24 *Autobiog*, no. 99. As a matter of editorial policy, throughout the present book *Spiritual Exercises* (in italics) refers chiefly to Ignatius' published book, and Spiritual Exercises (in roman, but capitalized) indicates chiefly the making

Two fundamental facts can be deduced from this brief declaration: First, the *Exercises* were the fruit of a prolonged period of elaboration; and second, Ignatius practiced them himself before he put them down in writing.

If Iñigo's first experience was that of the variety of the spirits which he perceived during his long convalescence, we must agree that the *Exercises* had their first origin at Loyola. There is question, we remember, of that alternation of motions which he experienced when, on the one hand, he felt himself attracted toward worldly ideals, and on the other towards the imitation of the examples of the saints whose lives he was reading. But the principal experiences, and above all the work of writing them down in the book that would be the *Exercises*, are chiefly the work of the months at Manresa. Diego Laínez, whose testimony is most authoritative, tells us that it was at Manresa that the book of the *Exercises* was written, at least "in its substance."[25] Polanco adds that there the Lord taught him the meditations which we call the *Spiritual Exercises* and the manner of going about them, although later on use and experience of many things made him improve on his first draft; further, that just as they had brought about a great transformation in his own soul, so he desired by means of them to help other persons."[26]

Attending to the trustworthy testimony of these contemporaries, we can state that from the period at Manresa come the fundamental meditations of the four Weeks, and the linking of them together into an order aimed at the attainment of the end of the Exercises, which is "to overcome oneself and to order one's life, without making one's decision through some affection which is disordered."[27] From Manresa, too, came the two examinations of conscience, the particular examination which Iñigo will teach from the beginning of

of the Exercises in a period of retreat. Since the book is intended as a guide to practice, the two usages often overlap. On this, see *ConsSJComm*, p. 357. For the similar problem with *Constitutions* and Constitutions, see ibid., pp. 356-357 and fn. 3 in ch. 17, below on pp. 233-234.

25 *FN*, I 82.
26 *PolSum*, no. 24, in *FN*, I, 163.
27 *SpEx* [21].

his apostolate, and the general examination which entails the moral norms for distinguishing between mortal and venial sin. Because of the experience in the discernment of spirits which Iñigo had possessed ever since his days at Loyola and which was confirmed at Manresa, we must assign to this period the rules on discernment which are more suitable for the First Week of the Exercises. All of this was still in a rudimentary form, such as could be seen and read a few years later, when at Salamanca the Pilgrim turned over to Bachelor Sancho Gómez de Frías "all his papers, which were the Exercises, for examination."[28]

6. The First Exercitant

Iñigo de Loyola himself was the first exercitant. The *Exercises* which he wrote were the fruit of his personal experiences at Manresa. He put them in writing to help others, by communicating to them the ideas and sentiments which had transformed him. For those persons who will decide to put them into practice in their entirety and are fit for this, he will prescribe a month of intense activity, with four or five hours of meditation daily, and also the examinations and reflections. The whole program is to be regulated by very precise norms—in his terminology, "annotations" (introductory observations), "additions" (additional directives), and "rules" (directives), all aimed at obtaining the greatest fruit possible. Ignatius does not tell us when he himself made the Exercises, but we have reasons to believe that he did this during his last tranquil months at Manresa.

We do not know with certitude the sequence through which Iñigo experienced the various themes of the *Exercises* in himself. In the realm of conjecture, we can suppose that, along general lines, the sequence was pretty much what he left us in writing.

His soul was well prepared to receive the lights from the Lord. At Montserrat he had purified himself with a general confession that lasted three days. At Manresa the frightful trial of scruples had completed this work of purification. His

28 *Autobiog*, no. 67.

soul was now in peace. He could devote himself in all tranquillity to the consideration of divine things.

From the days of his convalescence at Loyola his constant search was to put order into his life. He now realized that the first thing necessary was to know the purpose for which he had been created. What mattered most of all was to fulfil God's designs for him. To do God's will it was necessary, above all, to know it. The obstacle was to be found in the "disordered affections" which obscure the eyes of the mind and drag the will toward sin. He would have to fight against these disordered affections, and for this he would have to overcome himself. This was the end to which the *Exercises* would be a help, and their title synthesizes their whole content: "Spiritual Exercises to overcome oneself and to order one's life without making one's decision through some affection which is disordered."[29]

The work he was going to undertake demanded a generous and decisive will. Iñigo entered upon the Exercises "with great courage and generosity toward his Creator and Lord."[30]

Before all else, he placed before his eyes God's plan of creation: "Man is created to praise, reverence, and serve God our Lord, and by this means to save his soul."[31] The things of this world should help him toward attaining this end. Hence it follows that "he should make use of them in as far as they help him toward this end, and he ought to rid himself of them in as far as they impede him from it."[32] The truths of the Principle and Foundation are an orientation for the exercitant and a prologue giving light for the activities to be presented in the course of the Exercises—to such an extent that it is difficult to suppose that a document so important does not come from Manresa, at least in a rudimentary draft.[33] Aided by the

---

29 *SpEx*, [21]
30 Annotation 5, *SpEx*, [5].
31 Principle and Foundation, *SpEx*, [23].
32 Ibid.
33 *Exercitia spiritualia: Textuum antiquissimorum nova editio*, edited by J. Calveras and C de Dalmases, in MI of MHSJ (Rome, 1969), pp. 31-32, 426.

experience and studies of later years, Iñigo will succeed in giving it the perfect and harmonious formulation it now has.

In confrontation with God's plans arises the creature's rebellion, sin. Iñigo reviewed in his mind the course of his life, recalling the sins committed from year to year, the houses where he had lived, his dealings with others, the offices he had exercised. Two feelings overpowered his soul, shame and sorrow: shame for the loathsomeness of his sins, sorrow for having offended God. But the result was not despair. "Imagine Christ our Lord present before you on the cross, and begin a colloquy with him. Ponder how it is that from being Creator he has come to make himself man, and to pass from eternal life to death here in time, that thus he might die for my sins. I shall also reflect upon myself and ask: What have I done for Christ? What am I doing for Christ? What ought I to do for Christ?"[34] Iñigo's life will be an answer to this interrogation.

Another meditation on sins comes to a climax with a "colloquy of mercy,"[35] a confident and loving recourse to God's mercy, the sinner's only refuge.

From this first division or "Week" of the Exercises Iñigo emerged as one already inflamed with love for Jesus Christ viewed as liberator and redeemer. Not only will he not offend him again; he will endeavor also to follow him. Christ appears before him as a king, whom he must obey and serve with greater loyalty than he has shown to the lords of the world. Jesus calls him for a great enterprise, the restoration of lost mankind. To him sanctity appears as the conquest of a kingdom, to be won by the victory over all enemies of God's plans. Iñigo knew these enemies well, for he had been vanquished by them more than once. They are sensuality and carnal and worldly love.[36] Iñigo resolves to participate in this campaign with the utmost generosity. He will have only to follow the

34 *SpEx*, [53].
35 *SpEx*, [61].
36 *SpEx*, [97].

examples of Jesus, who will walk before him. His earnest desire will be to know Christ intimately in order to love him more and follow him. Meditating on the gospel scenes from the incarnation to the passion and resurrection of Jesus, he penetrated deeply into the divine Master's "intentions," that is, into his spirit and his principles, diametrically opposed to those of the world: poverty and humility against covetousness and pride.[37] He will find everything summarized in the sermon on the mount, in which Jesus taught his beatitudes to the world. Iñigo will embrace actual poverty and humiliations in order to imitate Christ poor and humiliated, thus enlisting himself under his banner. He will follow Christ in his passion and death in order to have part also in the glory of his resurrection.[38]

At the close of his Exercises, Iñigo has successfully resolved the problem of his life. The service of God will be his ideal, Jesus Christ his model, the wide world his field of action. For from this moment he will no longer be the solitary pilgrim totally given to meditation and penance, but he will devote all his strength to "the help of souls," that is, to helping men to the fulfillment of their end.

We can suppose that before leaving Manresa Iñigo paid a farewell visit to the *Seo*, the Dominican church, and the shrines (*ermitas*) where he had spent hours of devout prayer. It is probable that he climbed also to Montserrat to bid farewell to the Black Virgin and the Benedictine monks. To his Manresan friends he left the little he had: his wooden begging bowl, the rope girdle, and his pilgrim sackcloth. In exchange he was taking away the unforgettable memory of all he had received in that Catalan town. He had come here as a penitent and recent convert. He was now departing transformed into a spiritual man, launched upon the great enterprises for the greater glory of God to which he was destined, the germ of which was now incorporated into the *Exercises* he had made and written at Manresa. With the passing of time, the name of

---

37 Introduction to Considering States of Life, *SpEx*, [135; see also 142, 146].
38 See, e.g., *SpEx*, [97, 98, 167, 168, 261-312].

Manresa will remain universally linked with the memory of St. Ignatius. Thousands of visitors will flock to pray at the *Santa Cueva,* and Manresa will be the name of many a house of prayer and retreats throughout the world.

Chapter 5

IN THE FOOTSTEPS OF JESUS

"The time was drawing near that he had set for his departure for Jerusalem. Therefore, at the beginning of the year 1523 he left for Barcelona to take ship."[1] Thus writes the Pilgrim in his *Autobiography*. The only purpose of his journey to Barcelona was to embark for Italy. The timing was conditioned by the feast of Easter, during which pilgrims were accustomed to ask the pope's permission for their Jerusalem pilgrimage. That year Easter fell on April 5. According to the best calculations, Iñigo left Manresa on or near February 18 of that year of 1523.

1. A Stay in Barcelona

The Pilgrim entered Barcelona by the Puerta Nueva. Advancing along the streets called Puerta Nueva and Carders, he came to the Plaza de Marcús, where he made a brief delay to pray before the image of our Lady of the Way (*de la Guía*). Continuing along the calle de Corders, the Plaza de la Lana, and the calle de la Boria, he turned left along the calle de Febrers—today called calle de San Ignacio—where Inés Pascual had her home and shop. In the house of this benefactress of his he found hospitality for those days, and again during his second sojourn in Barcelona. Unfortunately, this house stands there no longer, as it was demolished in 1853 when the calle de la Princesa was opened.

Iñigo spent in Barcelona a little more than twenty days, the time required to arrange his sea passage to Rome. But he could not remain idle. As at Manresa, he was eager to find persons with whom he might converse on spiritual topics. From the process of his beatification we know that he visited the monastery of the Hieronymite nuns, dedicated to St.

1 *Autobiog*, nos. 34, 35.

Matthias and situated then in Padró square. On the outskirts of the city and at the valley of Hebron, there was a monastery of Hieronymite monks, of which some ruins still remain today. There also he went, as well as to some neighboring shrines (*ermitas*) scattered around San Ginés dels Agudells, for his same purpose of conversation. But we now know that his efforts to find spiritual persons here were but partially successful, as little as at Manresa.

One day in the church of San Justo he was sitting among the children near the choir steps, listening to the preaching of the word of God, when a lady named Isabel Ferrer, the wife of Juan Roser or Rosell, saw the face of the Pilgrim aglow with light. As she gazed, she perceived an inner voice telling her: "Call him, call him." After the sermon when she returned to her home, situated on the same square of San Justo and in front of the church, Isabel told her husband what she had seen. They decided to invite the devout Pilgrim to their home. After dinner they asked him to speak of things of God. From that day Isabel became so fond of the Pilgrim that she became his greatest benefactor in Barcelona, Paris, and Venice. Later, after the foundation of the Society, this attachment of Isabel to Ignatius issued into events which we shall relate at the proper time, in Chapter 18 below.

In his conversation he spoke of his projected voyage to Rome, mentioning that he intended to sail on a brigantine. They tried to dissuade him to take another larger ship, which one of their kinsmen intended to board. The Pilgrim took their advice; and it was providential that he did, for the brig went down a little after its departure from the port of Barcelona.

Iñigo had resolved to make his pilgrimage with the most absolute disregard of human means—alone and without any money. Many offered themselves as companions, but he courteously refused. To one who told him that, since he knew neither Latin nor Italian, it was rash for him to travel without a companion, he replied that even if he had the son or the brother of the duke of Cardona for a fellow passenger, he would not accept him. For his desire was to have three virtues:

faith, hope, and charity. A companion, if he had one, would come to his aid in hunger; and he would expect the companion to pick him up if he should fall. And this trust in creatures was what he wished to place in God alone.[2] For the same reason he wanted to embark without any provisions. But on this point he found himself obliged to yield in part. For, although the shipmaster gave him a free passage, he set the condition that he should bring with him the provisions of "ship's biscuit to maintain himself, and that otherwise by no way in the world would they receive him."[3] Now strong doubts came upon him. "Is this the hope and faith you had in God, that he would not fail you?"[4] He doubted much about what he ought to do. Finally, not knowing how to escape from that conflict, he decided to put himself in the hands of his confessor. He counseled Iñigo to beg what was necessary and take it with him on the ship.

And here is a curious anecdote from Iñigo's own account. As the Pilgrim begged help of a lady, she asked him the destination for which he was embarking. He doubted whether he had to tell her. At last he told her only that he was going to Rome. To this she replied: "So you would go to Rome? Why, those who go there, I do not know what they are when they return,"—meaning to say—Iñigo remarks—that those who go to Rome get little spiritual profit from it.[5] The reason why he doubted about revealing his plans to go to Jerusalem was his fear of vainglory, a temptation which haunted him so much during this period that he would never risk mentioning from what country he came or to what family he belonged. This indicates that his family was known even outside the Basque country.

Finally, having collected his rations, he went to the harbor to embark. But before going on board he discovered that he had some pieces of copper (*blancas*). He decided to leave these on a bench near the seashore.

2 *Autobiog*, no. 35.
3 Ibid.
4 *Autobiog*, no. 36.
5 Ibid.

2. **Toward Rome**

On or about March 20, Iñigo embarked for the port of
Gaëta. With a strong wind behind it, the ship completed the
crossing in five days and nights, in spite of the stormy weather
which all on board had to bear. A new problem faced the
passengers as soon as they landed: Fear of the plague was
threatening in that part of Italy. But Iñigo immediately took
off on the road to Rome. Among the travelers who joined him
was a mother with her son and a daughter dressed in boy's
clothes. The four travelers spent the night in an inn. It was
crowded with soldiers, who gave them food and wine in abundance, "in such a way that they seemed to want to warm them
up." Then they placed the woman and her daughter in an
upper room, and left the Pilgrim and the boy in a stable. In
the middle of the night loud screams were heard from the
women; they were trying to defend themselves from attackers
trying to violate them. The Pilgrim rushed to their defense,
shouting: "Do we have to put up with this?" His intervention
was so effective that it left the aggresors defenseless and unable to
carry out their designs. That very night, the Pilgrim abandoned
the inn with the two women. The young lad had already fled.[6]

They reached a neighboring town which, from all the clues
available, must have been Fondi. They found the gates closed,
with no one to come to their help with alms. Thus Iñigo spent
a day outside, exhausted with weakness and the hardships
of the voyage. On the morrow, learning of the arrival of the
countess of the city, Countess Beatrice Appiani, wife of Vespa-
siano Colonna, Iñigo accosted her, and asked her for permission to enter the town. This was granted. He spent two days
there and then continued his journey toward Rome, which he
reached on March 29, Palm Sunday. He applied to the pope,
Adrian VI, for permission to make the pilgrimage to the
Holy Sepulchre and the other holy places. The permission
bore the date of March 31, 1523.[7]

3. *In Venice, Waiting to Sail*

The Pilgrim spent the whole of Holy Week, the feast of

6 *Autobiog*, no. 38.
7 *FD*, p. 290.

Easter, April 5, and its octave, in the Eternal City. On April 13 or 14 he set out for Venice, following the route that went to the shores of the Adriatic Sea. Then, along the coast, he passed through Pesaro, Rimini, and Ravenna, up to Comacchio and Chioggia, south of the Venetian lagoon. From here he had to make a detour to Padua in order to secure a certificate of health, necessary for his entrance into Venice. He started toward Padua in the company of other fellow travelers, but soon he could not keep up with the group "because they traveled at a rapid pace and they left him at nightfall in an open field." While he was alone there, "Christ appeared to him in the manner he usually appeared...and comforted him exceedingly."[8] This was an apparition similar to the ones he received at Manresa. Henceforth all went well with him. While his companions were escaping the difficulty of the certificate by forgery, no one asked the Pilgrim for his, and he entered Venice without it. The guards, coming to the boat, examined all the passengers one by one and left only him unquestioned.

Iñigo maintained himself in Venice by begging. He slept at night in the colonnaded porticoes (*"procuratie"*) that surround the Piazza of St. Mark. One day a wealthy Spanish gentleman came upon him and asked him where he was going and what for. Learning his plans, he invited the Pilgrim to remain in his home until the time of departure. There Iñigo put into practice a method of conversation which he had begun already at Manresa. During the meal he spoke little but fixed his attention on whatever was being discussed, in order to find an occasion to speak about God. "And as soon as the meal was over, he did so."[9] The good man (*hombre de bien*) and his whole family that had been his hosts took such a liking to him that they did not want to let him depart from their house.

4. Pilgrim to the Holy Land

The pilgrimage to the Holy Land was from very remote times a pious practice of Christian people, which gained a noteworthy increase in the fifteenth century and the begin-

8 *Autobiog*, no. 41.
9 *Autobiog*, no. 42.

ning of the sixteenth. As we have seen, one requisite for it was a special permission of the pope, which he granted in a document issued by himself or by an authorized prelate. All the details were determined: the time of year, the pilgrim garment, the price to be paid, the place for lodging. Ever since the Turks had mastered the Near East, the governing council (*signoria*) of Venice was authorized to organize one pilgrimage each year. The pilgrims from all quarters assembled at Venice by Pentecost and participated in the procession of the feast of Corpus Christi. As soon as they set foot on Palestinian soil they came under the jurisdiction of the Franciscan friars, who since the year 1342 were entrusted with the custody of the Holy Land. They took care of pilgrims' lodging and arranged their itineraries.

About Iñigo's pilgrimage of 1523 we have abundant first-hand information, thanks to the travel diaries kept by two of his companions: Peter Füssly, a bell-founder and artillery-caster of Zürich, and Philip Hagen of Strasbourg. The latter begins his account with this observation: Whoever desires to go to see the Holy Sepulchre must provide himself with three large bags, one well filled with ducats, *marcelli*, and *marchetti* (Venetian silver coins), another full of patience, and a third full of faith. In fact, as experience amply proved, the pilgrimage was a very costly affair, because of the fares for trips, provisions, lodging, guides, and the like. Still more necessary was patience and endurance to bear not only the inconveniences of the traveling, but also the harassment from Turks and Bedouins. Without a lively faith such annoyances would have been obviously unbearable. Iñigo without the first of these three bags, made abundant provision for the other two. He had no money to pay for his travels, and for his maintenance he had nothing more than the trust he had placed in God.

Usually the group of pilgrims was very numerous, but in that year of 1523 many of those who had assembled to take the ship at Venice turned their steps homeward on learning of the fall of Rhodes into the power of the Turks in 1522. Those who did embark numbered only twenty-one: four Spaniards, three Swiss, one Tyrolese, two Germans, and eleven

Flemings and Dutch. Iñigo mentions only one name in his account, that of the Spanish nobleman Diego Manes, commander of the Order of St. John, who was accompanied by a servant. The other Spaniard was a priest, and the fourth, Iñigo.

The first need was to find someone who would admit him to a ship for his voyage, since he had no money to pay the passage. Since he had decided to place all his trust in God, he did not wish to apply to Alonso Sánchez, the ambassador of the emperor in Venice. But the generous Spaniard who was his host procured for him an audience with the newly elected doge of Venice, Andrea Gritti. This official listened kindly to the Pilgrim and gave orders that he should be given a free passage on board the ship, which was about to take Nicola Dolfin, the recently chosen ambassador of Venice, to Cyprus. The ship's name was *Negrona*, and seven other pilgrims, besides Iñigo, embarked on it. The other thirteen had found accommodation in a pilgrim ship that sailed earlier.

Before embarking the Pilgrim suffered a misfortune: "A grave illness with fevers" afflicted him for some days. It subsided in time, but the ship was to leave on the day he had taken a purgative. His host asked the doctor if the man could sail in such circumstances. The doctor answered that "certainly he could if he wished to be buried at sea. But he embarked and sailed that day. He vomited so much that he found himself relieved and soon completely recovered."[10]

The *Negrona* weighed anchor on July 14, and after a few setbacks reached the harbor of Famagusta, Cyprus, on August 14. There the pilgrims on it made arrangements with the captain of the pilgrim ship that had preceded them, who for twenty ducats per head agreed to transport them to Joppa. From Famagusta they proceeded overland to Salinas, (Larnaca today), from which they were to sail. For his sustenance on it Iñigo brought no more than "the hope he had in God, just as he had done on the first ship."[11] During all this

10 *Autobiog*, no. 43.
11 *Autobiog*, no. 44.

time, in the midst of so many hardships, "our Lord appeared to him often and gave him great consolation and strength." All the twenty-one pilgrims set sail from Larnaca on August 19 and reached Joppa on the 25th of the same month; but they got the permission to land only on the 31st.

Mounted on their little donkeys, they reached Ramla, twenty kilometers south-east of Joppa, where they spent the night. About two miles before reaching Jerusalem, the Spaniard Diego Manes suggested that "all should recollect themselves interiorly and travel in silence."[12] The moment they came in sight of the Holy City, they experienced a transport of enthusiasm, typical of all pilgrims on that occasion. Iñigo says that that joy did not seem natural. As they entered the city, the Franciscans came to meet them with their processional cross held aloft. It was Friday, September 4.

5. *In the Land of Jesus*

It is easy to guess Iñigo's sentiments at this time. At long last he saw realized his dream of Loyola, when, while reading the *Life of Christ*, he had planned that pilgrimage. In his plans, however, there was not question of a passing pilgrimage. He had no intention of departing from there.

The itinerary followed by the pilgrims in their visits of the holy places was the traditional one. On the morning of September 5, after hearing Mass at the convent of Mount Zion, they walked in procession, with lighted candles, to the Cenacle, where they recalled the Last Supper and the coming of the Holy Spirit. Then they moved to the church of the Dormition of our Lady. In the afternoon they visited the Holy Sepulchre, where they spent the whole night in vigil. Before dawn they made their confession and received Communion. At six in the morning the basilica was closed, and the pilgrims had to go back to their hostel for rest. That afternoon they walked the Way of the Cross, with its clearly indicated stations, from the Tower Antonia to Calvary and the Holy Sepulchre.

On Monday the 7th, they visited Bethany and the Mount

12 *Autobiog*, no. 44.

of Olives. The 8th and 9th were dedicated to Bethlehem. The 10th and 11th they spent in the Valley of Jehoshaphat and, crossing the torrent Kidron, they visited the Garden of Gethsemane. The night of the 11th was spent once more at the Holy Sepulchre. The 12th and 13th were rest days. On the 14th they took the road down to Jericho and the river Jordan. The road was bad and strewn with stones. At the Jordan, all would have gladly bathed in those waters sanctified by the baptism of the Redeemer, but their Turkish guards made them hurry, so that some of them had time only to wash their face and hands. On their return to Jerusalem they passed by the foot of the mountain of the Savior's forty-day fast. The Swiss and Spaniards in the group wanted to climb to the top of the mountain where Jesus fasted and was tempted by the devil, but the guards did not allow them time to satisfy that devotion.

The week of September 16-22 they passed in Jerusalem. Iñigo devoted those days to preparing his plan to "remain in Jerusalem, continually visiting these holy places and, in addition to this devotion, to be of help to souls."[13] He approached the Franciscan guardian of Mount Zion, to reveal his plan to him and showed him some letters of recommendation which he carried with him. The guardian explained the need which the friars were suffering. For Iñigo, the reply was easy: He would ask nothing from the house, except that someone should occasionally hear his confession. At this reply the guardian softened his reluctance but added that the provincial had to be the one to give the last word, and at the time he was at Bethlehem.

The Pilgrim believed he had now obtained what he had so much desired. Waiting for the provincial's return, he took to writing letters to his friends in Barcelona. We know that he wrote to Inés Pascual, but unfortunately this letter has not come down to us.[14] In it we would have found details about Iñigo's pilgrimage and about his intimate sentiments on finding himself in the land of Jesus.

13 *Autobiog*, no. 45.
14 *FN*, I, 1-4.

The provincial's reply was not what the Pilgrim expected. He told Iñigo that, after consideration of the matter, he thought that he could not comply with his wishes. His experience with other pilgrims led him to take this decision. Some who had desired to remain behind had been taken as captives, and others had been killed. Such a danger was not one to frighten a man as decisive as Iñigo. However, in the face of the Pilgrim's insistence, the provincial remained adamant, and told him that he could excommunicate him if he should stay without his permission. He indicated his readiness to show him the papal bulls giving him this authority. Then Iñigo had to surrender, seeing that this was God's will. There was nothing else for him to do but to make the return journey with the other pilgrims.

But before his departure he was seized with a strong desire to visit once more the Mount of Olives. Without informing anyone and without a guide, "he stole away from the others and went alone to the Mount of Olives. The guards would not let him enter, so he gave them a penknife from the writing-case he had with him. Then, after praying with deep consolation, he felt a desire to go to Bethphage. While there he remembered that he had not carefully noted on Mount Olivet the precise direction of the right foot and the left. So back he went and, I believe, he gave his scissors to the sentries this time, to move them to let him enter."[15]

When the friars discovered that the Pilgrim was missing, they took steps to find him and sent a servant to search for him. When he found Iñigo he threatened him with a cane; and making angry gestures amid signs of great anger, he gripped him by the arm and escorted him back to the convent. At that point the memory of Jesus came upon Iñigo, and "it seemed to him that he was seeing Christ above himself continually. This experience lasted in great abundance till they reached the monastery."[16]

6. The Return to Venice and Barcelona

On September 23, about two hours before midnight, the

15 *Autobiog*, no. 47.
16 *Autobiog*, no. 48.

pilgrims took the road to Ramla, which they reached about eleven o'clock the following morning, hungry and exhausted by their lack of sleep and fatigue. But all their troubles were not yet over. The governor of the town demanded from each pilgrim one ducat and one coat. They had to remain there for several days, in an unhealthy place made worse by the scarcity of drinkable water. Some of them fell ill. Finally on October 1 the governor gave them the order to depart.

The pilgrim ship sailed from the harbor of Joppa on October 3. The shipmaster had not laid in sufficient provisions and they began to fall short, more and more as the voyage dragged out through failure of the wind. Several passengers took ill and one of them died. It was October 14 when they disembarked at Larnaca in Cyprus.

The problem now facing the pilgrims was finding a ship to continue their voyage to Venice. The *Negrona* had departed some ten days earlier without waiting for them. Three other vessels remained. One, a large ship, belonged to the Contarini family, rich Venetian shipowners. The shipmaster was asking fifteen ducats per passenger. Diego Manes and his companion agreed to the price. Diego furthermore recommended the captain to give Iñigo a free passage, stating that he was not able to pay but was worthy of it because he was a saint. The captain replied with a sneer: "If he is a saint, he should go as St. James did, or in some way similar."[17] Other pilgrims, among them Füssly and the other Swiss, got a passage at a lower rate on another ship called *Malipiera*. Iñigo embarked, probably, on a *marana*, a type of ship used in Venice both for commerce and for war. He tells us only that he was admitted by the captain of a very small ship. During these days of waiting at Cyprus, the pilgrims made visits about the island. Among other places, they visited the church of the Franciscans at Nicosia.

At the beginning of November, the small vessel that carried Iñigo made to sea, as did also the other two ships. Iñigo calls

---

17 *Autobiog*, no. 49. According to a legend, St. James was miraculously transported to Spain.

one "the great ship" and the other "that of the Turks". They sailed one morning with a favorable wind, but in the evening a violent tempest struck. As a result, the great ship was wrecked on the coast of Cyprus and only the passengers were saved. The Turkish ship perished with all aboard. The small ship, however, on which Iñigo was traveling, had a hard time of it, but finally made port, a harbor of Apulia on the Adriatic, late in December. It was now mid-winter and bitterly cold, with snow falling "and the Pilgrim was clothed only in rough knee-breeches and shoes with bare legs; his doublet of coarse stuff was open and in rags on his shoulders, and he wore a threadbare coat."[18]

They reached Venice in mid-January, 1524. There Iñigo was welcomed by that Spanish gentlemen who had lodged him in his own house before he undertook the pilgrimage. He gave him fifteen or sixteen *giulii*—a coin worth one tenth of a ducat, so called after Pope Julius II who minted it—and a length of serge, in which Iñigo later made several folds to cover his stomach. Since he saw no reason to prolong his stay in the city of the lagoons, he began his journey to Genoa, where he would take ship for Barcelona.

He had to traverse the regions of Venetia, Emilia, Lombardy, and Liguria. The first stop mentioned by Iñigo in his memoirs is Ferrara.[19] He tells us this anecdote about his stay there. One day while he was in the cathedral to fulfill his devotions, a poor man asked him for an alms. He gave him a *marchetto*, a coin worth a few cents. Another beggar approached him and to this one he gave a larger coin. A third followed, and having no smaller coin, he gave him a *giulio*. By now the succession of beggars grew, until the Pilgrim had to tell them that he had nothing left to give them. Once more did Iñigo thus show that money had no importance for him and that for the future he would place all his trust in God's providence.

On his journey through Lombardy he had to go through the camping sites of both the imperial and the French troops.

---

18 *Autobiog*, no. 49.
19 *Autobiog*, no. 50.

It must be remembered that the war for the possession of the duchy of Milan was then at its highest, a conflict that in the following year was to culminate in the battle of Pavia and the capture of King Francis I. The Spanish soldiers advised Iñigo to make a detour in order to avoid the warring troops. But he did not heed their advice. At sunset he arrived at a besieged town. The sentries arrested him as a spy, then they stripped him and minutely searched his clothes and belongings. Learning nothing from this, they took him bound to their captain. What had happened in the Holy Land occurred again. While being dragged along by the soldiers, he had in mind a representation of how Jesus was seized at the beginning of his passion. He notes, however, that this time he was not treating of a vision, such as there had been on other occasions.[20] Standing before the captain, Iñigo began to doubt whether, to escape torture, he should address him, not in his customary informal manner as "you," but formally as "Your Lordship." This seemed to him to be a temptation, so he decided not to show any reverence, not even that of uncovering his head. During the interrogation he replied only in faltering phrases and long pauses. The captain dismissed him as a man with no common sense. Fortunately, a Spaniard who lived nearby took him home and offered him food and lodging for the night.

Setting off next morning he was again on the road, and at sunset the incident of the previous day took place again, but now in the French camp. This time Iñigo had better luck. The captain wanted to know from where he came. On learning that he came from Guipúzcoa, the French captain treated him well and said that Iñigo was almost a fellow countryman, since he was himself from the region of Bayonne. He ordered his soldiers to treat him well and to give Iñigo some supper.

When he arrived in Genoa, Iñigo was met in the street by Rodrigo Portuondo, whom Ribadeneira calls "admiral of the Spanish galleys."[21] In reality his office was to protect the

---

20 *Autobiog*, no. 52.
21 *RibVita*, I, xviii, in *FN*, IV, 169.

troopships arriving at Genoa. Portuondo recognized him from the days at Arévalo when they had served together in the court of Castile, and now gave him all he needed for his voyage to Barcelona. The crossing was a hazardous affair, for there was danger of falling into the hands of Andrea Doria, the Genoese admiral, who was then allied with the French.

Chapter 6

STUDENT IN BARCELONA: 1524—1526

"After the aforementioned Pilgrim understood that the will of God for him was not to remain in Jerusalem, his thoughts kept recurring to the question of what he ought to do. Finally he felt more inclined to study for some time so as to be able to help souls, and he made up his mind to go to Barcelona."[1]

The Pilgrim found himself faced with the need of making an important decision: What is he to do, since he sees that his plan of remaining in the Holy Land has been frustrated? He had ample time to turn over this question in his mind during his long return journey. Finally the decision was taken. To be able "to help souls," which was his ideal, he saw that he had to study. And he resolved to do this, at the age of thirty-three. Like all other students, he would begin with grammar and then study arts or philosophy. For the present his planning did not go beyond that. It is not groundless, however, to discover in this resolve of studying in order "to help souls" a vocation, at least implicit, to the priesthood. Ignatius never revealed when he first began to hear this call to the priesthood. We can place it in this period of his first studies.

Where would he take these courses? Remembering the bonds of friendship he had established at Manresa with a Cistertian monk of St. Paul's monastery, he thought that this religious would be the best man to have as his helper. So when Isabel Roser offered to defray his expenses, and Bachelor Jerónimo Ardèvol volunteered to teach him free of charge, he disclosed to them his plan of doing his studies at

[1] *Autobiog*, no. 50.

Manresa. He went to the town by the Cardoner River, but there he learned that this monk had died. Back in Barcelona, he gratefully accepted the offer of his benefactors. In the house of Inés Pascual he would find lodging; Isabel Roser would cover his expenses; and Jerónimo Ardèvol would be his teacher.

We are already acquainted with the two ladies. Ardèvol, a bachelor of arts, was a native of the little town of La Fatarella in the diocese of Tortosa. When Iñigo came to Barcelona, Ardèvol was one of the teachers of Latin in the high schools (*escuelas mayores*) of Barcelona. During the academic year 1525-1526 he held the chair of Latin, drawing a salary of forty Catalonian pounds.[2]

1. The Teaching of Humanities in Barcelona

What was the state of education then in Barcelona? Although already in 1450 King Alfonso V of Aragón had by a royal charter granted the faculty to create a university (*estudio general*) in Barcelona—a faculty confirmed the same year by Pope Nicholas V—the "city of the counts" (*Ciudad Condal*) did not in reality have a university until 1533. The *escuelas mayores* however, were in full operation as an amalgam of the schools of the city and the cathedral schools. In 1507 the schools of medicine joined the group. In 1508 the city brought out some ordinances on studies, still in vigor at the time of Iñigo's arrival.[3]

In these university ordinances are listed, among other things, the books prescribed for the teaching of Latin. Through them one discovers that the city of Barcelona had already abandoned medieval educational lines and fully adopted the new trends of humanism. Latin was being studied not only through Alexandre de Villedieu's Summary of Grammar (*Doctrinale Puerorum*) through which the schoolboys of Western Europe had been trained throughout three centuries, but also through the new Introductions to the Latin Grammar (*Introductiones*

---

2 C. Dalmases, "Los estudios de San Ignacio en Barcelona (1524-1526)," *AHSJ* X (1941), 283-293.
3 Ibid., 288-290.

in latinam grammaticen) produced by Antonio Nebrija and published in Barcelona. Among the authors explained were Vergil's *Aeneid,* Seneca's *Proverbs,* an anthology of Dionysius Cato's *Disticha moralia,* and the Contempt of the World (*Contemptus mundi*) by Bernard of Cluny (*Morlanensis*).

The leading promoter of humanistic studies in Barcelona was Martín de Ibarra, born at Logroño but of Basque origin. Besides holding the chair of grammar between the years 1510 and 1542 in the public school, he founded in 1532 a special type of academy for humanistic studies. His colleagues were Cosme Mestre, Arnaldo de San Juan, and Iñigo's teacher, Jerónimo Ardèvol. In the academic statutes approved by these four professors that same year, they allotted among themselves the materials which each one was to teach and agreed on the emoluments each should receive.

As a complementary note on Jerónimo Ardèvol, we may add that in 1535 he married Margarita Mestre, first cousin of his colleague Cosme Mestre. The second of their four children, baptized with the same name as his father, became a benefice holder of the church of Santa María del Mar and later parish priest of San Martín de Arenys. The Latin master of Iñigo made a will dated in Barcelona on March 12, 1551, the year of his death.[4]

2. *The Pupil of Master Ardèvol*

Under his master's guidance, Iñigo set himself to the study of the rudiments of Latin, following Nebrija's *Introductiones.* He soon met an obstacle. While he was beginning to memorize the declensions and other rules of grammar, new insights and delights on spiritual matters came into his mind, to such an extent that he could not study. Here, as on other occasions, his weapon was spiritual discernment. He reasoned that those motions could not be coming from God, since they hindered him in something so necessary as study. His reaction was

4 J. M. Madurell and C. Dalmases, "Jeroni Ardèvol, maestro de San Ignacio y la enseñanza de las humanidades en Barcelona de 1508 a 1544," *AHSJ,* XXXVII (1968), 370-407.

immediate and radical. He went to his teacher's house, which was close to the church of Santa María del Mar, and asked him to listen to him in that church. As they sat on a bench together, Iñigo recounted what had been taking place, and added: "I promise never to fail in attention at your lessons during these two years, provided that I can find in Barcelona bread and water to keep me alive."[5] After he made that promise "with strong resolve," he never again experienced that temptation.

Iñigo found himself in good health in Barcelona, free from the stomach pains that had afflicted him at Manresa. This led him to resume some of his former penances. He had become reconciled to the wearing of shoes. Without discarding them, he began to make a hole in the soles which gradually grew larger until, when the winter came, "he now wore only the upper part of the shoes."[6]

His firm resolve to devote himself fully to his studies could not check his desire to do good. His apostolic activities were, first of all, good example, then spiritual conversations and works of mercy for the poor and the sick. The desire to profit spiritually from his activity and to help him in his works of charity, drew to him the sympathetic favor of some of the most distinguished women of the Catalan nobility. Among them were: Leonor Sapila and her granddaughter Ana de Gualbes; Doña Estefanía de Requeséns, daughter of the Count of Palamós, who in 1526 married Juan de Zúñiga, major commander of Santiago and tutor of King Philip II; Isabel de Requeséns, married to Juan de Boixadors; Guiomar Gralla y Desplà, daughter of the chief treasurer of Catalonia Miguel Juan Gralla and of a niece of the archdeacon Luis Desplà; Isabel de Josa, wife of the nobleman Guillermo de Josa; Isabel Ferrer, married to Juan Roser, whom we already know.

It seems that during this time in Barcelona Iñigo made his first attempts at giving the Spiritual Exercises to others, and

5 *Autobiog,* no. 55.
6 Ibid.

it is probable that through them he attracted as followers those whom we might call his first three companions. Polanco tells us that "there he began to feel desires to associate some persons into his companionship to pursue the plan which he had from then on to help to reform the defects which he saw in the service of God and to become trumpeters of Jesus Christ."[7] The three companions were Calixto de Sa, Juan de Arteaga, and Lope de Cáceres.

3. The Convents of Nuns

The nuns could not remain outside the orbit of Iñigo's zeal. It was all the greater because with respect to them there was another element to stimulate his zeal: the desire to contribute to the reform, so necessary, of the convents.

This problem had been in need of attention at Barcelona throughout the fifteenth century. Of the convent of Hierony-mites it was said that its members were more like dames than nuns. The high point of conflict was that of enclosure, which had been relaxed to a scandalous degree. Not only were the nuns going out as they pleased, but also lay persons, relatives, and friends visited them with great facility. Of the eight convents of nuns in Barcelona, we know that Iñigo had com-munication with three: the Hieronymites of St. Matthias, the Benedictines of St. Clare, and the Dominicans of our Lady of the Angels. We have already treated of his dealings with the Hieronymites before his pilgrimage.

To describe a convent as dear to Iñigo as was that of St. Clare, it is worth our while to give it somewhat lengthier attention. By mentioning that its nuns were Benedictines, we have made a statement that contains a whole drama. In reality this convent of St. Anthony and St. Clare, situated in the suburb of Ribera near the Gate of St. Daniel, had since its foundation back in 1237 belonged to the Order of St. Clare. From it had come in 1326 the nuns who founded the convent of Pedralbes. Throughout the fifteenth century and at the beginning of the sixteenth, the nuns of St. Clare carried on a long battle in defense of their privileges. The Franciscan

7 *PolSum*, no. 35, in *FN*, I, 170.

superiors, both the Conventuals and the Observants, were unable to bring about the reform they considered legitimate and necessary. The Catholic Kings, Ferdinand and Isabella, also failed in the same attempt, when in 1493 they ordered a visitation of the convent. In the end the nuns opted for a radical decision—to abandon the Rule of St. Clare and embrace that of St. Benedict. A brief of Leo X, dated June 25, 1513, gave the seal of approval to this transformation, which in 1518 was considered as a finished matter.[8] After many vicissitudes of history, among which stand out the events of "the tragic week" of 1909, this monastery, placed under the patronage of St. Benedict, stands to this day in the heights of Montserrat, three kilometers from the Marian shrine on the road to Monistrol.

At the time when Iñigo arrived in Barcelona for his studies, only six years had elapsed since the convent had passed under the Benedictine rule. This fact should be taken into account by anyone reading Iñigo's correspondence with one of the nuns of St. Clare's, Teresa Rajadell. These letters to this fervent religious, rightly considered to be the best example of St. Ignatius' spiritual direction in the area of discernment of spirits, cannot be understood except within the historical context in which they were written. In that community there was still high tension. The change of rule had not brought peace to the members. The much desired reform was slow in coming. One group of the nuns, among whom Teresa stood out, was wholeheartedly in favor of that reform, but these had to confront the resistance of some of their sisters in religion. A moment came when Teresa and the prioress herself, Jerónima Oluja, proposed to place themselves under obedience to Ignatius. The general, who already in 1547 had had the unpleasant experience of the case of Isabel Roser, did not acquiesce to the proposal; but throughout his life he endeavored to foster a reform which he considered necessary for the divine service—the reform of this and the other feminine communities of Barcelona.

8 Tarsicio de Azcona, O.F.M.Cap., "Paso del monasterio de Santa Clara de Barcelona a la regla benedictina (1512-1518)," *Collectanea Franciscana*, XXXVIII (1968), 78-134.

These events go beyond the period of Iñigo's student days in this city, but this was perhaps the best time to refer to them. To complete the picture let us say that Ignatius, in his efforts to achieve his goal, set in motion all the means and persons within his reach: his own subjects in Barcelona, the viceroy of Catalonia, the bishop of Barcelona, the ambassador in Rome, and the prince Don Philip. All this should have contributed to bring the matter finally into the hands of the pope, the only one who could speak a definitive word on it.

But the longed-for reform was slow in coming. As late as in 1559, Father Miguel Gobierno, rector of the Jesuit college in Barcelona, informed Father Diego Laínez, St. Ignatius' successor in the government of the Society, about the state of that project. The best solution seemed to be not to admit new novices and to send back home those who had not yet made their profession. With this it was calculated that within four or five years, the situation would be on the right road for a solution. The rumor spread in the city that a papal brief had been received, according to which the convent of Santa Clara was to be closed down. The shock was enormous. But the result was positive, "because," as Gobierno adds, "never before had this monastery been so peaceful and subject to obedience as now."[9] Foremost in this desire for reform was the lady abbess.

4. Erasmianism

We do not have certitude that Iñigo came into contact, already in Barcelona, with the Erasmian group which existed there. In those years theological questions were inflaming minds throughout all Europe. A group of Barcelona citizens, who as high officials of the Supreme Council of Aragón had in 1520 followed Emperor Charles V first to Castile and then to Flanders and Germany, had occasion to acquaint themselves with the reformative ideas of Desiderius Erasmus. Some of the Barcelona clergy also became receptive to these ideas.

An item of interest is that Isabel Ferrer, who adopted her husband's surname of Roser, was a relative of the royal

---

9 *MonLain*, IV, 303-305; *LittQuad*, VI, 771.

officials Juan Ferrer and Miguel Mai. The latter was the best known Erasmian at Barcelona and from December, 1528, the imperial ambassador in Rome. Ribadeneira states that friends in Barcelona recommended the Handbook of a Christian Soldier (*Enchiridion militis christiani*) to Iñigo as something to read.[10] It is probable that Iñigo followed this advice. But it seems that the literary merit of the book, rather than the ideas expressed in it, was what had the greater weight in the recommendation. Iñigo was to have a later occasion to know Erasmianism, at Alcalá where this movement was more in vogue and had more followers.

10 *RibVita*, I, xiii, in *FN*, IV, 172-174.

Chapter 7

STUDENT AT ALCALA AND SALAMANCA: 1526-1527

At the end of Iñigo's second year of Latin study, his master told him that he could now study arts or philosophy, and he recommended him to go to Alcalá. To make doubly sure, Iñigo had himself examined by a doctor of theology, who gave him the same advice. The Pilgrim therefore set out for Alcalá.

1. *The Studies*

Iñigo said that "he studied at Alcalá almost a year and a half."[1] As on other occasions, his chronological calculations have only an approximate value. This sojourn at Alcalá de Henares may have lasted from March, 1526 to June, 1527 at the latest. But this period might have still to be shortened by two or three months.

In his account he despatched the matter of his studies in two lines: "He studied 'terms' of Soto (that is, the *Summulae* or Logic of Domingo de Soto), the physics of Albert (the *Physicorum libri octo* or Natural Philosophy of Albert the Great); and the Master of the Sentences (the *Sententiarum libri IV* by Peter Lombard).[2] Since these were the subjects taught at the university of Alcalá, founded in 1508 by Cardinal Cisneros, one must think that Iñigo studied them in the university lecture halls. There is, however, the deposition of a witness in the judicial processes conducted there, according to which Iñigo and his companions studied in private, under the guidance of a professor who was giving them lessons.[3] In either case, those studies were made hurriedly and "with little foundation", as Ignatius will acknowledge later.[4]

1 *Autobiog*, no. 57.
2 *Ibid.*
3 *FD*, p. 324.
4 *Autobiog*, no. 62.

The fact is, too, that he devoted himself more to his apostolic activities than to his studies. "And at Alcalá he busied himself in giving Spiritual Exercises and in explaining Christian doctrine; and by these activities he brought fruit to God's glory."[5] Many persons who associated with him made great spiritual progress. Others overcame troublesome temptations, "as the man who wanted to scourge himself but could not, just as if someone were holding back his hand."[6] His explanation of Christian doctrine always attracted large crowds.

According to Ribadeneira, "the first person with whom he came into contact was a young student from Vitoria, Martín de Olabe by name, from whom he received the first alms."[7] This Basque student, after receiving the doctorate in theology from the University of Paris in 1544, was later, when attending the council of Trent, to join the Society. He was also to become a brilliant professor of theology at the Roman College until his death in 1556, seventeen days after that of Ignatius.

At Alcalá Iñigo began a friendship with two priests who would also end by joining the Society. One was the Navarrese from Estella, Diego de Eguía, who was living in the house of his brother Miguel, "the owner of a printing house in Alcalá who comfortably had everything he needed."[8] Precisely this Miguel de Eguía brought out, in 1526 and 1527, two editions of Erasmus' *Enchiridion militis christiani* in a Spanish translation by Alonso Fernández, the "Archdeacon of Alcor." It was an unprecedented success in publishing. Also in 1526 he published the *De contemptu mundi libellus valde utilis* or Imitation of Christ, the *Gersoncito* of Ignatius in Latin. The other priest whom he befriended was the Portuguese Manuel Miona. He was chosen by Iñigo as his confessor. He is also the person who recommended him to read Erasmus' *Enchiridion*. The Portuguese Gonçalves da Câmara, to whom we owe this information, adds that Iñigo did not want to read that book, because there

5 *Autobiog*, no. 57.
6 Ibid.
7 *RibVita*, I, xiv, in *FN*, IV, 177.
8 *Autobiog*, no. 57.

were some preachers and other commendable persons who disapproved it; and also because there would be no lack of other books free from suspicion. These were the ones he desired to read.[9] We have already seen how, according to Ribadeneira, the reading of the *Enchiridion* had been recommended to him at Barcelona as a literary exercise more than as spiritual reading. But when he noticed that the reading tended to cool down his devotion, no doubt because of its criticism of the religious society of his time, he put the book aside. It is certain that during those years there was in Alcalá an environment full of enthusiasm for Erasmus; and Don Alfonso de Fonseca, the Archbishop of Toledo, was himself one of the professed advocates of the movement.

But Iñigo found himself involved in another movement which stirred up greater suspicions than the vogue of Erasmianism had raised. It was that of the Illuminati (*los alumbrados*). Both because of the odd costume he wore and the groups of persons which gathered around him, gossip was not slow in spreading. The matter reached the ears of the officials of the Inquisition at Toledo. Iñigo was warned by his host, who told him that he and his companions were being called "sack-wearers and also, I believe, illuminists" (*alumbrados*).[10] The connotations of this word are particularly significant, if one remembers that in September, 1525, the Inquisition had condemned forty-eight propositions of the *alumbrados*.

2. The Judicial Processes

Now began the long series of investigations and legal processes to which Iñigo was subjected until a little before his founding of the Society. In a letter to King John of Portugal in 1545 he enumerated eight of these processes.[11] Those instituted in Alcalá were, as attested by Ignatius himself, three.

Toward the end of 1526, there appeared in Alcalá Miguel Carrasco, a canon of the collegiate church of San Justo in that

9 *Memoriale*, no. 98, in *FN*, I, 585.
10 *Autobiog*, no. 58.
11 *EppIgn*, I, 296-298; *FN*, I, 50-54.

city, and Alonso Mejía, a canon of the cathedral of Toledo. These officials were not acting on their own initiative. By a letter dated April 29, 1526, the inquisitor general Alonso Manrique had commissioned them to traverse the cities of Toledo and Guadalajara, the towns of Pastrana and Escalona, and any other places they might deem opportune. They were to hear the deposition of witnesses who might offer information about pending cases of the *alumbrados*. By another letter of July 24, 1526, Don Fernando de Valdés, then a counselor of the Supreme Inquisition, pressed Mejía not to shirk in the execution of the mission entrusted to him. In their capacity as inquisitors, Mejía and his colleague fulfilled their mission. The evidence gathered by them must have been recorded in the Book of the Alumbrados (*Libro de Alumbrados*), which is no longer extant. But it should be noted that neither Iñigo nor his companions were ever summoned to trial by the inquisitors, as Iñigo himself has stated and as appears also from the minutes of the processes.

On November 19, 1526, the inquisitors began by interrogating the Franciscan Fernando Rubio. They asked him what he knew about "certain young men (*mancebos*) who go about in this town, clad in grey habits down to the ankles (*en unos hábitos pardillos claros y fasta en pies*), some of them barefooted, and who say that they live a life like that of apostles."[12] One of these "young men" was Iñigo, who was then thirty-five years of age. The others were his three companions whom he had won in Barcelona: Arteaga, Cáceres, and Sa. Another was added to these in Alcalá, a French youth named Juan Reynalde (Reynauld?), known as Juanico, a page of the viceroy of Navarre, Martín de Córdoba. Because of wounds he had received, the youth had to be interned in the Hospital de la Misericordia. He soon became fond of Iñigo, who was lodging there, and decided to follow him.

The inquisitors similarly interrogated Beatriz Ramírez, Julián Martínez, the manager of the Hospital de la Misericordia, and his wife María, a nurse.

After this the inquisitors left the matter in the hands of the

12 *FD*, p. 322.

episcopal vicar of Toledo in Alcalá, Juan Rodríguez de Figueroa. Later Ignatius will be able to affirm truthfully that he was never condemned, nor even interrogated, by the inquisitors, but at most only by their "vicars."

What immediately attracted the attention of anyone who first saw those young men was their attire—long gowns like cassocks, of a cloth called *pardillo*, the cheapest in the market. The one going barefoot was Iñigo. They were living in various houses. Iñigo found accommodation in the Hospital de la Misericordia, called also the Antezana after the name of the person who had founded it in 1483. There, as the manager testified, he was given food and drink, bed and candle.

After the first inquiries, the vicar Figueroa summoned Iñigo and his companions, to tell them that investigations had been made about them and that nothing blameworthy had been found in their life and teaching. Consequently they could continue as before. However, since they were not religious, it was not expedient for them to wear a uniform habit. Therefore he ordered that Iñigo and Arteaga should dye their gowns black, and Calixto and Cáceres theirs "lion-color" (*leonado*), and Reynalde could keep what he was wearing. This sentence was passed on November 21,[13] and it was the end of what we can call the first trial.

The second inquiry opened in the following year, with the interrogation of Mencía de Benavente on March 6, 1527. This time the point at issue was not the manner of dressing, but something more important. The facts are these. Among those frequenting the hospital premises to meet Iñigo were persons of all kinds: married and unmarried women, middle-aged and elderly men, friars and students. The interrogatories lead us to conclude that among them there were more women than men. To all, whether to individuals or to groups which numbered up to ten or twelve persons, Iñigo was giving instructions about spiritual matters. He called this activity "spiritual exercises" and also "Christian doctrine."

13 *FD*, p. 330.

To those familiar with the Ignatian Exercises it becomes clear that what Iñigo was preaching to his hearers were some "easy exercises" (*ejercicios leves*) such as he describes in the Eighteenth Annotation (*SpEx*, [18]). Mencía de Benavente expressed the matter as follows in her reply during the interrogatory: "And he has conversed with these [women], explaining mortal sins [that is, the capital sins], and the five senses and the powers of the soul; and he explained all this very well from the Gospels, St. Paul, and other saints. And he says that they should examine their consciences twice daily, recalling to memory anything in which they have sinned, as [if looking at] an image. He advises them to confess every eighth day and to receive the Holy Sacrament at the same time."[14] It is safe to state that the "Christian doctrine," such as Iñigo understood it to be in Alcalá, can be reduced to that summary.

In the deposition of María de la Flor there is a clearer reference to the Exercises in their lighter form (*ejercicios leves*) or to what Iñigo called "the service of God." "And Iñigo told her that he ought to speak with her uninterruptedly for a whole month; and that during this period she ought to confess and receive Holy Communion every eighth day; and that at first she would be very joyful without knowing whence this came, and that the following week she would be very sad; but that he hoped in God that she would perceive much progress during it. He told her that he would explain the three powers, in the way he explains them, and the great merit which is gained in temptation, and about venial sin and how it becomes mortal, and the ten commandments, and mortal sins [that is to say, the capital sins], and the five senses, and circumstances pertaining to all this."[15]

Iñigo's aim was to bring his hearers to renew their lives, by praying in the measure of each one's capacity, according to the first and second methods of prayer of the Exercises, and by examining their consciences, confession, and Communion. He explained also to them the rules for discerning spirits, more suitable for the First Week.

14 *FD*, p. 332.
15 Ibid., p. 334.

The results produced by these Exercises are more easily understood if we remember that some of the exercitants came from an evil life. The impact produced in the souls when they listened to Iñigo and submitted to his recommendations was at times violent, causing dismay and fainting spells. In these cases, by applying the rules of discernment he brought peace to such persons by explaining what was happening to them. As they decided to change their lives and abandon their sins, it was natural for them to experience a rebellion of nature. But he encouraged them in their resistance by telling them that if they persevered in it, within two months they would no longer feel any temptation.

The coming and going of persons to Iñigo's house and the meetings which took on the appearance of clandestine religious gatherings could not fail to attract the attention of the ecclesiastical authorities. It happened that "a married woman of quality was specially devoted to the Pilgrim. To avoid being seen, she used to come to the hospital at dawn, with her head covered as is the custom at Alcalá de Henares. On entering, she removed her mantle and went to the Pilgrim's room. But neither on this occasion did they do anything to them, nor even after the trial did they summon them or say anything to them."[16]

But four months later, after Iñigo had left the hospital and found accommodation in a little lodge (*casilla*) just outside, one day a constable (*alguacil*) came, summoned him to the door, and told him, "Come along with me,"[17] and left him in a jail. It was April 18 or 19, Holy Thursday or Good Friday of that year 1527. That confinement must not have been very severe, for the prisoner was able to receive many persons who came to visit him. "He acted the same as when he was free, teaching Christian doctrine and giving Exercises." He did not want to have an advocate or procurator, even though many persons offered him their services. One lady among others, Doña Teresa Enríquez, wife of Gutierre de Cárdenas and known as "the fool of the Blessed Sacrament" (*la loca del Sacramento*) because of her devotion to it, sent

16 *Autobiog*, no. 59.
17 *Autobiog*, no. 60.

visitors to him and "made many offers to obtain his release." But he did not accept them and said: "He for whose sake I entered this place will get me out of it, if it be to his service."[18]

What was the occasion which led to Iñigo's arrest? Two women, a mother and her daughter (Maria del Vado and Luisa Velázquez), accompanied by a maidservant (Catalina), had left the city on a pilgrimage to venerate the veil of Veronica, preserved at Jaén (215 miles south of Alcalá) and then another shrine of our Lady of Guadalupe (near Portugal). The vicar Figueroa suspected that these women had undertaken that rash pilgrimage on Inigo's advice.

After seventeen days of imprisonment without Iñigo's being told the reason for it, Figueroa came to interrogate him. His first question was: Did he know those ladies? He did. Did he know of their trip before they left Alcalá? He replied that not only had he known about it, but that they themselves had spoken to him of their desire to go about the world serving the poor in hospitals, and that he had constantly tried to dissuade them from such a project "because the daughter was so young and beautiful" (*la hija tan moça y tan vistosa*).[19] He pointed out to them that they could visit the poor in Alcalá, where they could also accompany the Blessed Sacrament. Figueroa went away with his notary, who had written down the whole interrogatory.

At that time Calixto de Sa was at Segovia, convalescing from a serious illness. On hearing of Iñigo's imprisonment, he hastened to Alcalá and spontaneously placed himself too in the jail. But Iñigo got him out through the influence of a doctor, a very good friend of his.

It was necessary to wait until the three pious women returned to Alcalá from their pilgrimage. It was then seen that Iñigo's answers were true. The notary entered the jail, where he read to the Pilgrim the definitive sentence and set him free. It was June 1, 1527.

18 Ibid.
19 *Autobiog*, no. 61.

3. The Sentence

The sentence contained two parts.[20] The first was a confirmation of that given on the previous November 11 regarding the attire of Iñigo and his companions. They were now ordered not just to dye their gowns, but to wear those customary for students. The Pilgrim replied that they would have been able to dye their gowns, but did not have money to buy new ones. Then the vicar supplied them with suitable garments and birettas and everything else that students at Alcalá required.

The second part of the sentence ordered them not to speak about matters of the faith until they completed four years of study. Iñigo acknowledged his own lack of studies. "This was the first thing he used to say whenever they examined him."[21]

He had been in prison forty-two days. As he left it, he was faced with the problem of his future. He could not reconcile himself to the idea that his interrogators were closing the door against his being able "to help souls," and this for the sole reason that he had not studied. He decided to appeal against this sentence before the Archbishop of Toledo, Alonso de Fonseca. Knowing that he was then at Valladolid, Iñigo went there to meet him. He told him that, although he was no longer within the territory of the archbishop's jurisdiction, he was ready to do whatever the archbishop would tell him. The prelate received him kindly and, learning of Iñigo's intention to go to Salamanca to continue his studies, he said that there too he had good friends and a college founded by himself which bore his name. He offered his services and as he dismissed Iñigo he gave him four *escudos*.

4. At Salamanca: 1527

Early in July, Iñigo arrived at Salamanca. His four companions had preceded him there. A lady informed him where they were lodging and thus they met again.

If he had studied little at Alcalá, even less was he able to study at Salamanca. Twelve days after his arrival he found

20 *FD*, pp. 342-343.
21 *Autobiog*, no. 62.

himself involved anew in interrogatories. It can be said that he himself gave the occasion for it. He chose for confessor one of the Dominicans of the Convent of San Esteban. His presence there was sure to arouse curiosity among the friars. His confessor told him that the fathers would like to speak with him, and therefore he invited him to dine with the community the following Sunday. Iñigo accepted the invitation and on the appointed day he went to the convent in company with Calixto. After the meal, the sub-prior Nicolás de Santo Tomás, who was in charge of the community because of the absence of the prior, Diego de San Pedro, took Iñigo to a chapel. To this meeting came the confessor and also, it seems, another friar. The conversation soon turned to a delicate point. The fathers had heard good reports about the conduct of Iñigo and his companions. They knew that "they were going about preaching in an apostolic manner." But what studies had they made? Iñigo replied frankly. He himself was the one who had studied most, but he had done this with little foundation (*con poco fundamento*).[22] The dialog continued in these terms.

Friar: "What is it, then, that you are preaching?"

Iñigo: "We do not preach, but we speak familiarly with people on the things of God, for example, after dinner with certain persons who call upon us."

Friar: "What things of God do you speak about? That is just what we should like to know."

Iñigo: "Sometimes we speak of one virtue, sometimes of another, and always to commend them; sometimes of one vice, sometimes of another, and always to condemn them."

Friar: "You are uneducated men and yet you speak about virtues and vices. Now, no one can do that unless in one of two ways: either through learning or through the Holy Spirit. You are not speaking through learning; therefore through the Holy Spirit."

At this the Pilgrim became somewhat on his guard, for that manner of arguing did not seem good to him. After a moment's silence, he said that there was no need to speak further about these matters.

The friar insisted: "Now when there are such great errors of Erasmus and others who have deceived the world, don't you desire to explain what you are teaching?"[23]

22 *Autobiog*, no. 64.
23 *Autobiog*, no. 65.

The subject of Erasmus could not be more up to date, for those very days, from June 27 to August 13, 1527, a conference of theologians was being held in Valladolid, convened by the inquisitor general Alonso Manrique, Archbishop of Seville, to discuss seventeen propositions taken from the works of Erasmus. Dominicans and Franciscans were showing themselves as adversaries of the humanist from Rotterdam.

The Pilgrim, knowing that his interrogator had no authority over him, replied: "Father, I will say nothing more than what I have said, unless it be in the presence of superiors who can oblige me to speak."[24]

The sub-prior could not get another word from the Pilgrim. He then had Iñigo and Calixto remain in that chapel. There they remained practically isolated, with all the doors shut. Meanwhile the friars went to speak with the ecclesiastical judges. Iñigo and Calixto remained in the convent for three days, having their meals in the refectory with the community. Their room was almost always full of friars who came to see them. The Pilgrim talked to them in his usual vein, and some of the friars took the side of the visitors, so that a division of opinions began to arise in the convent.

After three days a notary came to communicate to them the order of going to jail. There they were not placed together with the other prisoners, but in an upper room, dirty and poorly furnished. They were bound with the same chain. The following day the news of their imprisonment spread in the city, and sympathizers began to send them everything they needed. Visitors had access to the cell, so that Iñigo could continue his practices of speaking about God and the like.[25]

Bachelor Sancho Gómez de Frías came to examine them. He summoned each one of them separately and "the Pilgrim gave him all his papers, which were the Exercises, that they could be examined."[26] This is the first time that Iñigo speaks of his Exercises as something written. Frías asked them if they

24 *Autobiog*, no. 66.
25 *Autobiog*, no. 67.
26 Ibid.

had other companions. On their replying affirmatively, Lope de Cáceres and Juan de Arteaga were brought to the prison. The two were put with the common prisoners. Juanico was left free.

A few days later Iñigo was summoned before four judges, Alonso Gómez de Paradinas, Hernán Rodríguez de San Isidro, Francisco de Frías, and Bachelor Sancho Gómez de Frías. "They had all seen the Exercises."[27] They asked him many questions not only about the Exercises but also on topics of theology, such as the Trinity and the sacraments. The Pilgrim answered in such a manner that they found nothing with which to reproach him. The bachelor Frías, who took a leading part in the interrogations, put a canonical question. Iñigo answered in the manner which seemed best to him, but remarked beforehand that he did not know the opinion of the doctors on this matter. Next they brought up a topic on which he was well prepared. How did he explain the First Commandment? His answer was so ample that the judges had no desire to continue further.

Regarding the Exercises, the only point on which they fastened was that in which he explained when a sin is mortal and when venial.[28] Their doubt was always the same: If he had not studied theology, why did he try to determine points so delicate? Iñigo's way out was obvious: It was their part to judge. If any of his statements was wrong, they should condemn it. But "in the end they went away without condemning anything."[29]

During these days of imprisonment something happened which shows how Iñigo lived out the truths of the Exercises. One of his visitors was Don Francisco de Mendoza y Bobadilla, later bishop of Coria, and cardinal archbishop of Burgos. He asked Iñigo whether he was well during his imprisonment and whether he found it hard to bear. Iñigo replied: "I will answer what I answered today to a lady who expressed words of sympathy at seeing me thus locked up. I told her:

27 *Autobiog*, no 68. For the identification of the four persons who judged Iñigo at Salamanca, see Benigno Hernández Montes, "Identidad de los personajes que juzgaron a San Ignacio en Salamanca," *AHSJ*, LII (1983), 3-51.
28 *SpEx*, [35-37].
29 *Autobiog*, no. 68.

'In this you show that you have no desire to be a prisoner for the love of God. Or, does imprisonment seem to you so great an evil?' Then I say to you that there are not so many fetters and chains in Salamanca that I would not desire to bear still more, for the love of God.' "[30]

A few days later he had an occasion to prove that these were not merely empty words. It happened one night that all the prisoners escaped from the jail. Only Iñigo and his companions remained inside. There is no need to describe the impression which this fact made in the city. The reaction was such that "then they gave them the whole neighboring palace as their jail."[31]

After twenty-two days of imprisonment the judges communicated the sentence to the prisoners: Nothing had been found reprehensible in their life and doctrine. They were, therefore, free to continue teaching the doctrine and speaking about the things of God. But they should not explain whether something is a venial or a mortal sin until they have completed four years of studies. As is evident, this was a repetition of the sentence pronounced at Alcalá. The judges gave their verdict amid signs of sympathy for Iñigo. But he did not let himself be softened by that. He replied that he would do what they ordered him but that he did not accept the sentence; for they were closing his mouth so that he could not help others, although they had found in him nothing blameworthy. And even though Doctor Frías "showed himself very benevolent,"[32] Iñigo insisted that he would comply with their order as long as he remained in the jurisdiction of Salamanca, but not afterwards.

Then he was released from the jail. But he saw that at Salamanca the door to his "helping souls" was closed for him by that decision which forbade him from explaining what was a mortal and what a venial sin. Hence "he decided to go to Paris to study."[33]

30 *Autobiog*, no. 69.
31 Ibid.
32 *Autobiog*, no. 70.
33 *Autobiog*, no. 71.

Chapter 8

_____

STUDIES IN PARIS

1. *At the Crossroads Once More*

Iñigo found himself at a crossroad in his life. Even his decision to go to Paris to pursue his studies did not solve the problem of his future. Already in Barcelona when he decided to enter upon studies, a doubt came into his mind: How far would he go in them, and what would he do after he had completed them?

Two solutions occurred to him. One was to embrace the religious state, the other "to continue wandering about the world."[1] He put off the decision for a later time. But on the hypothesis of becoming a religious, he was more inclined to enter some relaxed and unreformed order and that for two reasons: He would have more occasions to suffer for Christ, and he might be able to contribute to the reform of the order he embraced. "God gave him a great confidence that he would bear well whatever affronts and indignities they might inflict on him."[2]

Two reasons contributed to his choice of Paris as the place for his studies. One was that he would be able to dedicate himself seriously to study since, not knowing how to speak French, he would have less occasion to speak with others on spiritual things. The other reason was a confidence that at that celebrated university he could win over other students to follow his way of life, since there were many Spaniards and Portuguese among them. One thing we know for certain: He desired to avoid his initial mistake of trying to combine serious study with works of the apostolate. In later years, this experience was to help him in the composition of the Consti-

1 *Autobiog*, no. 71.
2 Ibid.

106

tutions of the Society, in which he will demand that Jesuit scholastics devote themselves completely to their studies, since these "in a certain way require the whole man."[3]

There was another point in which we observe a radical change of procedure. At Manresa, Barcelona, and Alcalá his apostolic activities had been directed preferentially to feminine audiences, more available and docile. In Paris his interlocutors will be university students.

Fifteen or twenty days after his release from prison, he departed from Salamanca alone, "with some books loaded on a little donkey,"[4] on his way to Barcelona. It was there that his greatest benefactors lived, from whom he expected the financial aid he needed for his plans. He did find his friends prepared to help, but this did not keep them from showing their worries about his proposed journey. Spain and France had been in a state of permanent war against each other. Reports were circulating that the French "put Spaniards on roasting spits."[5] But because of the temper of Iñigo's will, it was clear that such objections would not make any impression on his mind. In fact, when the date he had fixed arrived, alone and on foot he took to the road from Barcelona to Paris, where he arrived on February 2, 1528.

Iñigo was now in his thirty-seventh year. This notwithstanding, he resolved to take his studies seriously. Recognizing that he had made little progress in his studies in Barcelona, Alcalá, and Salamanca, he decided to repeat them, by taking the course in the humanities for a year and a half. Thus he was studying "with the small boys, going through the order and method of Paris."[6] This is tantamount to saying that he experienced in his own case the "method of Paris" (*modus parisiensis*), which he would eventually select as the model for the colleges of the Society of Jesus.

To this personal conviction of his own were added the require-

3 *Cons*, [340; see also 362].
4 *Autobiog*, no. 72.
5 Ibid.
6 *Autobiog*, no. 73.

ments laid down by the University of Paris. There access to the study of philosophy was not permitted to any student who had not proved, by a previous examination, that he possessed the necessary knowledge of Latin.

2. Humanistic Studies in the College of Montaigu

For this initial lap of his studies Iñigo chose the College of ·Montaigu, founded by Gil Aycelin de Montaigu, Archbishop of Rouen, in the middle of the fourteenth century, restored by Jan Standonk at the end of the fifteenth, and updated in 1509 with new statutes by Noël Bédier (Beda), the staunch opponent of Erasmus. Bedier was succeeded by Pierre Tempête (1514-1528). On February 5, 1528, three days after Iñigo's arrival, Jean Hégon assumed the directorship of the college, which he retained until his death in 1546. Everything in Montaigu breathed an atmosphere of the archaic, which brought down on it the satires of Erasmus and Rabelais. The very plan of studies of 1509 seems more antiquated than the one in force at Barcelona according to the statutes of 1508. For the teaching of Latin the textbook chiefly in use was the *Doctrinale puerorum* of Alexandre de Villedieu, which in Barcelona had been supplanted by the *Institutiones* of Nebrija. Cato's *Disticha moralia* and Donatus' *Ars minor* were the common patrimony of all European schools.

Iñigo enrolled at Montaigu as a *martinet*, that is, an extern student, who had to fend for his own lodging. This he was easily able to secure, at least for a time, thanks to the twenty-five escudos which he received from a merchant for a note of exchange from his friends of Barcelona. In that boarding house there were other Spanish students. With his habitual unconcern for money, Iñigo entrusted that amount to one of his fellow boarders, who squandered the money in a short time.

By Easter Iñigo was again a beggar on the streets, obliged to live on alms. He sought refuge in the hospice of Saint-Jacques, intended for pilgrims to Compostella, situated on rue Saint-Denis, 133, just beyond the church and cemetery of Les Innocents. Its main inconvenience was the distance to Montaigu. In order to go from the hospice, on the right bank (*rive droite*) to the college on the left bank (*rive gauche*) by crossing the island of Cité and climbing up the rue Saint-Jacques to the hill of Sainte-Geneviève, where the college stood, he needed a good half-hour's walk. Besides, since the hospice did not open its doors until sunrise, whereas the first classes in the college began at five in the morning, Iñigo was forced to forego some of them. In the evening he had to be back before the Angelus bell, so that he also lost time from the evening exercises. And since he still had to beg for his sustenance, he had little time left to study.

He came to know that some students remedied this need by placing themselves at the service of a university regent or professor. He opted for this solution, just as if this post were easy to find, and in his imagination he built up a whole plan of service: In the person of his master he would recognize that of Jesus Christ, and in each of his fellow students that of one of the Apostles. One would take the place of St. Peter, another that of St. John, and so on. But, however much he searched for such a master, he did not find one—not even with the recommendations of the bachelor Juan de Castro and of a Carthusian monk who knew many of the professors.

3. To Flanders in Search of Funds

Finding no other solution, he followed the advice of a Spanish friar who recommended him to go on a begging tour to Flanders every summer. There he could find wealthy Spanish merchants residing at Bruges and Antwerp, who would certainly help him with enough money to see him through his whole course.

The Pilgrim made this trip three times: the first during Lent of 1529, the second in August and September of 1530, and the third during the same period in 1531. On this last occasion he crossed over to England, reached London, and returned to Paris with more money than ever before. Thanks to the generosity of his benefactors, he was able not only to cover his expenses for the whole year but also to help other needy students.

During his first begging tour, at Bruges Iñigo met the celebrated Spanish humanist and educational reformer Luis Vives, who invited him to his table. It was the season of Lent, as we have mentioned, and the fare had to be fish. This provided an occasion for an objection which the Valentian humanist proposed to him with a touch of skeptical humor. The Church, he thought, had not hit the right target when she prescribed, as an act of penance, abstinence from meat, for sea-food too could be eaten with great relish. Iñigo's reply did not long keep him waiting. "You and others who have the means for it can dine very well on fish, but this is not the case with the majority of people."[7] Polanco, who related this anecdote for us, observes that in Flanders one could eat excellent fish, which was cooked in highly appetizing ways. We do not know how Vives reacted; but according to the testimony of the doctor Pedro de Maluenda, the humanist said later of Iñigo: "This man is a saint and he will be the founder of a religious order."[8]

On his return from this first journey, Iñigo intensified his spiritual conversations, and in May and June, 1529, he gave the Exercises to three Spanish students: Juan de Castro, Pedro de Peralta, and Amador de Elduayen. Castro, from Burgos, had been studying at the College of the Sorbonne since 1525. Peralta, from Toledo, and Amador, a Basque, had matriculated in 1525 in the Faculty of Arts. Those Exercises transformed their lives, but none of them decided to follow Iñigo in a steady manner. At the end of his studies, Castro entered in 1535 the Carthusian monastery of Vall de Cristo at Altura, near Segorbe, where he received a visit from Iñigo; and in 1542 he was appointed prior of the monastery Porta Coeli, near Valencia.

Peralta graduated as a master of arts in 1530. He made an attempt to go on pilgrimage to Jerusalem, but in Italy he was detained by a kinsman who had the pope order him to return to his country. There he became a famous preacher and canon of the Toledo cathedral. Amador studied in the College of Sainte-Barbe. There he irritated the principal

7 *FN*, II, 557.
8 Ibid.

Diogo de Gouveia, who complained that Iñigo had transformed this student into a fool.

In September of the same year 1529, a letter came from that Spanish youth who had squandered Iñigo's money. He told Iñigo that he was ill in Rouen, where he was detained on his return journey to Spain. He was a man in need, and this was enough to put Iñigo's charity into action, as he still hoped to win him to his cause. His first impulse was to travel the twenty-eight intervening leagues from Paris to Rouen barefooted and without eating or drinking. He reflected in the church of St. Dominic and his decision to travel in the manner mentioned above came to maturity. But as he arose the next morning, he had fears so great that he was scarcely able to put on his clothes. But he did not give up his plan because of these fears. He set out and they remained with him continually until he had walked the first three leagues, as far as Argenteuil. From there on all his repugnance was transformed into consolations so great that as he walked through the fields he spoke in a loud voice with God. He arrived in Rouen, consoled the sick youth, and procured the means for him to continue his journey to Spain. He also gave him letters for his friends whom he, Iñigo, had left there.

On his return to Paris he found an atmosphere openly hostile on the part of the university authorities, because of the change in manner of life observable in the three students who with him had gone through the Spiritual Exercises. It tended to draw them away from serious application to their work of study. Those most preoccupied with this concern were Diogo de Gouveia, principal of the College of Sainte-Barbe, and Doctor Pedro Ortiz, who was a relative of Pedro de Peralta. Gouveia threatened to give Iñigo, as soon as the academic year commenced, a flogging called "the hall" (*sala*). It consisted of many blows inflicted on the culprit, stripped to the waist, by the masters in the presence of the students congregated in a hall of the college.

On hearing that he was a wanted man, Iñigo presented himself of his own accord before the inquisitor of Paris, the Dominican Matthieu Ory. He requested him to despatch his case promptly, as St. Remigius' day, October 1, on which the course of arts began, was fast approaching. The inquisitor informed Iñigo that he had received complaints against him, but that he did not intend to take any punitive action. The storm subsided and Iñigo began to live as a boarder (*portionniste*) in the College of Sainte Barbe, to start his course of arts or philosophy under the direction of Master Juan Peña, of the diocese of Sigüenza in Castile.

4. Philosophy at Sainte Barbe

The College of Sainte Barbe still stands on rue Valette, 4. To be a boarder (*portionniste*) in a Parisian college was to get for rent a "portion of a room"—in other words, to share it with others. Iñigo had as roommates his master Juan Peña and two students who were to be his intimate companions: the Savoyard Pierre Favre and the Navarrese Francisco de Javier. At Peña's suggestion Favre undertook to repeat the lectures for the newcomer Iñigo.

Iñigo's proselytizing urges were kept in check by his firm intention to study seriously. He tried, however, to get the three companions whom he had left behind at Salamanca to come and join him in Paris. We have seen that he gave letters for them to that Spanish youth whom he had visited at Rouen. In his letters, he expressed his desire to have them near him, but he also told them of the difficulty of their having to meet their own expenses. This problem was less in the case of the Portuguese Calixto de Sa, because the king of Portugal granted fifty scholarships for subjects wishing to study in Paris. Iñigo secured one of these scholarships for Calixto through the noble Portuguese Leonor Mascarenhas, lady-in-waiting of the Empress Isabel, the wife of Charles V. In addition, Lady Leonor offered to supply him with a mule to make the journey to Paris. In the end, however, he did not make use of these facilities.

Calixto's later life was to be unusual. In his *Autobiography* Iñigo tells us only that "he set out for the Indies" in the company of a certain spiritual woman; also that after returning to Spain he went back to Mexico, whence he finally

112

returned to Salamanca as a wealthy man, thus causing wonderment in those who had known him earlier. These words conceal a drama on which we are well informed today. The name of the spiritual woman was Catalina Hernández, and she was one of those devout ladies (*beatas*) or members of the Third Order of St. Francis who were sent to Mexico to help in catechizing the neophytes. To observers Calixto seemed to be excessively familiar with Catalina. The matter reached the ears of the magistrates of the high court of justice (*Audiencia*) of Mexico. The judges, after fruitlessly warning Calixto to stop those dealings, gave him the choice between breaking up that friendship and returning to Spain. He opted for the second solution. To judge by appearances, he had become a merchant; and this explains his return to Salamanca as a wealthy man and with a plan of life much different from that he had followed some years earlier.[9]

Lope de Cáceres returned eventually to his native Segovia, where he lived in such a way as to give the impression that he had forgotten his former resolutions.

Juan de Arteaga was named a knight commander (*comendador*) and then designated bishop of Chiapas in Mexico. Out of veneration for his former master, Ignatius, he wrote to him offering that bishopric for one of the first Jesuits. Ignatius refused the offer. After his ordination as a bishop Arteaga went to Mexico, where he died through a tragic accident. In an illness he was given, instead of water to refresh him, a poison which brought about his death.

The fourth youth, Juan Reynalde, had joined the Franciscans.

In Paris, besides the three Spaniards we have mentioned, Iñigo worked with other students. He induced them to meet on Sundays at the Carthusian convent where, besides holding familiar conversations on spiritual subjects, they went to confession and received Holy Communion. But the time of those Sunday get-togethers happened to coincide with the scholastic disputations in the college which were from week to week more

9 *Autobiog*, no. 80.

poorly attended. The master, Peña, warned the leader of the group, who was Iñigo; and when this proved ineffective, he had recourse to the principal of Sainte Barbe. Gouveia decided to impose on the offender the punishment with which he had already threatened him at the beginning of his studies—the "hall". Iñigo does not relate this episode in his *Autobiography*, but we know it from the testimony of Ribadeneira, who said he heard it in Paris in 1542.[10]

When the sentence was communicated to Iñigo, he deliberated seriously about the reaction he ought to take. Neither the pain of the lashings nor the humiliation of the punishment were important for one who was disposed to suffer all for Christ. But he feared that that severe correction might be a scandal for the other students. He therefore went to Doctor Gouveia and fully explained his problem. The principal, a severe man but at the same time a deeply religious person, was convinced of the validity of the objection. When the time came to execute the punishment, to the great surprise of all those present, the principal fell on his knees before Iñigo's feet and begged his pardon.

These friendly relations between Doctor Gouveia and Iñigo, which began then, were enduring. From them arose the proposal made in 1538 by the principal of Sainte Barbe to his sovereign John III, that some of those who had joined Ignatius during their Paris days should be sent as missionaries to India.

Meanwhile Iñigo was able to continue his Sunday retreats with the students and the time table of the scholastic disputations was changed.

These apostolic activities were not an obstacle to his study of philosophy, which constituted his primary occupation. But to his external vicissitudes were soon added the same interior disturbances which he had experienced in Barcelona. While he was trying to apply his mind to his studies great lights and spiritual consolations came to him. With the experience in

10 *RibVita*, II, iii, in *FN*, IV, 221-227; see also *FN*, II, 382-384.

discernment which he had acquired, it was not difficult for him to detect the tactics of the evil spirit. His reaction was the same as that in Barcelona. He approached his master and promised his attendance and attention to his lectures, as long as he would find bread and water for his sustenance. The moderation which he imposed on himself regarding his apostolic activities had the beneficial result that he was no longer molested because of them. The Aragonese Doctor Jerónimo Frago observed this change and Iñigo gave him this explanation. The reason why they leave me in peace is that I no longer speak to people on the things of God; but when this course of studies is over, I shall return to my former practice.[11]

The students of arts or philosophy made their way through three courses, each of which lasted one year; and according to the subject matter they were pursuing they were called "summulists," logicians, and physicists. In the first two courses the students, through the dry study of logic, learned how to reason, to formulate their ideas with precision, and to defend them against the objections of an adversary. In the first course the textbook was the *Summulae* of Pedro Hispano, along with a variety of commentaries. But Master Juan Peña directly explained Aristotle's *Organon;* and when he found a difficulty in the interpretation of the text, he had recourse to Pierre Favre, who knew Greek.

The matter studied in the second course was the *Logic* of Aristotle, as explained by its commentators. Among these, Juan de Celaya was Peña's preference. The chief academic exercises consisted of the disputations, which were protracted almost throughout the day. At the end of the second year the candidate was admitted to an examination, known as "the determinations" (*determinantiae*), which allowed him to proceed to the baccalaureate. This examination was conducted in the schools on the rue de Fouarre (of the Forage), so called from the fodder or hay spread on the floor as sitting accommodation for the students. Here Iñigo obtained his Bachelor of Arts degree in 1532.

The third course was devoted to the study of Aristotle's

11 *Autobiog*, no. 82.

Physics, Metaphysics, and *Ethics.* At the close came the examination leading to the licentiate. This final examination consisted of two parts: one held in public, and another, much more severe, held in the private dwelling of the chancellor of Notre-Dame or in the Abbey of Sainte-Geneviève. It took place in the presence of four examiners, one from each of the four "nations" into which the university students were divided. The Spanish students were grouped in the "venerable Gallic nation" (*veneranda natio Gallicana*). The candidates were summoned for the second examination in accordance with the classification they had won in the first. Iñigo was ranked 30th on a roll of a hundred candidates.[12] For the second examination, the students were divided into groups of 16, wherefore Iñigo found himself in the second group. There is evidence that he and his companions appeared for their examination in the Abbey of Sainte-Geneviève. Once the examinations were completed, the university chancellor announced the date for the ritual of conferring the degree of licentiate. The day appointed for Iñigo was March 13, 1532, according to the manner of calculating in which the year starts with Easter; but this means March 13, 1533 according to the way of reckoning current now in which the year starts with January.[13] Starting from the church of the *Mathurins* (Trinitarians) on the rue Saint-Jacques, the candidates marched in solemn procession to the Abbey of Sainte-Geneviève. There the chancellor solemnly pronounced the formula whereby the candidates received the license to teach, dispute, and "determine" (*docere, disputare, et determinare*) at Paris and anywhere else in the world.

The reception of the licentiate carried with it considerable expenses, for the new graduate, besides paying the academic fees and taxes, had to offer a banquet for masters and students.

12 *FD*, p. 391.

13 It is important to notice that in Ignatius' era, the method of computation which begins the new year with Easter Sunday was in vigor in France. Hence the days which fell between January 1 and Easter Sunday, and which according to our present-day method of computing the new year were considered to be in 1533, were in France then considered to be still in 1532. In accordance with this, the date on which Ignatius received his licentiate in theology is March 13, 1533 when it is reckoned according to our present-day computation; but in French documents it is given as 1532. See *FD*, 390-391.

On this occasion Iñigo ran out of funds and was obliged to recur to the generosity of his Barcelona friends.

More costly was the conferral of the degree of Master of Arts, equivalent to the doctorate. Consequently, Iñigo postponed the ceremony for a year, and Pierre Favre for six years. Francis Xavier, on the other hand, obtained the degree a few days after his licentiate.[14]

The conferral of the degree of Master of Arts (*magister artium*) was celebrated with great solemnity in the halls of the *natio Gallicana*, on the rue de Fouarre. It consisted of an inaugural lecture delivered by the candidate which for being his first was called the inception (*inceptio*) or commencement. Next the president asked the attending masters if they approved of the granting of the biretta (*biretta*) to the candidate. Hence the ceremony of *incipere* came to be the same as *birretari*. The master of the beginner (*incipiens*) delivered an allocution, after which he imposed on the new master a four-cornered biretta as insignia of his new academic degree. Thereby the University added his name to the roll of its professors and authorized him to hold the office of "regent" or professor in any of its affiliated colleges in Paris.

In a subsequent assembly, celebrated in the convent of the Maturins, the secretary of the faculty handed over to the master the diploma in a parchment sealed with the great seal of the University. The diploma granted to "Master Ignatius of Loyola, of the diocese of Pamplona," has been preserved. It bears the date of March 14, 1534; but according to the way of reckoning current now this means March 14, 1535.[15] From then on Iñigo could be called Master Ignatius (*Maestro Ignacio*), as in fact he ordinarily was.

5. *Friends in the Lord*

It was in Paris that those young men who were to become Ignatius' companions in founding the Society of Jesus entered into close association with him. All of them decided to take

14 *FD*, pp. 386, 388.
15 *FD*, pp. 387, 395-397.

this step and join him after they made the Spiritual Exercises under his direction, except Francis Xavier who, because of his classes as a regent in the College of Dormans-Beauvais, did not make the Exercises until after the vow of Montmartre on August 15, 1534.

The first of Ignatius' permanent followers was Pierre Favre (*Petrus Faber* in the Latinized form of his name). He was born in the village of Villaret, in Savoy, on April 13, 1506. Already in the spring of 1531 he had thought of following in the footsteps of his fellow student Iñigo at the College of Sainte-Barbe. In the fall of 1533 he undertook a journey to his native place to visit his father and relations and settle some family affairs. Back in Paris early in 1534, he made the Spiritual Exercises for a month, after withdrawing to a house in the suburb of Saint-Jacques, where Iñigo, his director, visited him from time to time. The cold was so severe that the Seine was frozen, to such a point that wagons could be driven over it. But instead of heating his room Favre slept in a plain shirt upon the logs he had been given to kindle a fire. To this mortification he added fasting; he went six days without taking a mouthful. When Iñigo was given an account of this, he obliged him to stop those extremes, light a fire, and eat some food. Favre made a decision to be a priest totally dedicated to God's service, and this freed him from all the doubts which had tormented him regarding his future. His soul, agitated till then, was flooded with light and peace. On May 30 of that year 1534 he received the priestly ordination, and on July 22, the feast of St. Mary Magdalene, he celebrated his first Mass.

The Portuguese Simâo Rodrigues, a native of Vouzela in the diocese of Vizeu, and the Navarrese Francis Xavier decided to cast their lots with Iñigo in 1533. Xavier was Iñigo's most difficult conquest. Like Iñigo himself, Xavier had felt the allurements of a bright future in the world. To the insinuations of his·older companion in studies he offered long and stubborn resistance. Gradually however, a change was taking place in his soul and in the end the grace of his vocation won out. Once he made his decision, only the insistent pleas of his friends succeeded in persuading him to carry on his classes until the end of that academic year at the College of Dormans-

Beauvais where, after receiving his degree of Master of Arts in 1530, he had secured a place as a professor.

Little by little the rest of the companions joined the group. Diego Laínez from Almazán, Soria, and Alfonso Salmerón from Toledo, made the Exercises later than Favre in 1534. Both of them came from the University of Alcalá, whence they had moved to Paris to continue their studies. Another reason for their going there was, it seems, their desire to know Ignatius, of whom they had heard great praises at Alcalá.

Soon a youth from the kingdom of Castile, after going through the experience of the Exercises, joined Ignatius' band, Nicolás Alonso from Bobadilla del Camino in the diocese of Palencia. He was always known by the name of his native place. He had studied philosophy and theology at Alcalá and Valladolid, when in 1533 he decided to move to Paris. Here he learned that a student called Iñigo was giving help to some students in their material needs. Thanks to the support of this protector, Bobadilla secured a post as regent in the College of Calvi. But he was able to accomplish only a little in this occupation, for in 1534 he made up his mind to leave all for Christ and join Ignatius' group.

With Bobadilla there were in addition to Iñigo six who— as one of them, Diego Laínez, writes—"through prayer had resolved to serve our Lord, leaving behind all worldly things."[16] The idea of divine service recurs, with the persistence of leit-motiv, in the accounts of the vocations of the first companions. There is no doubt that Iñigo had inculcated it in each one's mind in the course of the Exercises. Starting with this initial decision, those generous youths formed a closely knit group of "friends in the Lord,"[17] as Ignatius himself called them in a letter to his Barcelona friend Juan Verdolay. They persevered in their resolution through prayer, the reception of the sacraments of penance and the Eucharist, and by pursuing the same studies. Since these were theological studies, they helped them to deepen their knowledge of divine things.

16 *FN*, I, 100.
17 *EppIgn*, I, 119.

6. *The Vow of Montmartre: August 15, 1534*

In this constant sharing of ideals the project which was to orientate their life for the future matured in the minds of all of them: to devote themselves to the welfare of their neighbor while living according to a plan of strict poverty, in imitation of Christ. First of all, they would undertake a pilgrimage to Jerusalem. For this purpose they would all assemble at Venice, the necessary port of embarkation. If after waiting for a whole year it should become clear that the pilgrimage was not possible, they would present themselves to the pope, that he might send them where he thought best. Such was, in its general thrust, the matter of the vow which Iñigo and his first six companions pronounced on Assumption day, August 15, 1534, in the little chapel dedicated to the Blessed Virgin Mary, on the hill of Montmartre at the place of the martyrdom of St. Denis and his companions.

On this solemn day, Pierre Favre, the only priest among them, celebrated the Mass. Just before communion time the celebrant turned to his companions, holding the sacred host above the paten, heard each one of the six recite his vow, and gave them Holy Communion. Then he himself pronounced his own vow and consumed the Blessed Sacrament.

The precise formula of the vow is not known. To arrive at its contents we have to recur to the testimony of those who pronounced it and of other contemporaries. A careful reading of the earliest accounts which have been preserved enables us to discover the deep root of the vow and all its modalities; and they can be summarized in the manner used above in the first paragraph of this section.[18]

There was one point which remained still to be determined: Once they were in Jerusalem, would they remain there permanently, or would they return? It is easy to suppose that Ignatius inclined to remain permanently. Let us recall that this had been his firm determination when he journeyed to the Holy

18 Among the earliest formulations of this vow, that of Favre can be seen in *FN*, I, 36-39; of Lainez, ibid., 102-104; of Polanco, ibid., 184, 190; of Ignatius, in *Autobiog*, no. 85, in *FN*, I, 480.

Land in 1523. But whether because the companions did not reach unanimity on this point, or because the possibility of the pilgrimage always turned out to be problematical, they left the decision for the time when they would be in Jerusalem.

In the vow they did not formally include that they would live in chastity, but it is clear that all were resolved to observe it. At least Ignatius and Favre had made the vow of chastity in a private form. All promised it in 1537 before their priestly ordination.

It is not difficult to discover in this vow a prolongation of the program that Ignatius had set down for himself since the days of his conversion at Loyola and of the illuminations he received at Manresa. From Loyola came his plan of journeying to Jerusalem to live in the land sanctified by the life and death of Jesus Christ. From Manresa stemmed his plan decidedly apostolic, which he proposed to execute in the strictest poverty with his other companions who shared his ideals.

Within the plans of Ignatius and his companions, in this vow there appeared for the first time the figure of the pope, considered as the vicar of Christ and his representative on earth. If the companions should not be able to spend their lives in the land of Jesus, they would place their persons at the disposal of him who holds his place on earth. Here were laid the foundations of what was to be the fourth vow of special obedience to the pope in what pertains to "missions," which the professed of the Society will pronounce. This vow, according to the felicitous expression of Blessed Pierre Favre, was virtually "the foundation (*fundamentum*) of the whole Society" and "its most manifest vocation."[19]

The Society of Jesus was not born at Montmartre. When they were taking their vow, Ignatius and his companions did not have any intention of founding a new religious order. Nor did they even decide at the time whether or not they would give a stable form to their group. But it is clear that on that feast of the Assumption and on the hill of Montmartre,

19 *FN*, I, 42.

the first foundation stones were laid of what was to be the Society of Jesus.

The vow taken in 1534 was renewed on the same feast of the Assumption in the two following years. There were two differences, however. First, Ignatius was not present at these two renovations, for he had returned to his native country, as we shall see; and second, to the original six companions three more were added, the Savoyard Claude Jay, and the Frenchmen Jean Codure and Paschase Broët. With them was completed the number of the ten who, including Ignatius, founded the Society of Jesus in 1539.

7. The Student of Theology: 1533-1535

On completing his three years of philosophical studies, Ignatius began those in theology, which he was unable to complete in Paris. From that time on he did not aspire to the doctorate in theology, because twelve years of study were required for it, nor even to the baccalaureate, which took five or six years. After he had already left Paris, a diploma, dated October 14, 1536, was sent to him from the Faculty of Theology. It testified that Ignatius of Loyola, Master of Arts, had studied Theology for a period of one year and a half.[20] This term "one year and a half" was a protocol expression which is found also in the diplomas of other students who had devoted to theology much more than eighteen months. But in Ignatius' case this was the exact time he had given to the study of the sacred sciences in Paris.

He did his theology by following the lectures in the Dominican convent of Saint-Jacques and in that of the Franciscans (*cordeliers*) nearby. To the lectures he had to bring the Bible and the commentary on the book of the *Sentences* by Peter Lombard. Outstanding among his professors were the Dominican Jean Benoît, who enjoyed great prestige, and the Franciscan Pierre de Cornes (*de Cornibus*). Ignatius' formation was essentially Thomistic. In his *Constitutions*, [464], he will prescribe that students of the Society be taught "the scholastic doctrine of St. Thomas," and "in positive theology

20 *FD*, p. 523.

those authors should be selected who are more suitable for our end."[21]

With regard to his proficiency in these theological studies, Nadal repeats the generic phrase which he had already used in respect to those in philosophy, that Ignatius did them "with great diligence." His words are: "And after [the Arts] he studied sacred theology also with great diligence, according to the doctrine of St. Thomas. On most of the days he went before dawn to the monastery of St. Dominic to hear a lecture given especially to the friars at that early hour."[22] Laínez gives the following global judgment on Ignatius' progress in studies: "In regard to his studies, although he happened to have more impediments than anyone else of his time, he showed diligence as great as his contemporaries or, with other things being equal even greater than they. In learning he made a median progress (*aprovechó medianamente*), as could be judged by what he showed when he answered in public and when he conversed with his fellow students during the time of his studies."[23] The expression *medianamente* is equivalent to "with much profit." This appears from the fact that Laínez applies the same expression to himself and to his other companions, among whom were some who were very good theologians.

To Ignatius' tenacity must be added his qualities of intelligence. These enabled him to answer in theological matters with a competence that attracted attention even from some who had done more studies than he. According to Nadal, "One doctor, a distinguished person, said in admiration of our Father that he had not seen anyone who could discuss theological matters with such mastery and dignity."[24] Polanco adds: "And with Dr. Martial [Mazurier] something curious happened. When Iñigo was not yet even a bachelor of arts, the doctor proposed to make him a doctor in theology, saying that since Iñigo was teaching him who was a doctor, it was but fair that he should have the same degree, and that he was considering how to make him a doctor."[25]

21 *Cons*, [464].
22 *FN*, II, 196.
23 *FN*, I, 100.
24 *FN*, II, 198.
25 *PolSum*, no. 51, in FN, I, 181.

Ignatius' theological studies could not fail to have an influence on the composition of the book of the *Exercises*. In it there are some parts, such as the meditation on the Three Classes of Men and the entire series of meditations on the life of Christ toward the end of the book, that seem to come from his years in Paris. Also from that period is a general revision of the text.

To Paris we must attribute the Eleventh Rule "toward acquiring the genuine attitude (*sentido*) which we ought to maintain in the Church." We ought "to praise both positive and scholastic theology. For, just as it is more characteristic of the positive doctors such as St. Jerome, St. Augustine, St. Gregory, and the rest to move the affections toward our loving and serving God our Lord in everything, so is it more characteristic of the scholastic doctors such as St. Thomas, St. Bonaventure, the Master of the Sentences, and the rest to define or explain for our times the things necessary for eternal salvation, and also to combat and explain better all errors and fallacies."[26] The words "or explain for our times" are a later addition made in the Saint's own hand, which reveals his concern for adaptation to the changing needs of the Church.

8. The Inquisitor Liévin and the Exercises

The book of the *Exercises* was formally approved by the Inquisitor of Paris, the Dominican Valentin Liévin, in March, 1535.[27] As Ignatius was near the time of his departure from Paris for Spain, he learned that rumors were spreading against him, surely because of the Exercises. Seeing that he had received no summons and that, on the other hand, he could not long delay his departure, he went on his own accord to the inquisitor and asked him to pronounce sentence on his case. He did not want to leave a dispute pending. The inquisitor told him that complaints against him had come in to him, but no measure had been taken against him, because he did not believe that these were matters of importance. Yet, he did wish to "see his writings of the *Exercises*." Ignatius gave them to him. After examining them, the inquisitor praised them highly and asked for a copy of them. We may suppose that

26 *SpEx*, [363].
27 *FN* I, 33*.

Ignatius complied with this order, but that copy of the *Exercises* has not been preserved. If we had it, and if also the text presented by Iñigo to the judges at Salamanca had come down to us, all the doubts regarding the process of elaboration of the *Exercises* would vanish. We would know in the concrete what they contained at the stages of such importance as those of Salamanca and Paris. Ignatius was not content with that oral approbation given by the inquisitor. He desired him to pronounce a formal sentence clearing these writings from anything blameworthy. The inquisitor offered excuses; but Ignatius came back accompanied by a notary who took down notes of the entire discussion. Thus the matter was considered closed.[28]

The inquisitor Liévin had known Ignatius earlier. Polanco relates how Ignatius had introduced before the inquisitor many who, touched by heresy, wished to retract their errors which stemmed from the "affair of the placards." This had exploded at the end of 1534. The Protestants, who had seen their numbers swell in France, desired to make a show of strength. On the morning of October 18, 1534, a great number of posters appeared, attached to the walls of the houses of Paris and displaying words depreciatory of the sacrifice of the Mass. The entire city was in commotion and a vigorous reaction followed. On January 21, 1535, a procession of atonement was organized that moved along the streets from the Sainte-Chapelle to the cathedral of Notre-Dame. This demonstration marked the beginning of a severe repression against heretics. Some were condemned to be burnt alive after they had their tongues pierced. King Francis I himself participated in this campaign, in the course of which he pronounced a discourse in the cathedral of Paris, in the presence of the clergy, the University, Parliament, the members of his private Council, and the ambassadors.[29]

28 *Autobiog*, no. 86; see also *PolSum*, 50, in *FN*, I, 180.
29 See G. Schurhammer, *Francis Xavier: His Life, His Times*, Vol. I, *Europe, 1506-1501* (Rome, 1973), translated by M. Joseph Costelloe, pp. 225-234.

Chapter 9

APOSTLE IN HIS OWN COUNTRY: 1535

Toward the end of his sojourn in Paris Ignatius was afflicted with those pains which throughout his life he described as stomach trouble, and which only the autopsy after his death showed to have been gallstones (biliary lithiasis) with referred pains to the stomach. The climate of Paris was disadvantageous for him. All the remedies employed proved ineffective. Finally the physicians advised a return to his native air. His companions supported this opinion, all the more so because of another reason. Since the Spaniards did not intend to return to their country, they thought it well that Ignatius should go there in order that, besides recruiting his strength, he should pay visits to the relatives of each one of them and settle some family affairs still pending.

There was another reason, not mentioned by the person most concerned but which, based on testimony from Polanco, we may consider as decisive: Ignatius wished to spend some time at Azpeitia to make amends with apostolic works for the bad examples he had given there during his youth.[1]

The decision was taken. Ignatius would leave for Spain and, after completing his projects there, he would journey to Venice, where he would wait for the arrival of his companions to embark on their pilgrimage to Jerusalem. Meanwhile the companions would continue their theological studies and leave Paris by the feast of the Conversion of St. Paul, January 25, 1537. As things turned out, the hazards of the war between France and the Emperor forced them to make an early departure on November 15, 1536.

---

1 *FN*, II, 568.

1. From Paris to Azpeitia

It was probably early in April, 1535, that Ignatius, mounted on a horse which his companions had bought for him, set out from Paris on the way to his native land. Already during the journey his health began to improve.

Ignatius tells us that on reaching Bayonne near the frontier, he was recognized by someone who hastened to bring the news to his brother Martín García at Loyola.[2] On crossing the border into Guipúzcoa, Ignatius did not keep to the ordinary route which would have taken him straight to Azpeitia, but he ventured into the more solitary mountains. Obviously he feared being identified, which actually happened. For he soon saw two armed men riding to meet him. The reason why they were armed was that those roads had a bad reputation for being infested with brigands. Then a pursuit began. The men followed Ignatius' footsteps, while he kept on trying to evade them. Finally they came together. They told him that they belonged to the household of Loyola; and they had come from his brother who had ordered them to go to meet him. But Ignatius had no desire whatever to follow them and slipped away. But a little before he arrived at Azpeitia he met these same men again, who were searching for him. They pressed him anew to go with them to his brother's house. But they were not able to force him.

In the process of beatification of Ignatius, Potenciana de Loyola, a niece of Ignatius, gives a different version of what happened. She states that the person who first recognized Ignatius was Juan de Eguíbar, the supplier of the meat shops (*bastecedor de las carnicerías*) of Azpeitia, who on his way to Behobia, stopped at the inn of Iturrioz, which "is a desert place, two leagues from the town."[3] There the innkeeper's wife told him of the arrival of a traveler who had strongly attracted her attention. Then Eguíbar, peeping through a crack in the door of Ignatius' room, saw him praying on his knees. Back at Azpeitia, Eguíbar informed Martín García de Oñaz how he had recognized Iñigo. Then the lord of Loyola

2 *Autobiog*, no. 87.
3 *SdeSI*, II, 190.

sent the priest Baltasar de Garagarza to search for his brother and accompany him to Loyola. Don Baltasar did find the traveler, but he could in no way convince him to accept his brother's invitation. Ignatius continued on his way alone through those mountains, following a route which we today can reconstruct. Starting from the inn of Iturrioz, which still exists, he passed near the inn of Etumeta, and from there he continued past those of Aritzain and Elaritza (which witness Potenciana calls Errarizaga) toward Lasao. Descending from there by the road that snakes along the bank of the Urola, he reached the hospital of La Magdalena, some 300 paces before the entrance of Azpeitia. There he begged for and received hospitality. The day was a Friday of the month of April, 1535, at five in the afternoon.

3. In the Hospital of La Magdalena

The administrators of the hospital and of the neighboring shrine of La Magdalena, situated on the other side of the road, were since 1529 Pedro López de Garín and his wife Emilia de Goyaz. In 1545, ten years after Iñigo's visit to Azpeitia and while a certain Joaneyza de Loyola was administrator, an inventory was drawn up of items belonging to the hospital and the shrine.[4] Naturally enough, bed linen and kitchen utensils were predominant among the items belonging to the hospital. In 1551 there was still kept there "the same old horse which Your Paternity left at the hospice now sixteen years ago, and it is very stout and very fit, and still rendering good service to the people in the house." Father Miguel Navarro, a companion of St. Francis Borgia in his journey through the Basque country, wrote this in a letter to Ignatius dated January 8, 1552.[5] It is clear that he was referring to the horse which Ignatius' companions had procured for him to make his journey through France to Azpeitia.

Ignatius tells us nothing about his efforts to recover his health. The documents are silent too. In contrast, they are prodigal in recounting the works of moral and social improvement which Ignatius undertook for the welfare of his native town.

4 *FD*, pp. 659-662.
5 *LittQuad*, I, 494.

In the process for the beatification of Ignatius, held at Azpeitia in 1595, the majority of the twenty witnesses summoned to make depositions remembered his sojourn at Azpeitia sixty years before.[6] Among them we may single out these few: Domenja de Ugarte, who was a servant girl of the hospital administrators when Ignatius lodged there; Catalina de Eguíbar, from the house of this name, near that of Loyola where Iñigo was born and raised; and Potenciana de Loyola, the daughter of his brother Pero López, the parish priest of Azpeitia.

All the witnesses agree in recalling that Ignatius stubbornly refused to lodge in the house of Loyola, in spite of very strong pressure brought to bear on him. All stressed that he lived by begging from door to door, and that he distributed among the poor the abundant alms he received, and that he carried on a life of great austerity, sleeping on the floor and wearing a hair shirt.

The reports of the witnesses in these processes confirm all that had been related by Ignatius himself in his *Autobiography* and by the writers contemporary to him. We can be sure nothing escaped his zeal in regard to anything he could do for the welfare of Azpeitia.

By his conversations he edified all those who came to visit him. His first care was to teach catechism to the children every day. He paid no attention to his brother, who tried to dissuade him by stating that no one would come to listen to him. Ignatius replied that for him it would suffice if he had only one hearer. A little later those who gathered around him were many, and among them was his brother. He also preached to the adults in the shrine of La Magdalena. Those attending ceased to fit within it and it became necessary for all to take to the open air. Some climbed the mud walls and trees to be able to hear him. On Sundays he customarily preached in the parish church.

Among his sermons stands out one which he preached in front of the shrine of our Lady of Elosiaga on St. Mark's day,

6 *SdeSI*, II, 167-259.

April 25. On the occasion of the rogation days, large crowds used to flock to that shrine, not only from Azpeitia but also from the nearby towns, Régil, Vidania, Goyaz, and the rest. Ignatius took that occasion to deliver a sermon. Mounted in a cherry tree in order to be seen and heard by all, he forcefully deplored vices and sins. He himself saw the fruit which came from his words. Ana de Anchieta states that "he castigated one vice practiced by the women in those places mentioned above, their [manner of] wearing yellow bonnets and fair hair (*tocas amarillas y cabellos rubios*). And during the sermon itself they covered them, and they wept with deep feelings."[7]

For a man so zealous for the glory of God, his chief preoccupation clearly had to be the reform of customs. He brought about the reconciliation of the estranged, achieved the conversion of three women of ill repute, put order into some marriages, and cut short some cases of concubinage. Ignatius relates a concrete case. The custom was prevalent in Azpeitia, he says, for the young unmarried girls of Azpeitia to go about with their heads uncovered until the time when they married. But some of those women who were living in concubinage were not ashamed to cover their heads, and say that they were doing this for this or that man. Ignatius brought it about that the governor was to enact a law in virtue of which all those women who would cover their heads for someone who was not their husband would have to be punished by a court of law. Thus that abuse began to be abolished.[8]

We have seen that Ignatius stubbornly refused to go to his ancestral home of Loyola. One night he made an exception, though not to sleep there. His sister-in-law, Magdalena de Araoz, had on one or another occasion requested him to go to Loyola. After some time, on one day she made her petition on her knees and "for the sake of the souls of your ancestry, and by the Passion of our Lord." Domenja de Ugarte, who informs us about this fact, does not state the strong reason which Magdalena brought forward. But it was so weighty that for

7 Ibid., 206.
8 *Autobiog*, no. 89.

130

this time Ignatius acceded to it, with these words: "You tell me this? Then for this I shall go to Loyola, and even to Vergara and anywhere else."[9] Years later Ignatius himself was more explicit when he was conversing with Father Pedro de Tablares. One of his relatives, he told Tablares, had a concubine, and every night she made her entrance through a secret door. Ignatius "waited for her one night, came face to face with her, and asked, 'What are you looking for here?' She told him what was going on. Ignatius put her into his own room and, to keep her from going farther and sinning, remained on guard over her there until the morning. He put her out then, as there was no way of doing it earlier. When he said, 'I put her into my own room,' Tablares remarked, 'I would not have done this.' And the Father replied, 'I did do it, because I knew that I could.' " Ignatius, as though he regretted his having told the story, ended by saying: "May God forgive you, who have made me tell what I had not wanted to mention."[10]

4. Works of Beneficence Promoted by Ignatius

One initiative of Ignatius destined to become lasting was his bringing about that every day at noon the bells of the parish church and of the ten shrines within its jurisdiction should be rung, in order that those hearing them might kneel down and recite one Our Father and one Hail Mary to obtain that all those who might be in mortal sin might repent from it, and then another Our Father and Hail Mary that they themselves might not fall into grave sin.[11] It was his desire that the house of Loyola should undertake this obligation in perpetuity. As a matter of fact, his brother Martín disposed in his will that this custom should be observed, and that for it two ducats should be paid each year to the parish sacristan, and a Castilian silver coin (*real*) to each of the sisters-in-charge (*seroras* or *freilas*) of the ten shrines.[12] He stipulated that two ducats and ten silver coins should be charged to the farm-

---

9 *SdeSI*, II, 188.

10 *FN*, III, 333.

11 *Autobiog*, no. 89; *FN*, I, 104, 187; *EppIgn*, I, 163; *FD*, p. 582. Concerning the charitable works promoted by Ignatius at Azpeitia, see N. Brieskorn, "Ignatius in Azpeitia 1535. Eine rechthistorische Untersuchung," *AHSJ*, XLIX (1980), 95-112.

12 *FD*, p. 582.

house (*caserío*) of Aguirre, which was part of the property of the lord of Loyola. In his will Martín García added also that he wished to "bequeath to my brother another memorial" (*otra memoria*), in other words, another recompense to his brother Ignatius, who however wanted nothing more than that previous one.[13] Here, as we have seen also on other occasions, it clearly appears once more that for Ignatius money was something superfluous.

It was greatly due to his exertions that abuses of gambling were eradicated. According to the account of one witness, many packs of playing cards were discarded along the Urola River.[14]

During the sojourn of Ignatius at Azpeitia a work was initiated of which he was an ardent promotor. On May 23, 1535, the town council, in plenary session, approved an ordinance whereby, on the one hand mendicancy was checked, and on the other, provision was made for the necessary assistance to the poor of the town.[15] Begging was forbidden except in case of genuine necessity. To replace it, two delegates were to be elected each year, one a cleric and the other a lay man. Their duty was to collect on every Sunday and feast day the alms for the poor and to supervise its distribution. The needy were to apply to these delegates of the town. To stop the abuse of those who merely feigned poverty or were able to work, a list of those truly in need was to be drawn up. The delegates were to give the alms to these but refuse it to cheats. The administrators of the hospitals were not to give lodging to any persons other than those truly poor.

Ignatius took a leading part in the foundation of this charitable work, as he himself recognized in these words of his *Autobiography*: "He saw to it that the poor were to be helped publicly and regularly."[16] This is expressly confirmed by an ancient *Account of the first origins of the remembrance of the poor*

13 *FD*, p. 583.
14 *SdeSI*, II, 220.
15 *FD*, p. 456.
16 *Autobiog*, no. 89.

who are ashamed to beg.[17] This report links the foundation of this work of relief with the arrival of Ignatius at Azpeitia in 1535. Among other good works which he undertook, he "labored as much as he could that those truly poor in his country, who suffered from hunger and other needs, would receive help."[18] He exposed his ideas to the councilors and other leading persons of Azpeitia and gave his full collaboration in drawing up the statutes for this work. The chief animators of the enterprise were Juan de Eguíbar, the first one who recognized Ignatius in the Iturrioz inn, and his wife María de Zumiztain. This couple put 160 ducats on deposit in order that the income from them might increase this fund for the poor. They were also the first administrators of the "box for the poor" (*bacín*).[19]

5. Settlement with the "Isabelitas"

May 18, 1535, marked the end of a controversy that for over twenty years had kept two ecclesiastical parties at loggerheads with each other: the parish clergy of Azpeitia and the church patron on the one side, and on the other the nuns of the convent of the Immaculate Conception, who belonged to the Third Order of St. Francis, locally known as the "Isabelitas." The foundation of that "monastery of the Immaculate Conception" in 1497 was due to María López de Emparan, a cousin of Ignatius since she was a daughter of his aunt Catalina, and to her companion Ana de Uranga. This foundation encountered difficulties from the start. Its proximity to the parish church, only 150 paces away, raised problems of rights in the matter of Masses, sermons, funerals, and other acts of worship. More than once the lay patron of the church had recourse to the protection of the king, who considered the church of Azpeitia as part of the crown patrimony.

The most publicized episode was that of the funeral of Juan de Anchieta. This celebrated musician, who had been choir master (*maestro de capilla*) of the infante Don Juan, son of the Catholic Kings, had been a great protector of the nuns as

17 *FD*, pp. 441-443.
18 Ibid., p. 442.
19 See the documents on this matter in *FD*, pp. 439-462.

rector of Azpeitia. In his last will he had disposed that his body should be interred in the convent church.[20] When he died on July 30, 1523, the rector of the parish, Andrés de Loyola, a nephew of Ignatius, with the rest of the clergy seized by force the body of the deceased for burial in the parish and not in the convent.[21] We should mention in passing that the Anchieta family, whose manor-house (*casa solar*) is still at Urrestilla, from where came the apostle of Brazil José de Anchieta, was habitually at odds with the families of Loyola and Emparan. When rector of Azpeitia, Juan de Anchieta had proposed to resign his office in favor of his nephew García de Anchieta, thus overriding the patron's right of presentation. García de Anchieta was assassinated on September 15, 1518, by Pedro de Oñaz and Juan Martínez de Lasao.[22]

The quarrels between the parish and the convent gave rise to a court-case that reached the Roman curia. This court decided in favor of the parish clergy and its patron and imposed a fine of 180 ducats on the nuns. Several attempts at reconciliation came to naught, one of them being that made in 1533 by Martín García de Oñaz.[23] During his stay at Azpeitia, Ignatius resolved to put an end to the conflict in which his brother was implicated with so much harm to the common peace. His efforts were successful. As indicated above, on May 18, 1535, the writ of agreement between the two parties (*escriura de acordio*) was signed. The first of the witnesses who signed the document was "Ynigo."[24]

It seems that Ignatius could do nothing further for his native town. All that he accomplished sprang from his well-ordered but intense love of his land and its people. His fellow Azpeitians must have been astonished at the examples of virtue given by their fellow countryman. One can truly say that those three months of heroic life altogether obliterated the traces of a past which had been scarcely edifying.

20 *FD*, 287-289.
21 Ibid., p. 292.
22 Ibid., pp. 367-373.
23 Ibid., pp. 392-395.
24 The complete text of the agreement is in *FD*, pp. 397-439.

Ignatius will never again return to Azpeitia, but even from faraway Rome he will maintain his concern for the welfare, especially the spiritual good, of his native town. This is shown by his letters to the town council and to his nephew Beltrán, the new lord of Loyola. Writing to Beltrán in 1539, he beseeched him "for the love and reverence of God our Lord," to remember what he had often recommended to him by word of mouth, that is to say, to endeavor "to work for peace and reform especially of the clergy of the town." This, he said, would be the best proof that he deserved the "trust" he had placed in him since his father's death.[25]

A concrete example of his love for Azpeitia was given by Ignatius when, in 1538, the Italian Dominican Tommaso Stella founded in the Roman church of Santa Maria sopra Minerva a confraternity of the Blessed Sacrament, confirmed on November 30, 1539, by Paul III. Ignatius took the trouble of sending at once a copy of the bull of foundation of the confraternity extended to Azpeitia. The bull went astray but Ignatius sent in 1542 a fresh copy of the document.[26] Thus the confraternity, commonly known as of Minerva, replaced the one founded in 1508 by Doña Teresa Enríquez, the great devotee of the Eucharist (*"la loca del Sacramento"*), which also had been extended to Azpeitia in 1530.[27]

The recovery of his health had been the expressed reason for Ignatius' journey to his native land. At the beginning of his stay there he felt well, but later he fell into a serious illness. Once he felt better, he decided to carry out the second part of the project on which he and his companions in Paris had agreed while planning his journey.

6. *Journey through Spain*

Toward July 23, 1535, he took to the road from Azpeitia to Pamplona. That very day he had acted as a witness in the sale of a chestnut horse, made by Beltrán López de Gallaiztegui to his cousin Beltrán de Oñaz for the payment of "thirty ducats

---

25 *EppIgn*, I, 148-151.
26 FD, pp. 655-657.
27 *FD*, pp. 375-383.

of old gold and full weight" (*de oro viejo e de peso.*)[28] Was this horse a parting gift made by the lord of Loyola to his pilgrim uncle?

At the village of Obanos in Navarre he met Captain Juan de Azpilcueta, brother of Francis Xavier, to whom he delivered the latter's letter. Francis was asking his brother to be a good host to Ignatius and to disregard prejudices he might perhaps harbor against him, founded on false information. He asked him also to send him, through his companion, some money "to alleviate my great poverty."[29]

From Obanos he made his way toward Almazán in Soria, where he delivered a letter of Diego Laínez to his father. Other stops were at Sigüenza, Madrid, and Toledo, the home town of Alfonso Salmerón. In Madrid he was seen by Prince Philip, then a boy of eight, as the king himself recalled in 1586, when he saw the Saint's painting by Alonso Sánchez Coelho.

He then turned east toward Segorbe. In the nearby village of Altura stands the Carthusian monastery of Vall de Cristo, which Juan de Castro, his former exercitant and friend of Paris days, had entered. It is not difficult to imagine the fond memories they would recall as they conversed. Castro would have been, no doubt, a faithful follower of Ignatius, but his vocation was not to the active life but to one of contemplation.

Ignatius pushed on to Valencia. There by the river Turia stands a house where a tradition exists that it had been used by Ignatius as his lodging. At the Grao or port of Valencia he embarked for Genoa. Though historical sources are silent about this, it is probable that the ship called at Barcelona. There he would make concrete arrangements with his friends and benefactors for the remittance of pecuniary resources to help him complete his studies in Italy, which surely reached him, we know. At Valencia his friends did all they could to

28 *FD*, p. 466.
29 *EppXav*, I, 10-11.

dissuade him from undertaking the sea voyage to Italy, because of the hazards posed by the presence of the Turkish pirate Barbarossa (Khair-ed-deen) in Mediterranean waters. But dangers of this kind, we know, would not have weight enough to change the plans of a man so firm in his resolves as Ignatius.

Chapter 10

EVANGELICAL LIFE IN ITALY: 1535-1538

1. Route across Italy

By the month of October or November, 1535, Ignatius started his voyage to Italy. Fortunately, in the crossing the ship did not encounter the pirate Barbarossa; but it did run into a violent storm. The rudder of the ship was broken. The situation reached the point where it seemed that, humanly speaking, shipwreck was inevitable. Ignatius, preparing himself for death, now had no fear because of either his sins or the coming judgment. What he did feel was great confusion and sorrow for his past failure to make better use of the graces and gifts which God had communicated to him. Providence watched over him. The danger passed and the ship reached a pier in the harbor of Genoa.

Ignatius planned to devote the year or more which remained to him before the arrival of his companions at Venice, scheduled for the beginning of 1537, to a continuation of his theological studies. The city he chose for this was Bologna. Therefore, once he had landed at Genoa, he took the road to that city of Emilia. His most probable route was that followed by the post horses. Through Chiavari and Sestri Levante along the coast, he would move toward Varese Ligure. Through the mountain pass of Centocroci he would come to Borgo di Val di Taro. Following the course of the river Taro by way of Fornovo, he would reach the Emilian Way near Parma. From there the journey to Bologna on this ancient Roman road was easy.

It was necessary for him to cross the Appenines, and this was a difficult undertaking. At a certain point, he lost his way. A moment came when he was unable either to advance or go back. For a time he had to make his way by crawling on all fours. Ignatius will state later that this had been the greatest fatigue and bodily labor which he incurred in his life. But hardly knowing how, he escaped from it.[1]

But his changes of fortune did not end there. While entering Bologna, he fell from a small footbridge into one of the ditches or canals which run through the outskirts of the city. He arose completely wet and muddy, causing laughter among those who saw him so unfortunately dressed. He begged for a little bread to recover his strength; but he found none, even though, as he himself states, "he went through the whole city."[2] Ribadeneira marveled at that, since there was question of "so great, wealthy, and charitable a city"[3] as Bologna.

In these straits, he remembered that there was at Bologna the College of San Clemente, founded for Spanish students by Cardinal Gil de Albornoz. He sought lodging there, where, as Polanco relates, "he found persons whom he knew, who helped him to wash up and eat."[4] We do not know who these friends may have been. In that year of 1535 the rector of the college as well as of the University of Bologna, was Pedro Rodríguez, a professor of canon law who was a native of Fuentesaúco in Zamora. The chaplain was Francisco López, a native of Gómara in the diocese of Osma. Ignatius, to be sure, was not a student in this College of San Clemente. It is most probable that during his brief sojourn at Bologna he put up in one of the boarding houses in which the Spanish students lodged.

When he had passed through these first difficulties and could begin on his plan of studies, he fell ill before Christmas. He had to remain in bed for seven days with stomach trouble and alternations of chills and fever. It was becoming clear that Bologna was not the right place for him. He then decided to move on to Venice, which he did at the end of 1535.

1 *Autobiog*, no. 91.
2 Ibid.
3 *Rib-Vita*, II, v, in *FN*, IV, 245. See also C. Dalmases, "El paso de San Ignacio por el Real Colegio de España en Bolonia," *Studia Albornotiana*, 12 (1972), 403-410.
4 *PolSum*, no. 61, in *FN*, I, 188; see also *FN*, II, 572.

2. In Venice: 1536

Ignatius spent the whole of 1536 in Venice. There everything went well with him. His health gave him no trouble. He had no problems about lodging, since he was received "in the house of a man who was very learned and good."[5] There seems to be reference here to Andrea Lippomano, prior of the Trinità, a future benefactor of the Society. He had no lack of money. Isabel Roser had promised him at Barcelona that she would send whatever he needed to complete his studies. We know already that he was satisfied with little. Isabel had arranged that twelve escudos should be waiting for him on his arrival at Bologna. Now further money reached him from the archdeacon of Barcelona, Jaime Cassador. Meanwhile he was waiting for Lent to arrive "in order to put aside his literary labors to undertake others of more importance and of higher rank," as he wrote to an unknown Doña María, a benefactress of his in Paris.[6]

The labors to which he referred were, above all, spiritual conversations and the Exercises. Among the persons to whom he gave these Exercises, he himself enumerates Pietro Contarini, a noble Venetian cleric, procurator of the Hospital of the Incurables; Gasparo de' Dotti, vicar of Girolamo Verallo, the apostolic nuncio to Venice; a Spaniard named Rozas, about whom we know nothing. Another Spaniard who also made the Exercises was Diego de Hoces, a priest from Málaga. But he had problems at the start, for besides conversing with Ignatius, he dealt also with Gian Pietro Caraffa (Carafa), bishop of Chieti (Theate), who together with St. Cajetan (Gaetano) of Thiene had founded in 1524 the first order of clerks regular, called the Theatines. In all probability it was Caraffa who put Hoces on guard against dealing with Ignatius. In spite of this Hoces decided to make the Exercises, although he took the precaution of putting into his bag some books by which he might refute the errors his master might perhaps teach him. Three or four days sufficed for him to see that his fears were unfounded. He not only remained free from doctrinal problems but also decided to follow his master's

---

5 Letter to Jaime Cassador, dated Feb. 12, 1536. *EppIgn*, I, 94.
6 *EppIgn*, I, 724.

way of life. Unfortunately, he was not able to increase the number of those who founded the Society of Jesus, as he died at Padua in 1538. Ignatius, who at that time was at Monte Cassino giving the Exercises to Doctor Pedro Ortiz, saw his soul going up to heaven.

While in Venice, Ignatius entered into communication with the aforementioned Gian Pietro Caraffa who in 1555 was to become Pope Paul IV. It is clear that these two great men were not born to understand each other. They did not have the same ideas about what a life of apostolic poverty ought to be. We have already indicated that Caraffa was the cofounder of the Theatines. Ignatius observed the tenor of life which these religious followed—at least in Venice at that precise time—and it did not come up to his likes. We can infer that there were frictions with Caraffa from an autograph letter written to him by Ignatius, though in all probability it was never sent.[7] If we prescind from the contingent circumstances that inspired it, this letter is of the highest interest to us. For it reveals to us what, according to Ignatius' mind, the plan of life of the Society of Jesus ought to be, three years before its foundation and when it was still far from being formally decided upon. Ignatius saw that the Theatines in Venice did no begging even though they were lacking in means of subsistence; they hoped to obtain everything necessary from voluntary offerings. They shut themselves in their houses and did not go out to preach. They were not practicing the corporal works of mercy. These practices were in contrast with Ignatius' ideas. He envisaged a life in poverty but also dedicated to the apostolate and to works of mercy. These would stimulate the charity of the faithful, in such a way that what was needed for living would not be lacking. Ignatius wrote to Caraffa: "St. Francis and the other saints hoped and were confident in the Lord; but notwithstanding this they would not omit employing the most convenient means to maintain and enlarge their houses to the greater glory of God and the greater praise of his Majesty."[8] St. Francis and other saints acted in this manner. They did not fail to use suitable means to support their houses.

7 *EppIgn*, I, 114-118. Critical edition in *AHSJ*, XLIV (1975), 139-152.
8 *EppIgn*, I, 117.

To act otherwise would seem to be tempting God. That is why Ignatius feared "that the society which God has given you will not spread."⁹ Caraffa was not in agreement; and from this began the difficulties which Ignatius had with the future Paul IV. They soon separated from each other, for the Theatine was summoned to Rome by Pope Paul III on September 27, 1536, to work at the preparation of the Council of Trent, and on December 22 of the same year he was elevated to the cardinalate.

3. Reunion of the Companions in Venice

The companions set out from Paris on November 15, 1536. They wore their long and rather threadbare student gowns, held up in front by a belt to enable them to walk more freely. Their heads were covered with a broad-rimmed hat. They carried a rosary hung about their necks and also, by straps slanting across the shoulders, a leather knapsack containing their books and notes. Each carried a tall pilgrim's staff in his hand.

Apart from the distance, enormous for a journey to be covered all on foot, two circumstances made it especially difficult: the state of war between France and the Emperor, and the intense winter cold. It should be remembered that in that same year of 1536 Francis I invaded Savoy and he even captured the city of Turin. On his part, Charles V had entered Provence where he was repulsed by Montmorency. It was clear that the companions had to recede as far as possible from the fields of battle. Hence they chose the route through Lorraine and Alsace, and from there they would enter Switzerland and proceed via Bolzano and Trent to the Venetian territory.

To be less noticed as they left Paris, they divided into two groups, which were to converge in Meaux, some forty-five kilometers from the capital. While they were travelling on French soil, since several of them were subjects of Charles V, they had to conceal their nationality. Therefore when they needed information, only those who spoke French well did

9 *EppIgn*, I, 115.

the speaking. If someone asked them who they were and where they were going, they replied simply that they were students of Paris who were going on a pilgrimage to Saint-Nicolas-de-Port, a shrine near Nancy. On one occasion when some soldiers importuned them with further questions, fortunately for them a passerby happened along and said, "These fellows are on their way to reform some country."[10] This was a remarkable intuition from an unknown person.

On French territory they were rained on almost every day. Later they encountered the rigors of an extremely severe winter. But nothiug could stop their advance. They placed their confidence in God alone, for whom they were submitting to this hard test.

Their manner of travelling was the following. Periods of silent prayer alternated with the singing of psalms and spiritual conversations. The three priests, Favre, Jay, and Broët, celebrated Mass and the others heard it, confessed, and received communion. When they came to an inn, before going to bed they thanked God for the day's blessings. On the next morning, before continuing their march they made a short prayer. "In eating," Laínez writes, "we took enough, and rather too little than too much."[11]

They missed no chance to speak of God with those they met. When travelling through areas which had become Protestant, they took more than one occasion to defend their faith with vigor.

From Strasbourg they made for Basle, which had accepted the teaching of Zwingli. Here, on the night between July 11 and 12, 1536, Erasmus had died. Other stops on their journey were Constance, Feldkirch, Bolzano, and Trent. From there they had a direct route to Venice through the pass of Val Sugana. Moving through Bassano del Grappa, Castelfranco, and Mestre, they finally reached Venice. The day was January 8, 1537. They had been on the road for fifty-four days.

10 *FN*, I, 108, 189.
11 *FN*, I, 108.

In Venice they were heartily received by Ignatius, who had been waiting for their arrival. He remained in the house of his benefactor, and the newcomers found accommodation in two hospitals, that of Sts. John and Paul and that of the Incurables. There they devoted themselves to the service of the sick. In this way they awaited the coming of Easter, the time appointed to ask in Rome for the permission necessary for the pilgrimage to Jerusalem.

On March 16 they set out for Rome for the purpose of asking this permission. All went, except Ignatius. To the original group of nine two had been added in Venice, the priest Antonio Arias and the former servant of Francis Xavier in Paris, Miguel Landívar. Ignatius stayed behind in Venice for fear that his presence in Rome would create difficulties from two influential persons at the papal court. One was Doctor Pedro Ortiz who, as we saw above, had in Paris taken offense at the change of life taken up by his relative Pedro de Peralta after he had made the Exercises. The other person was the new Theatine Cardinal Gian Pietro Caraffa, from whom he had become estranged in Venice because of their differing criteria with respect to religious life.

Following the Via Romea which runs along the Adriatic coast, the travelers passed through Ravenna, Ancona, and Loreto. After they had satisfied their devotion at the Marian shrine, they penetrated into the interior of the peninsula by way of the Marches and Umbria. By keeping to the Flaminian Way through Trevi, Terni, and Civita Castellana they drew near to their goal.

At sunset on Palm Sunday, March 25, they crossed the Milvian bridge and entered Rome through the Porta del Popolo. They found lodging in the various hospices of their respective nationalities. The Spaniards stayed together in the hospice for them, next to the church of St. James of the Spaniards in the Piazza Navona. One of the council members of the hospice that year was Doctor Pedro Ortiz. After celebrating the Holy Week services devoutly, they prepared themselves to accomplish the purpose of their journey to Rome, which was to obtain the permission for their pilgrimage to the Holy Land.

Contrary to what they had expected, Doctor Ortiz not only failed to show himself hostile to the group but he even helped them to obtain an audience with the pope, Paul III. This took place on Easter Tuesday, April 3, in the Castel Sant' Angelo. Along with cardinals, bishops, and theologians, the recently arrived Parisian Masters found themselves among those invited. During the meal the pope heard them discourse on theological topics. He was much pleased and showed himself willing to grant them their desire. They told him that they wanted only two things: his blessing and the permission to go to Jerusalem. He orally granted what they asked. He also gave them sixty ducats for their voyage, an example which was imitated by some cardinals and other members of the Roman curia. The sum gathered amounted to 260 ducats.[12]

A few days later two documents were issued, both bearing the date of April 27, 1537: the permission to proceed to Jerusalem, and the dimissorial letters, sealed and signed by the chief penitentiary himself, Cardinal Antonio Pucci, granting to those among them who were not yet priests permission to receive sacred orders from any bishop, even though he be outside the territory of his jurisdiction. And this could be done even outside the Ember Days, on three Sundays or feast days.[13] On April 30, Pierre Favre, Antonio Arias, and Diego de Hoces, who were already priests, received the faculty to absolve any of the faithful even from censures reserved to a bishop.[14]

Early in May they undertook their return journey to Venice, where they resumed their helping services in the hospitals. On May 31, the feast of Corpus Christi, they participated with the other pilgrims in the solemn procession which started from St. Mark's basilica. As it ended they were presented, in the ducal palace, to the Doge Andrea Gritti, then eighty-three years old, the one who in 1523, fourteen years earlier, had helped Iñigo to make his pilgrimage possible.

The month of June was the time set for the departure of the

12 *EppIgn*, I, 120; *FN*, I, 116, 192; *FN*, III, 80.
13 Text in *FD*, pp. 526-529.
14 *Fabri Monumenta*, pp. 7-8.

pilgrims. But this year of 1537 not a single ship sailed from Venice with destination to the Holy Land. It was the first time in thirty-eight years that this had happened. Insistent rumors of war went the rounds and there was talk that the Republic of Venice had secretly tightened its alliance with the pope and the emperor against the Turks. These, with their galleys, were invading the waters of the Ionian Sea and there was fear that they would attack the Apulian coast and the papal states. In this situation so tense it was obvious that no pilgrim ship could set out to the sea.

4. Holy Orders

While they waited, Ignatius and his companions thought of making use of the permission they had received in Rome to be ordained. Two bishops offered to ordain them: the papal legate in Venice, Girolamo Verallo, and Vincenzo Nigusanti, Bishop of Arbe. It was the latter who proceeded to the ordinations. This prelate, a native of Fano, was since 1515 at the head of the diocese of Arbe, an island off the Dalmatian coast, known today as Rab. Nigusanti resided habitually in Venice, and there in the chapel of his own house he conferred the orders on Ignatius and those of his companions who were not yet priests. He stated later that never in his life had he performed an ordination which brought him consolation as great as that one. He did not ask the newly ordained for any money, not even a candle. They were seven in number: Ignatius, Bobadilla, Codure, Xavier, Laínez, Rodrigues, and Salmerón. Landívar was not ordained; he and Arias had already left the group. Salmerón received all the orders up to the diaconate; but he had to postpone the priestly ordination till October of that year, because in June he was not yet twenty-two years old.

The program they followed was this. Before receiving orders they all pronounced, on their own initiative, the vows of poverty and chastity in the hands of the nuncio, Verallo. On June 10, a Sunday, those who had not yet done so, received the minor orders. On the 15th, the feast of Sts. Vitus and Modestus, a day of obligation in Venice, they received the subdiaconate; on Sunday the 17th, the diaconate; and on the 24th, feast of St. John the Baptist, the priesthood.

146

5. Awaiting a Ship to the Holy Land

Without giving up their hope of being able to sail, they decided to distribute themselves meanwhile into various cities of the Republic of Venice, "La Serenissima," that they might assemble quickly in its capital if a propitious opportunity should arise. The various fields of their apostolate were these. Ignatius, Favre, and Laínez went to Vicenza; Xavier and Salmerón to Monselice; Codure and Hoces to Treviso; Jay and Rodrigues to Bassano del Grappa; Bobadilla and Broët to Verona. Their plan was to prepare themselves to celebrate their respective first Masses, to preach in the piazzas, and to exercise other works of the apostolate in the measure which their knowledge of the language made possible. Each one would choose his own date for his first Mass. They had faculties to celebrate it any day from July 5 onward, as well as to preach and administer the sacraments, granted by the nuncio Verallo for the entire territory of his jurisdiction.[15]

Their departure from Venice was fixed for July 25. Ignatius, Favre, and Laínez betook themselves to Vicenza, where they took up their abode in a ruinous building without doors or windows. It was the abandoned monastery of San Pietro in Vivarolo, situated in the outskirts of the city. Throughout this whole period Ignatius lived out, as he himself avows, a second Manresa.[16] In contrast to what occurred during his years of study, he experienced at Vicenza many spiritual visions and he had almost continuous consolations. The priesthood was their most important focus.

The companions dedicated the first forty days wholly to prayer. Two of the three went out to beg for their food. This was so meager that it was barely sufficient to sustain their lives. They were ordinarily satisfied with some cooked bread, which they had to use in a mash or soup. It was prepared by the third, who remained at home. Almost always this was Ignatius.

After these forty days Codure joined them, and then they

15 Text in *FD*, pp. 533-534.
16 *Autobiog*, no. 95.

began to preach in the piazzas. By shouting and waving their birettas they assembled a congregation. Many persons were moved by their preaching. What they had experienced before on similar occasions was further confirmed: When they engaged in works of mercy, they received more abundant alms. In this way the prediction which Ignatius made to Gian Pietro Caraffa in Venice was fulfilled.

An urgent summons from Bassano came to interrupt that solitude. Simão Rodrigues was seriously ill. Although he himself then had a fever, Ignatius decided to go immediately to console his companion. With Favre he covered the thirty-five kilometers of the road so fast, that his companion could hardly keep pace with him. Engaged in prayer as he traveled, he knew, through a divine illumination, that Simão was not to die from that illness. But Ignatius did not for that reason turn back from the intended visit. Rodrigues and Jay had taken lodging in the hermitage of St. Vitus, still existent outside the city, as guests of a hermit named Antonio. The joy which Simão felt at the presence of Ignatius was enough to make him well.

6. All Reunited in Vicenza

In October, 1537, all were again together in a house in Vicenza, except Xavier and Rodrigues who were sick in a hospital. The external circumstances were developing in this manner. On September 13 of 1537 Venice concluded a first treaty of alliance with the pope. As a result, the republic found itself in a state of war against the Crescent. It was clear that in those circumstances a pilgrimage was unthinkable. Yet the companions did not give up as vanquished but decided to await developments. It is unclear whether the twelve months they had promised to wait, in virtue of their vow at Montmartre, were being counted from the arrival of the companions at Venice, and therefore from January of 1537 to January of 1538; or rather from June, the month in which the pilgrim ship ordinarily departed, to June. What is certain is that, even though the period stipulated in the vow expired in January 1538, they agreed to prolong it by a few months more.

In the meantime all had celebrated their first Masses, except for Ignatius, as we shall see. They decided, therefore, to distribute themselves anew through various cities; but this time to cities not limited to the region of Venice. They chose cities in which there were universities, with the hope that some young university student would desire to join their group. They also wished to observe whether any focus of Lutheranism was forming in these centers. This second distribution was the following: Ignatius, Favre, and Laínez went to Rome, from which they had been called, probably by Doctor Ortiz; Codure and Hoces to Padua; Jay and Rodrigues to Ferrara; Xavier and Bobadilla to Bologna; Broët and Salmerón to Siena. The mixture of nationalities should be noticed except in the case of Bologna. It was not by accident but by design.

7. The Company of Jesus

A question arose which at first sight had only a circumstantial and secondary character but gave rise to an answer which was to mark for all times the destiny of that little band of men. What were they to reply to those who asked them who they were? Their decision was this: They were to answer that they were the company of Jesus. It is worthwhile to cite an important text of Polanco about the origin of this name:

> The name is the Company of Jesus (*Compañia de Jesús*). The name was taken before they reached Rome. When discussing among themselves what they should name themselves in reply to someone who asked what was their congregation, made up of nine or ten persons, all immediately betook themselves to prayer and to thinking what name would be most fitting. And, seeing that they had among themselves no other superior except Jesus Christ whom alone they desired to serve, it seemed to them most fitting that they should take the name of him whom they had as their head, by calling themsleves the company of Jesus (*la compañía de Jesús*).[17]

The name of *compañía* did not have a military connotation. It was a noun applied to brotherhoods or associations whether religious or cultural. Among such cases, one of the most significant is that of the Company of Divine Love (*Compagnia*

---

17 *PolSum*, no. 86, in *FN*, I, 204.

del Divino Amore), an association of persons determined to live according to the principles of the Catholic reformation.

This was the origin of the name Society of Jesus, at a time when Ignatius and his companions had not yet decided upon the foundation of a new religious order.

However, that Ignatius was thinking of founding a "company" was something which he had already communicated confidentially to his nephew Beltrán in their intimate conversations at Azpeitia in 1535. When, four years later, the foundation of the Society of Jesus had become a fact through the oral approval of Pope Paul III granted on September 3, 1539, Ignatius informed Beltrán of this pleasing news in a letter written in that same month: "Since I well remember that when I was with you there in our country you requested me earnestly to keep you informed about the society which I was hoping to form, I also believe that God our Lord expected you to distinguish yourself in it, that you might leave behind something more memorable than our ancestors have left. And, coming to the point of the matter, I, though most unworthy, have succeeded, by means of the divine grace, in laying firm foundations for this Society of Jesus, which we have thus entitled and which has now been approved by the pope."[18]

The company (with a small c) of Paris and Vicenza had now already become the Company of Jesus (with a capital C) of Rome. Ignatius would have been pleased if his nephew were to join it in order to "distinguish himself" in undertakings of greater moment than those of their forbears of the house of Loyola. But this was not to be, for Beltrán had married Juana de Recalde in 1536 and since his father's death in 1538 was the new lord of Loyola.

The name "Company of Jesus" (*Compañía de Jesús* in Spanish, *Societas Iesu* in Latin, *Society of Jesus* in English) received a decisive confirmation in the vision of La Storta, of which we shall treat below; and it gained a formal approbation in the deli-

18 Letter of Sept., 1539, in *EppIgn*, I, 150.

berations which the companions held in 1539, out of which the new religious order was born. Ignatius desired that this name should be applied to the order as an irrevocable mark. He would never change it; and in view of the fact that all the companions had decided that in regard to the most important points they would not be able to introduce changes unless it was by unanimity, the name of the Society would remain fixed forever.[19]

Before the companions returned to Venice, Ignatius had been accused before the ecclesiastical authority. His detractors, lacking any specific transgression of faith or morals with which to reproach him, spread the rumor that he was a fugitive from Spain and Paris, where he had been prosecuted and burned in effigy. The papal legate Verallo empowered his vicar Gaspare de' Dotti to hold an investigation. The latter, though convinced that the accusations were false, set up a regular inquiry with the summoning of witnesses and the presentation of accusers and advocates. The verdict of not guilty was announced on October 13, 1537. That Ignatius might hear it, he was summoned to Venice. The sentence characterized the accusations against him as "frivolous, vain, and false." Still further the accused person was declared to be a priest of good life and doctrine.[20]

Free of that trial, Ignatius could now undertake his journey to Rome with peace of mind. At the end of October or beginning of November he made the journey with his companions Favre and Laínez.

8. The Vision at La Storta

During this journey to Rome a supernatural event occurred which is of enormous and lasting importance both for the spiritual life of Ignatius and for the foundation of the Society of Jesus. It is now commonly called the vision of La Storta, an area close to Isola Farnese, situated on the Via Cassia which leads from Siena to Rome and sixteen and a half kilometers distant from the capital. What Ignatius experienced on that

19 *Cons*MHSJ, I, 47; *FN*, I, 204.
20 Text in *FD*, pp. 535-537.

occasion we can piece together from a brief declaration made by him, complemented by further details given by Laínez, a witness present at the time, to whom Ignatius himself made reference.[21] His contemporaries Nadal, Polanco, Ribadeneira, and Canisius also contributed clarifying data which will be taken into account.

The facts took place in this manner. During the journey Ignatius experienced many spiritual emotions, especially while receiving Communion administered to him by Favre or Laínez during the daily Mass. One sentiment prevailed above all the others: A firm confidence that God would protect these companions in the midst of the difficulties they might encounter in Rome. The words he heard interiorly were these, according to the formulation of Laínez: "I shall be propitious to you in Rome."[22] Nadal and Ribadeneira repeat the sentence but omit the reference to Rome. The same Nadal, in another writing, employs the formula "I shall be with you" (*Io saró con voi*)[23]. And this is the expression preferred by Canisius, who considered it as the most meaningful.[24] The fact is that there is question merely of nuances of one and the same reality. Laínez sought to allude to the problems they would have to face on their arrival in Rome. The other biographers saw in the words addressed to Ignatius a promise of the divine assistance in regard to the enterprise they were about to undertake, the foundation of the Society.

But during the course of these divine communications there was a peak moment. Ignatius tells us that after his priestly ordination he had decided to wait for a full year before celebrating his first Mass, preparing himself and begging our Lady to deign "to place him with her Son."[25] This aspiration, experienced for so long a time, found its fulfilment when Ignatius with his two companions tarried to pray "in a church," which tradition has identified with the chapel of La Storta.

21 Declaration by Ignatius, *Autobiog*, no. 96; by Laínez, *FN*, II, 133-134.
22 *FN*, II, 133.
23 *FN*, I, 313. See the various versions of this formula in footnote 37.
24 Censor's report by St. Peter Canisius on the Life of St. Ignatius by Ribadeneira, in *FN*, IV, 946-947.
25 *Autobiog*, no. 96.

There "whilst in prayer, he experienced such a change in his soul and saw so clearly that the Father was placing him with Christ, His Son, that he could not doubt that the Father was placing him with His Son."[26] It was now no longer our Lady but the Father himself who was effecting the mystical union of Ignatius with Jesus.

Laínez, of whom Ignatius himself said that he remembered further details about what happened there, gives important additions.[27] Jesus with the cross on his shoulders appeared to Ignatius, and by His side the Father, who said to Him: "I desire you to take this man for your servant." Jesus then turned to Ignatius and said to him, "It is my will that you serve Us." The pronoun in the plural, *Us*, imparts to this vision a seal clearly trinitarian. The Father unites Ignatius closely with Jesus bearing the cross, and expresses His will that Ignatius should dedicate himself to their service. Ignatius is called to a mysticism of union, to be "placed with Christ," and also of service, by being invited to consecrate his life to the divine service. A seal of all this was the divine protection, promised for him and for the entire group, against the trials which were coming.

The mystical phenomenon experienced by Ignatius had, as we have already indicated, a clear repercussion upon the foundation of the Society of Jesus. With deep feeling Ignatius perceived himself as one intimately united with Christ; and he also desired that the society which was soon to be founded should be totally dedicated to Him and bear His name. It was a name which was a whole program: to be companions of Jesus, enrolled under the banner of the cross in order to devote themselves to the service of God and the good of their fellow men. This program would later on be expressed more concretely in the Formula of the Institute of the Society.

9. Definitively in Rome

Ignatius, Favre, and Laínez entered Rome through the Porta del Popolo on a day in November, 1537. For a short

26 Ibid.
27 *FN*, II, 133-134.

while none of their foreseen difficulties were verified. Everything went well for them. They found lodging in a house on the property of Quirino Garzoni, situated on the slopes of the Pincio and on the street today named San Sebastianello. A stone's-throw away was the church of the Order of Minims, the Trinità dei Monti. Pedro Ortiz showed himself ready to help them. Apparently it was he who suggested that Favre and Laínez should be invited to lecture in the University of Rome, housed in the palace of *La Sapienza*. The two Masters took up their tasks immediately. Favre taught positive theology, explaining the Sacred Scriptures; Laínez lectured on scholastic theology, explaining the commentary of Gabriel Biel on the canon of the Mass. From time to time Paul III invited them, along with other theologians, to hold a disputation in his presence whilst he was seated at table.

Ignatius concentrated his activities on giving the Exercises to qualified persons. Each day he went to visit his exercitants, even when these lived in houses far distant from one another. Once he gave the Exercises simultaneously to one who was living near St. Mary Major and to another living near the Ponte Sisto. Any person familiar with the topography of Rome will have an idea of the distance between these two points in the city. Illustrious exercitants were the Spanish physician Iñigo López, who from that time on amiably offered his services to the companions and was treated as one of the household; Lattanzio Tolomei, Ambassador of Siena in Rome, a member of the group of Vittoria Colonna and Michelangelo; Cardinal Gaspare Contarini, president of the pontifical commission for the reform of the Church.

Doctor Ortiz merits separate treatment here. To ensure greater tranquillity, both director and exercitant traveled to the abbey of Monte Cassino for the Lent of that year, 1538. There for the space of forty days, the theologian and Scripture professor of Salamanca placed himself under the guidance of one who had hardly completed his theological studies but who, on the other hand, possessed an experiential knowledge of the things of God and a long approved practice in the direction of souls. At the end of the Exercises, Ortiz was able to state that in them he had learned a new theology, different from that one learns in books; for it was one thing to study in order to teach others, and another to study in order to put into practice what one has learned.[28]

It was during Ignatius' stay at Monte Cassino that Bachelor Diego de Hoces died at Padua—the first of the Society to die, when it was not yet canonically established. Ignatius had a divine illumination about his companion's death. He beheld his soul going up to heaven surrounded by rays of light; and he perceived this with such clarity that he could not doubt it, and with so much consolation that he could not hold back his tears. Hoces was of a brown complexion and none too handsome, but after his death his countenance was so comely that Jean Codure, his companion, never tired of gazing on him, for he looked like an angel.

That sorrowful loss was compensated by the addition of two new members to the group. One was Francisco Estrada, a native of Dueñas, near Palencia. He had been in the service of Cardinal Gian Pietro Caraffa in Rome when he was dismissed along with others. On his journey to Naples in search of another employment, he met Ignatius and Ortiz, who were returning from Monte Cassino. Ignatius invited him to join them. In Rome he made the Exercises and decided to become a member of the group. In the course of time he was to become a renowned preacher. The other recruit was a priest from Jaén, Lorenzo García, whom Ignatius had known in Paris during his studies. Now in Rome he joined Ignatius but did not persevere. When the storm of persecution which we shall soon relate burst upon them, he took fright and abandoned the camp. However, we are indebted to Lorenzo for two testimonies in favor of Ignatius. One was that given in Paris by the inquisitor Thomas Laurent on January 23, 1537. Ignatius and his companions had already left Paris and they availed themselves of the mediation of Lorenzo García and Diego de Cáceres to obtain from the inquisitor the testimony of their innocence.[29] The second testimony was given by the same García at Otricoli,

28 *RibVita*, II, xii, in *FN*, IV, 277.
29 Text in *FD*, pp. 524-525.

when he passed through there after he had separated from the companions.[30]

After Easter, April 21, with the arrival in Rome of those who had remained in northern Italy, the group was again together. Six months had passed since they had separated.

[30] Text in *FD*, pp. 540-541.

Chapter 11

THE BIRTH OF THE SOCIETY OF JESUS

The foundation of the Society of Jesus was preceded by a persecution which put it in jeopardy before it was born, and then by a period of profound reflection on the part of the companions in the group which was to bring it to life.

1. The Judicial Inquiry in Rome

When the life of this group seemed to be developing smoothly, a very serious obstacle arose which endangered its very existence.

It all started during the Lent of 1538. The lenten sermons in the church of Sant' Agostino were being preached by the Piedmontese Agostino Mainardi. The sermons drew large congregations. Among the listeners were also Favre and Laínez; and they soon noticed with astonishment that the celebrated preacher was teaching doctrines which were clearly Lutheran. They were not wrong in their diagnosis. In fact, two years later Mainardi openly embraced Protestantism and fled to Chiavenna in the Valtellina, where he founded a reformed community and died in 1563. Favre and Laínez paid a visit to the preacher and tried in a fraternal manner to bring him to retract his erroneous statements. Their efforts were unsuccessful.

The conflict was aggravated by the intervention of some Spaniards, influential in the papal court, and favorable to Fra Agostino. Their names are known to us: Mudarra, a certain Barrera, Pedro de Castilla, and Mateo Pascual. But the one who fanned the blaze was Miguel de Landívar, changed from a friend into an enemy because he had been excluded from the group. These persons began to spread the idea that those "reformed priests" were in reality disguised Lutherans, who were seeking to make disciples through their Exercises.

157

Because of their immoral lives and doctrinal errors they had been hailed into court in Spain, Paris, and Venice, whence they had fled and taken refuge in Rome.

The false rumors spread like fire in stubble and the results were soon perceived. The faithful began to withdraw themselves from association with those suspected men.

One of those who allowed themselves to be influenced was Cardinal Gian Domenico De Cupis, dean of the Sacred College. He was a friend of Quirino Garzoni, the host of Ignatius and his companions; and he advised Garzoni to dismiss them from his home. Garzoni replied that he had asked Antonio Sarzana, his servant and gardener, to observe them and that Sarzana considered them as saints. He had provided them with beds, but they were not using them, sleeping instead on mats on the floor. The food they collected, and also other things of their own, they distributed among the poor. The cardinal then told Garzoni that they were not to be trusted, as they were wolves in sheeps' clothing, whose intention was to mislead the populace.

Ignatius then initiated a move very much in keeping with his character. He went to visit the cardinal in his palace, located on the street of Santa Maria dell' Anima, and succeeded in obtaining an audience. He spent two hours with Cardinal De Cupis, while others waited impatiently in the antechamber, The cardinal was finally convinced by Ignatius' reasons and ended by casting himself at his feet and asking pardon. Henceforth he showed himself ever a friend and benefactor of the little group.

Then Ignatius struck another blow still more decisive. He sought and obtained an audience with the governor of Rome, responsible for the administration of justice. His name was Beendetto Conversini. As a proof in his favor, he showed him a letter which Miguel Landívar had previously sent to him, in which this former servant of Francis Xavier was all praises for Ignatius and the other companions. With this letter in hand it was easy to show the hopeless contradictions in which the Navarrese had entangled himself and the lack of any foundation for his accusations. The upshot of the trial was that Landívar was banished from Rome.

This brought the first phase of the conflict to an end, and the companions were able to dedicate themselves to their priestly labors in peace, by distributing themselves to various churches of the city. Ignatius preached in Spanish in the national church of the Crown of Aragón, Santa Maria de Montserrato. The others preached in Italian, as best they could, Favre in San Lorenzo in Damaso; Laínez in San Salvatore in Lauro; Jay in San Luigi de' Francesi, the French national church; Salmerón in Santa Lucia del Gonfalone; Rodrigues in Sant' Angelo in Pescheria; Bobadilla in San Celso e Giuliano, near the bankers' quarter. Xavier, however, had to remain at home, as his weakened health required attention and rest.

To be nearer to the field of their activities, in June of 1538 all of them moved from the Pincio to a house near the Ponte Sisto in the center of the city and not far from the residence of Dr. Ortiz. Some friends had rented it for them for four months.

In the meantime Mudarra and his friends did not relax in their smear campaign. Ignatius showed himself firm. On July 7, he formally presented a request for a trial to Cardinal Vincenzo Caraffa, whom Paul III had left as his delegate in Rome when on May 20 he set out for the city of Nice to try to bring about peace between the emperor and the king of France. What Ignatius asked from him was a formal investigation into the case, followed by a judicial sentence.[1]

Faced by this attitude which was so determined, his adversaries reversed their tactics and withdrew their charges against the "reformed priests." They even changed their accusations into praises. There were some persons, even among the companions themselves, and some undoubting friends such as Dr. Ortiz, who thought that this was enough and that the case

1 For the documentation on this judicial trial, see *FD*, pp. 542-558. A historical reconstruction of it is to be found in M. del Piazzo and C. de Dalmases, "Il processo sull' ortodossia de S. Ignazio e dei suoi compagni svoltosi a Roma nel 1538," *AHSJ* XXXVIII (1969), 431-453.

could now be considered closed. Ignatius was not of this opinion. He thought that the sanction of a judicial sentence was necessary in order that his innocence might be definitively recognized. Short of this, the apostolic activities of the group would remain under suspicion.

There was another reason, not mentioned by the biographers, which certainly had great influence on his conduct. The hopes which they had of realizing their pilgrimage to Jerusalem had vanished. This was true above all since February 8 of that year 1538, when the league between the republic of Venice, the emperor, and the pope was now an accomplished fact. Therefore the moment was drawing near when Ignatius and his companions had, in virtue of the vow at Montmartre, to present themselves to the pope and place themselves at his disposal. The foundation of a new religious order had not as yet been formally decided upon, but it was already visible on the horizon. For it was evident, as developments soon showed, that this compact group was not destined to be dissolved but, on the contrary, to perpetuate itself by receiving an organization which would guarantee its stability and development. Now, with what peace of mind would they be able to present their projects to the Holy Father if their situation should not be clarified? Today we are able to state that the foundation and approbation of the Society of Jesus depended on the solution of that conflict. Hence the importance which Ignatius attached to this inquisitorial process and the official declaration of innocence which marked its end. This is also proved by the abundance of information we possess regarding this case. It has turned out to be one of the best documented incidents in the life of Ignatius.

To support their cause, Ignatius and his companions left no stone unturned. They despatched letters to the authorities of those cities where various ones of them had been working, requesting them to send to Rome written testimonies about their life and doctrine. In fact, laudatory testimonies came in from Ferrara, Bologna, and Siena.

Ignatius took still another step. When the pope returned to Rome on July 24 from his trip to Nice, Ignatius did every thing possible to have an interview with him. In the second half of August, Paul III moved to Frascati. Ignatius followed him there, and was so fortunate that he was received in audience the very day of his arrival. He himself later gave abundant details of the meeting in a letter to Isabel Roser: "...I went thither [to Frascati] and talked alone with His Holiness in his apartments a whole hour [Polanco adds that he spoke in Latin]. Then, while speaking at length to him about our designs and intentions, I related clearly how many times judicial proceedings had been taken against me....I begged His Holiness, in the name of all my companions, to have a remedy devised, in order that our doctrine and manner of life should be investigated and examined by whatsoever ordinary judge His Holiness would appoint.[2] The pope acceded to Ignatius' wishes and gave orders to the governor of Rome to conduct the desired legal investigation at once. In the text of the petition addressed by Ignatius to Paul III on July 7, there is at the end this autograph note of Cardinal Vincenzo Caraffa which, translated from the Latin, states: "By order of our Lord the pope, let the governor hear the petition, cite witnesses, set up the process, as is petitioned, and let him administer justice."[3]

A set of highly favorable circumstances was present which Ignatius did not hesitate to call providential. In that summer and fall of 1538 all those who had investigated and judged him at Alcalá, Paris, and Venice happened to come to Rome for different reasons. From Alcalá had come Juan Rodríguez de Figueroa; from Paris, the inquisitor Dr. Matthieu Ory; from Venice, the vicar general of the legate, Gaspare de' Dotti. All of them were summoned to make depositions in the presence of the governor. Their testimonies were a brilliant demonstration of innocence. No doctrinal or moral error had been proved against the accused men; and further still, their lives were shown to be holy and their teaching sound. To the testimony of these former judges was added that of other personalities of still greater prestige: Dr. Pedro Ortiz, the ambassador

---

2 Letter of Dec. 19, 1538, in *EppIgn*, I, 137-144 and *FN*, I, 4-14. Polanco's statement is in *PolSum*, no. 85, cited in *FN*, I, 202.
3 *FD*, p. 545.

of Siena Lattanzio Tolomei, and the celebrated Dominican theologian Ambrosio Catarino.[4]

In the end, on November 18, 1538, the governor, Benedetto Conversini, pronounced the accused not guilty.[5] In the sentence he declared that Ignatius and his companions not only had not incurred infamy but that their innocence had been proved by clear testimonies, whereas the accusations of the calumniators had been shown to be groundless and false. At Ignatius' request the names of the accusers were omitted from the text of the sentence. This, however, did not free them from incurring severe penalties.

Ignatius showed enormous care to make sure that the sentence would become known in those places where the rumors about the false accusations might have reached. This accounts for the great number of authentic copies of the sentence which are preserved in archives. One copy was sent by Ignatius to his relatives at Loyola, who preserved it like a relic.[6]

After the sentence declaring innocence, peace and serenity returned to the persons involved. Ignatius and his companions could with tranquillity look forward to the future which now appeared cloudless. The longed-for pilgrimage to the land of Jesus had turned out to be impossible. The stipulated term for waiting had indubitably expired. No other course remained except that of placing themselves entirely at the pope's disposal, in accordance with what they had vowed at Montmartre.

The act of offering themselves must have taken place between November 18, the date of the acquittal, and November 23, the day on which Favre, whose testimony is the only one we have about this fact, in a letter addressed to Diogo de Gouveia speaks of the offering as a recent event.[7]

Paul III gladly accepted the sincere offer made of their persons by these apostolic men who were seeking nothing

---

4 Their declarations can be seen in *FD*, pp. 545-556.
5 *FD*, pp. 556-557.
6 FD, p. 825.
7 *EppIgn*, I, 132; *Fabri Monumenta*, p. 198; in *FN*, I, 42.

else than to serve God and his Church. On an earlier occasion, during one of the theological disputations carried on in his presence, the pope had already remarked to them: "Why do you have such a desire to go to Jerusalem? Italy is a good and true Jerusalem if your desire is to bring forth fruit in God's Church."[8] From these words the inference can be drawn that the pope's chief intention was to retain them in Italy.

2. *Ignatius' First Mass*

For Ignatius the moment had arrived, so ardently wished for and for which he had prepared himself with prayer and longing for a year and a half—the celebration of his first Mass. Apart from his desire of diligent preparation, the reason for so long a postponement must be sought, it seems, in his intention to celebrate his first Mass in Bethlehem or some other place in the Holy Land. Now that this was impossible, he chose for his first Mass the night of Christmas in that year of 1538, and also the altar of the manger in the basilica of St. Mary Major. This altar had been renovated by Arnolfo di Cambio about the year 1289; and from antiquity it had recalled to the faithful the memory of the Savior's birth. This altar which with its own chapel is now situated in the crypt of the Sistine Chapel in that basilica, was then some sixteen meters away from its present location, to which the chapel was transported as a unit by Domenico Fontana. There Ignatius offered his first Mass "with the help and grace of God," as he himself wrote in a letter to his relatives at Loyola on February 2, 1539.[9]

3. *In the House of Antonio Frangipani*

By October of that same year the group had moved to a house of Antonio Frangipani, next to the Tower of Melangolo and not far from the Capitol. It was not difficult for them to acquire it, as it was uninhabited. There was a rumor, too, that it was haunted. But they scorned that fear, which some nocturnal noises seemed to confirm. Later on that house became the property of a certain Mario Delfini, after whom

---

8 Bobadilla says it in his Autobiography; see *FN*, III, 327.
9 *EppIgn*, I, 147.

the street was named. Today it bears the number 16 on the Via de' Delfini. Important events took place in that house. There the sentence of acquittal was received on November 18, 1538. There took place, in the first half of 1539, the deliberations which led to the founding of the Society. From this house Francis Xavier departed for India in March, 1540. And there, in September of the same year, was received the first bull of approval of the Society of Jesus.

In the winter of 1538-1539 the Frangipani house became the scene of the charity of Ignatius and his companions. That was a winter extremely severe; nothing equal to it was remembered in Italy for forty years. The harvest had all but failed. As a result there was scarcity of food which led to an unprecedented rise in prices in the city. The companions had a good occasion to exercise the works of mercy, by using their house to give assistance to the hungry. There they gave such aid to as many as some 300 at one time. They tried to procure for them shelter, fire, and all the sleeping places they could locate. For them too they procured sufficient food. And in order that spiritual food might be united with their bodily nourishment, the companions gathered them into a large room where one of them instructed the crowd in Christian doctrine. It is calculated that during the whole time this scarcity lasted, the companions gave aid to a total of some 3,000 persons, in a city which then counted scarcely 40,000 inhabitants.

Besides these corporal works of mercy, the Parisian masters devoted themselves to those priestly ministries enumerated in that Formula of the Institute of the Society which Ignatius was to draw up during that year 1539 in that very house of Frangipani: cathechesis, preaching of the word of God even outside the usual seasons of Advent and Lent, the administration of the sacraments, and the giving of the Spiritual Exercises.

4. The Deliberations of 1539

All these activities just mentioned took place in Rome. But requests began to come in from other cities of Italy and beyond. The ambassador of Charles V manifested the desire that some of the companions should be sent to America. The King of Portugal, for his part, asked that some should be destined to India.

In these circumstances, the time was foreseen to be near when the group would have to disperse. There arose, too, the question that could not be postponed: When the pope sent them to one place or the other, were they to answer the summons as independent individuals or as members of a stable body? And in the latter case, ought they to oblige themselves under vow to obey one of their number elected as superior? These questions were virtually equivalent to this other one: Ought they to found a new religious order? A decision was pressing because the pope, acceding to the requests coming from Siena, had destined Broët and another as companion to that Tuscan city to work toward the reform of the monastery of Benedictine nuns, San Prospero e Sant' Agnese. This was the first mission entrusted to the Society in virtue of the offer made to the pope in 1538.

To deliberate on these questions facing them, the companions decided to meet together in common for as long as would be necessary. This is how those deliberations arose which lasted from March to June 24, 1539.[10]

To avoid interruption of the activities already initiated, they agreed to follow this working plan. Each day one point would be proposed for discussion. During the day each one, without interrupting his ordinary work, would recommend the matter to God at Mass and in prayer. In the night session, each one would present reasons which he saw pro and con. Once the discussion was ended, a decision would be taken by unanimity.

The first question was this: Now that they had dedicated their persons to Christ our Lord and his true and legitimate vicar on earth so that he might dispose of them and send them wherever he judged that they could produce fruit, would it be expedient that they remain united and bound together,

10 The text of the Deliberation of the First Fathers is in *Cons*MHSJ, I, 1-7.

thus forming one body, or was the contrary better? The decision was easy and raised no controversy: That union and congregation had been brought about by God and ought not to be undone; on the contrary, it was proper to confirm and strengthen it. This was all the more true because, in the case of any difficult undertaking, their forces would be stronger and more effective when united in one body than they would be if dispersed. Naturally, however, this whole matter ought to be submitted to the pope for his approval.

More difficulties were encountered in the second point. Since all had pronounced the vows of poverty and chastity in the hands of the papal legate at Venice, Verallo, would they now also take the vow of obedience to one of their number who would be elected as superior? Before deliberation began on this theme of such great importance, a preliminary question was proposed: In order to reflect with greater tranquillity, and to obtain more light from God, should they all, or at least some of them, retire into some place of solitude for thirty or forty days? The decision was negative. They would all remain in Rome, and this for two reasons: to avoid attracting the attention of the faithful, who might interpret that departure as a flight, and to avoid interruption of the works of zeal which kept them occupied.

In order to reach a successful decision, they planned to apply to this case the rules for making a good election which are found in the book of the *Exercises:*

First, all would dispose themselves at Mass and in prayer to find more spiritual relish and a greater inclination toward obeying rather than commanding, even when the one or the other procedure would lead to equal glory to God.

Second, they would not discuss a topic with one another, but each one would endeavor to form his own opinion in accordance with what seemed more fitting to him during prayer.

Third, each one would act as if he were a person outside the group, so that each might give his own independent conclusion.

When the time for discussion in common arrived, each member set forth the reasons for and against which occurred to him. The reasons against the vow of obedience were these: Through our sins, the words "obedience" and "religious life" (*nomen religionis et obedientiae*) do not in our day evoke such good connotations as they did in the past. If we decide to take a vow of obedience, it is probable that the pope will compel us to incorporate ourselves within some one of the orders already existing. It is possible that the idea of the vow of obedience will deter some who might feel inclined to follow our way of life.

On the following evening the reasons in favor of the vow of obedience were put forth: Without obedience, the necessary cohesion within the group would be lacking, with each one casting a task and responsibility for it upon another, as experience has already shown. Without the vow of obedience, our congregation could not last long, but sooner or later it would be dissolved. Obedience offers an opportunity for the exercise of many virtues and even of heroic acts. Nothing is so effective as obedience to keep pride within proper bounds.

The greatest difficulty against the vow of obedience arose from the area of practice. Since they had decided to place themselves at the pope's disposal, obedience to another superior appeared superfluous and even harmful. The answer to this objection was that, realistically, the pope could not be expected to take under his responsibility the numberless details and contingencies which would occur. And even if he could, it would not be expedient to put him under such an obligation.

After many days of debates, prolonged during Holy Week and Easter Week, they unanimously decided that it would be better to give obedience to one of their number. In this way they would be able to carry out better and more exactly their original design, which was to fulfil the will of God in all things; the Society would be preserved with greater security, and all could better carry to completion the spiritual and temporal works entrusted to them.

Once these two points were decided upon, it can be said

that the project of founding the Society of Jesus stood as something settled by the group. Nothing further remained necessary except approval by the pope. The companions were fully conscious of the importance of this first step resulting from their discussions, and they wished to seal it with a solemn ceremony. This took place on April 15, 1539. After making a general confession, they assisted together at a Mass celebrated by Pierre Favre, who was recognized as the spiritual father of them all. After receiving Communion from his hands, they all signed a document in which they declared that they thought it more conducive to the glory of God and the more secure preservation of the Society that its members should take the vow of obedience. At the same time they bound themselves, though without a vow, to enter the Society. Those signing the document were Cáceres, Jean Codure, Laínez, Salmerón, Bobadilla, Paschase Broët, Pierre Favre, Francis Xavier, Ignatius, Simão Rodrigues, and Claude Jay.[11]

In the course of May and June some of the general lines of the new religious order were sketched in writing. Besides the usual three religious vows of poverty, chastity, and obedience, one who wishes to enter the Society is to pronounce a special vow of obedience to the pope, binding himself to travel to any part of the world where the pope may send him. He will be obliged to teach Christian doctrine to children. Before the year of probation he will have to employ three months in making the Spiritual Exercises, undertaking a pilgrimage, and rendering service in hospitals. In the Society there will be a superior general, elected for his entire life. The Society will be able to possess houses but without exercising the right of ownership over them. The general will have authority to admit novices and to dismiss those who show themselves unfit, but only after he has listened to the opinion of his consultors.[12]

In regard to the manner in which the teaching of Christian doctrine to children should be regulated, Bobadilla expressed his disagreement. This was the occasion for the decision that

11 Ibid., 8.
12 The text of the *Determinationes Societatis* is in *Cons*MHSJ, I, 9-14.

ın future the criterion of unanimity would no longer be followed in the voting but, instead, the majority of the votes.[13]

The deliberations were considered as terminated on June 24, 1539.

During those days, some other companions, in addition to Broët and Rodrigues who were destined to Siena, had to leave Rome. According to the desires of Ennio Filonardi, called the cardinal of Sant' Angelo, apostolic legate in Parma and Piacenza, the pope had sent to these two cities Favre and Laínez, who departed on June 20. In July, Codure went to Velletri and Bobadilla to Naples.

5. The First "Formula" of the Institute

Ignatius then set himself to the task of composing the first "Formula" or sketch, which in its five chapters (*quinque capitula*) contained the essential lines of the new institute, a true Magna Charta of the new order which was equivalent to the "Rule" of the older religious orders. In it the following main points were touched on: the name of the Society, its end, its vows of poverty, chastity, and obedience, the vow of special obedience to the pope in what pertains to "missions" or occupations, the admission of novices, the formation and maintenance of the scholastics, the composition of the Constitutions, the authority of the general, the renunciation of every kind of property and fixed revenue, the recitation of the divine office in private, the use of penances determined not by rule but by each one's personal devotion. The undertaking laid upon those who desired "to serve as a soldier of God beneath the banner of the cross" was arduous. Wherefore, each one, before laying this heavy burden on his shoulders should carefully ponder if he feels strong enough to bear it. On the part of the Society, no one ought to be admitted to definitive incorporation if it has not become clear, after many probations, that he is fit for it.[14]

By the end of June or beginning of July, Cardinal Gaspare Contarini presented the "Five Chapters" to Pope Paul III for

13 Ibid., 12-13.
14 Critical edition of the Formula of the Institute of 1539, is in *Cons*MHSJ, I, 14-21.

for his approval. The pope submitted these chapters to the Dominican Tommaso Badia, Master of the Sacred Apostolic Palace, for his examination. He retained them for some two months and then certified them as pious and holy.

Ignatius immediately dispatched the young Antonio de Araoz, who had recently joined the group, to bring these documents, the Five Chapters and the opinion of Tommaso Badia, to the pope. The pontiff was then at Tivoli, spending a few days of rest in his castle (the Rocca Pia built by Pius II) in the company of Cardinal Contarini. The cardinal read the Five Chapters to the pope, who approved them orally (*vivae vocis oraculo*) and added: "The finger of God is here" (*Digitus Dei est hic*).[15]

This happened on September 3, 1539. That same day Contarini hastened to communicate the good news to Ignatius in a note which Araoz took to Rome on the following day. Simultaneously with his oral approval the pope issued an order that Cardinal Girolamo Ghinucci, the secretary for papal briefs, should draw up the suitable document, but without specifying whether this was to be a bull or a brief.

This seemed to be a matter of protocol; but it turned out to be otherwise. Ghinucci, an expert in the practices of the Roman curia, perceived that the matter was one of such importance that it would require not a mere brief but a bull, and that thus it came under the competence of the papal chancery. There it would have to be reexamined to see whether the project was in conformity with the norms of that curial office. Besides this technical obstacle, Ghinucci objected to some items in the contents of the Five Chapters which had been presented to him. The exclusion of choir and of the singing of the divine office was an innovation which could be interpreted as a concession to the Reformers, who were criticizing the Church for those traditional practices. The exclusion of penitential acts imposed by rule constituted too great a novelty from the style of religious life then current. Ghinucci found his chief difficulty, it seems, in the fourth vow of special

---

15 *Cons*MHSJ, I, 21-22; see also *FN*, I, 312.

obedience to the pope. He considered this as superfluous, since, according to him, it was evident that all the faithful, and more particularly the religious, were bound to render obedience to the Supreme Pontiff. Ignatius and his companions had sought to forestall that objection by employing in the draft a phrase which clarified the peculiarity of this vow. But they soon had to convince themselves that Ghinucci was, for his part, definitely opposed to giving his official approval to this foundational document of the Society.

In an effort to escape this obstacle, the pope placed the matter in the hands of Cardinal Bartolomeo Guidiccioni. The cardinal found no objection in the content of the Five Chapters, which he considered to be "just and holy." But he did have a difficulty with the fact itself of founding a new religious order. Already on earlier occasions he had shown himself against the multiplication of religious institutes. The prescriptions in this line of thought which emanated from Lateran Council IV (1215) and the Council of Lyons II (1274), he alleged, should be urged anew. His contention was that all the religious orders should be reduced to the ancient four: the Benedictines, the Cistertians, the Franciscans, and the Dominicans.

In defense of their cause, Ignatius and his companions went personally to visit Cardinal Guidiccioni. At first he was unwilling either to receive them or read the Five Chapters. Finally he did, but only to repel them. If it had not been for the order of the pope, he said, he would not even have taken them into consideration.

Upon seeing that the doors were closing for him, Ignatius had recourse to his two habitual resources: prayer and human means. In addition to other prayers and acts of penance, he promised that he and his companions and other friends would offer 3,000 Masses in honor of the Blessed Trinity to impetrate the wished-for grace. Further still, he started to send out messages to influential persons in various cities of Italy where the companions had already begun to work, hoping that these persons would recommend the happy conclusion of his concern to the pope. At last Cardinal Guidiccioni relented and came to terms, and even ended by praising the project of founding the Society of Jesus, suggesting a solution which was certain to facilitiate matters: The number of men admitted to profession should be limited to sixty.

Pope Paul III accepted the cardinal's proposal and finally, on September 27, 1540, the bull *Regimini militantis Ecclesiae* issued from the Palazzo di San Marco on the Piazza Venezia. It solemnly confirmed the foundation of the Society of Jesus, with the limitation to sixty in the number of its professed members.[16] In the bull were included, with some modifications, the Five Chapters or "Formula" of the Institute of the Society. It had been necessary to hope and work for an entire year after the oral approval granted by Paul III at Tivoli. But in the end the Society of Jesus, solemnly confirmed, had been added to the number of religious Orders canonically erected in the Church.

6. Ignatius the First General of the Society

Up to this time the group of companions had no superior. This role had been exercised by each one of them in weekly turns. As a matter of fact, however, all looked up to Ignatius as the soul and leader of the community. He had won them for Christ. But, once the Society had been approved, the moment had come to give it a superior.

When the bull of confirmation of the Society was issued only three of them were in Rome—Ignatius, Codure, and Salmerón. Xavier and Rodrigues were at Lisbon and Favre was at Parma, whence in October he left for Germany with Doctor Ortiz. Ignatius sent notice to the four who were working in Italy to assemble in Rome with a view to giving to the newly founded Order a first beginning of legislation and proceeding to the election of the general.

At the beginning of Lent of 1541 Broët, Jay, and Laínez arrived in Rome. Bobadilla was detained by the pope at Bisignano, a city in the kingdom of Naples.

---

16 The text of the bull *Regimini* is in *Cons*MHSJ, I, 24-32.

On March 4, Ignatius and Codure were entrusted with the task of working out the first plan of Constitutions of the Society. Thus, during the month of March was prepared the draft of the Constitutions of 1541, which partly modified and partly complemented the Determinations composed two years earlier.[17] These Constitutions, which Ignatius considered as such though not definitive, touched in forty-nine articles on a variety of points concerning the manner of life of the Society, ranging from poverty, with which most of the articles were concerned, to the form of dress. Points included were the office of the general, which was to be for life, the teaching of catechism, and the foundation of colleges in which the scholastics of the Society were to live.

Once these Constitutions had been drawn up and signed by the six members present, nothing remained to be done except to proceed to the election of the general.[18] For three days the six companions gave themselves to prayer and reflection. Then on April 5 the six assembled and deposited their written ballots in an urn. In it were also placed the sealed votes of those absent, Favre, Xavier and Rodrigues. These last two had left their ballots behind before they departed from Rome. After another three days of recollection, on April 8, the Friday in Passion week, the examination of the ballots took place.

The election of Ignatius was unanimous, with one sole exception, his own ballot. On his ballot slip he had written: "Ihs. Excluding myself, in regard to there being a superior I give my vote in our Lord to him who will receive a majority of votes for that office. I have given my vote indeterminately, considering this as good. But if the Society thinks otherwise, or judges that it is better and more to the glory of God for me to designate one person, I am ready to do so. Done in Rome, April 5, 1541. Iñigo."[19]

Favre had sent two ballots, one from Worms signed on December 27, 1540, and a second from Spiers on January 23,

17 The text of the Constitutions of 1541 is in *Cons*MHSJ, I, 33-48.
18 The account, by Ignatius himself, is in *FN*, I, 15-22.
19 For the Spanish text of Ignatius' ballot, see *SdeSI*, II, 5, fn. 4.

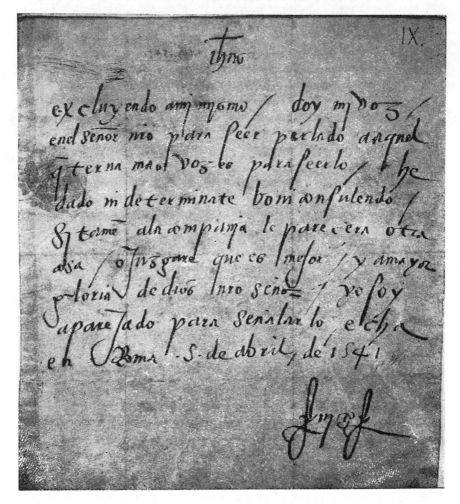

Facsimile of Ignatius' Ballot, April 5, 1541

The text reads: "Ihus. Excluyendo a mí mismo, doy mi voz en el Señor nuestro para seer perlado a aquel que terná mas vozes para seerlo. He dado indeterminate, boni consulendo. Si tamen a la Compañía le parecerá otra cosa, o juzgare que es mejor y a mayor gloria de Dios nuesro Señor, yo soy aparejado para señalarlo. Echa en Roma, 5 de Abril de 1541. Inigo."

1541. In both he gave his vote to Ignatius, "and in his absence by death(which may God forbid), to Master Francis Xavier."[20] On March 15, 1540, the day before Xavier's departure for Portugal and India, he specified that he was giving his vote "to our old leader and true father, Don Ignacio, who, since he brought us together with no little effort, will also with similar effort know how to preserve, govern, and make us advance from good to better, since he knows each one of us best."[21] In case Ignatius should be dead, he gave his vote to Master Pierre Favre. Salmerón gave the reason for his choice of Ignatius by writing that "as he begot us all in Christ and fed us with milk as babes, so now he will nourish us with the solid food of obedience."[22] Bobadilla did not send his vote or it did not arrive in time. In his Autobiography he wrote that he had voted for Ignatius.[23]

In spite of so clear a consensus, Ignatius did not accept the appointment. In some very sincere words addressed to the assembled group, he declared that he felt more inclined to be governed than to govern, and that "because of his many and bad habits, past and present, with many sins, and other faults and miseries,"[24] he thought that he ought not to accept the charge unless it should become evident with great clarity that he ought to do so. Therefore he begged his companions to take some days for further reflection.

The companions yielded to his wishes, although they had no desire of their own to do so. The new election, set for April 13, Wednesday in Holy Week, yielded exactly the same result as the first. But Ignatius did not yet give up as one overcome. He said he would leave the decision in the hands of his confessor.

That same day, crossing the Tiber by the Ponte Sisto and going toward the lofty Janiculum, he directed his steps to the Franciscans' convent of San Pietro in Montorio, founded by

20 *Fabri Monumenta*, pp. 51-53; also in *Cons*MHSJ, I, 14-21.
21 *EppXav*, I, 26.
22 *Epistolae P. Alphonsi Salmeronis*, I, 1, in MHSJ.
23 *FN*, III, 330.
24 *FN*, I, 18.

the Catholic Kings. There he repeated what he had done at Montserrat at the beginning of his conversion. In a general confession that took three days of Holy Week, he described to his confessor, Fra Teodosio da Lodi, his whole life and all his infirmities and bodily miseries. On Easter Sunday, the confessor gave him his definitive opinion. This was that Ignatius ought to accept the election, and that to refuse it would be to resist the Holy Spirit. There was nothing for him to do but submit. The one thing he begged of the friar was to put down his opinion in writing. This Fra Teodosio did by sending to the group a sealed letter which confirmed his opinion in writing. Thereupon Ignatius accepted the office. It was the Tuesday within the octave of Easter, April 19, 1541.

In that same session another momentous decision was made. The following Friday, April 22, they would make a visit to the seven churches, and in the basilica of St. Paul outside-the-Walls they would make their religious profession in accordance with the papal bull.

On the appointed day, in that basilica of St. Paul outside-the-Walls, after the companions had confessed to one another, Ignatius celebrated the Mass. Just before Communion, holding the body of Christ in one hand and a paper containing the formula of his profession in the other, he made his profession in the following words translated from the Latin:

"I, the undersigned [Ignatius of Loyola] promise to Almighty God and the Supreme Pontiff, his vicar on earth, in the presence of his Virgin Mother and the whole heavenly court, and of the Society, perpetual poverty, chastity, and obedience, according to the manner of living which is contained in the bull of the Society of our Lord Jesus and in its Constitutions adopted or to be adopted. Moreover, I promise special obedience to the Supreme Pontiff in regard to the missions as contained in the bull. I likewise promise to procure that children will be instructed in the rudiments of the faith in accordance with the same bull and Constitutions."[25]

25 The Latin text is in *FN*, I, 20-22.

Thereupon he received the body of the Lord. Then taking five consecrated hosts on the paten, he turned toward his companions. Each one made his profession and then received the Eucharist from the hands of Ignatius.

This moving ceremony took place at an altar attached to the right pillaster (as seen by one entering the principal door of the basilica) of the triumphal arch of Empress Placidia. At this altar the Blessed Sacrament was kept. At it, too, was venerated a byzantine image in mosaic of the Blessed Virgin Mary, attributed to the times of Pope Honorius III in the thirteenth century. That altar has now disappeared and the Virgin in mosaic is venerated in the chapel of the Blessed Sacrament.

After the Mass and their prayer at the privileged altars of the basilica, all assembled at the central papal altar of the Confession, where the relics of the Apostle St. Paul are kept. There they all gave one another the embrace of peace "with no lack of devotion, feeling, and tears."[26] With these emotions of interior consolation they continued their visit of the "seven churches" of Rome.

The young Pedro de Ribadeneira was a witness of these proceedings, and towards evening he prepared a meal for them in a place near St. John Lateran. The teenager from Toledo was particularly struck by the extraordinary devotion of Jean Codure, "who could in no way keep it inside himself, so that it simply bubbled out of him."[27] Four months later, on August 29, Codure entered into the joy of the Lord.

The absent companions made their profession in various places and on different dates. Favre did it at Ratisbon on July 9 of the same year of 1541; Xavier at Goa in December 1543 or January 1544; Rodrigues at Evora, on December 25, 1544. Bobadilla, giving once more signs of his restless character, at first refused to follow his companions' example. Ignatius

26 Ibid., 22.
27 *RibVita*, III, i, in *FN*, IV, 371.

became much preoccupied about this and spent three days without eating that his companions might not fail in what was hoped for from him. Finally, after consulting three persons of his confidence, Bobadilla made his profession into the hands of Ignatius in the same basilica of St. Paul, in September, 1541.

Chapter 12

THE APOSTLE OF ROME

St. Ignatius deserves in all justice the title of Apostle of Rome. Shortly after his arrival in that city we see him preaching in the church of Our Lady of Montserrat and teaching catechism to children in the streets and public squares. We have already seen how on the occasion of the famine that gripped the city in the winter of 1538-1539 Ignatius and his companions labored beyond their duty and with great personal abnegation to bring material and spiritual relief to a large number of needy persons.

Once the Society was founded and the responsibility devolved on him of organizing and governing the new religious order, Ignatius did not relinquish his concern for the works of direct apostolate. His companions were leaving Rome, sent out on various missions by the pope. For him, the field of direct apostolate was Rome. One can hardly think of any apostolic enterprise, either in the religious or in the social plane, in which he did not work zealously and with self-abnegation. Abundant proof is found in the works in which he participated, either by founding them or by collaborating in those already existent.

In general, as we shall see presently, his plan was the following. He gave life to a new charitable or social work. An organization made up of charitable persons was created to finance and direct it. An effort was made to have the work erected as a confraternity by means of a papal bull. As long as his collaboration was necessary, he offered it with personal self-sacrifice. When his presence was no longer necessary he withdrew, leaving the work in the hands of others. And then he addressed himself to some other work that needed his presence and collaboration. This is what happened in the works which we shall now succinctly sketch.

1. The Work for the Catechumens

One of these works was that for the catechumens who were converts from Judaism. In this connection it is helpful to recall what Ignatius thought of the Jews in an era in which they were looked on with caution and suspicion. Moreover, what he did merits attention all the more because of the reply he made to the vicar Figueroa in Alcalá. When he asked Iñigo whether he had the custom of observing the Sabbath, he replied that "in his country there were no Jews."[1] For him the only thing that mattered was the human being. Race had no importance. Still further, he considered it to be a privilege of the Jews that they were relatives, according to the flesh, of Christ and his Virgin Mother. Ribadeneira relates this anecdote: "One day when we were eating with many present, because of a remark dropped by another he stated about himself that he would consider it as a special grace from our Lord to come from a line of Jewish ancestors. He gave the reason by stating: 'Why! —to be able to be a person related, according to the flesh, to Christ our Lord and to our Lady, the glorious Virgin Mary! These words he uttered with such a countenance and such feeling that tears flowed from his eyes, and this was something which was extensively noticed."[2]

Ignatius showed great concern for the spiritual and material welfare of the Jews who wanted to receive baptism. In August or September, 1541, a young Jew thirty-two years of age was baptized in the little church of Our Lady of the Way. Others followed him. Ignatius sought to help these converts in two ways. In the first place he obtained from the pope the brief *Cupientes Judaeos* of March 21, 1542. By it the long-standing practice, already condemned by the popes Nicholas III in 1278 and John XXII in 1320, was forbidden anew. This practice was that Jews who became converts had what goods they previously possessed confiscated and their children declared disinherited. Obviously, this new measure removed a barrier which was making their path to conversion difficult.

In the second place, with the help of Margaret of Austria,

---

1 *FN*, II, 548; *PolSum*, no. 39, in *FN*, I, 174.
2 *FN*, II, 476. See also J. W. Reites, "St. Ignotius and the Jews," *Studies in the Spirituality of Jesuits*, XIII, no. 4 (Sept., 1981), 1-48.

daughter of Charles V, and Girolama Orsini, duchess of Castro, the mother of Cardinal Alessandro Farnese, Ignatius obtained two houses where the Jewish catechumens could be received, one for the men and another for the women. The pope approved this institution by the bull *Illius qui pro dominici,* issued on February 19, 1543. The work was attached to the church of San Giovanni del Mercato, commonly known as "Del Mercatello."

The chaplain of this church was the priest Giovanni da Torano, called also, because of his office, John of the Market-place. When the institution was solidly established, about the year 1548, Ignatius withdrew from it.

Some years later, in 1552, Giovanni da Torano, moved by envy and ambition according to Ribadeneira, turned from friend to enemy of the Society and accused the Fathers before the Pope of heresy and violation of the seal of confession. An inquest was made and proved the accusations to be completely false. At the same time some secret crimes of the accuser were discovered for which he was condemned to life imprisonment. This sentence was later commuted to banishment from Rome.[3]

2. The House of St. Martha

Ignatius worked very hard to check the evil of prostitution which was ravaging the city of Rome. There existed since 1520, founded by the Oratory of Divine Love, a monastery of "converted women" in the street known to this day as Via delle Convertite, at the corner of Via del Corso. In 1543 some eighty such repentant women lived together in that house. But the institution did not meet all the needs because it had been founded only for single women who intended to take religious vows. There was still need to solve the problem of the married women and of those unmarried ones who wished to contract matrimony. Ignatius carried on his work of St. Martha to give help to both these classes. To begin the raising of funds he charged Father Codacio, the treasurer of the Society's house, to sell some relics of stone or marble which came from buildings of the Roman era. These were discovered during

3 Minutes of the judicial trial, in *FD*, pp. 724-731.

the excavations for the foundations of the house of Our Lady of the Way. From this sale a hundred escudos were gained, which Ignatius applied to the work he was planning. Other donations from devout persons followed. In this way the house of St. Martha was begun. Its church, used now for expositions, still stands in the present Piazza del Collegio Romano.

As had been done already in the work for the catechumens, Ignatius arranged that a confraternity should be formed. It took the name of *Compagnia della Grazia* and was approved by a bull of Paul III on February 16, 1543. The work was supported by fourteen cardinals, several prelates and religious, and some distinguished ladies of the Roman society. Prominent among them was Doña Leonora Osorio, the wife of Juan de Vega, the Spanish ambassador at Rome.

Ignatius assumed the spiritual care of this work and also the temporal care of it. Until 1546 he was assisted in this by Father Diego de Eguía. In 1543 the women living in St. Martha's were nine, with two or three more seeking admission. In the next six or seven years some three hundred of them received help. Ribadeneira recounts these humanitarian feats of Ignatius, who was seen more than once walking through the streets of Rome followed by one of these unfortunate women whom he was escorting either to the house of some lady he knew or to the House of St. Martha.

Ignatius' biographer adds that someone objected that that work was useless, since these unfortunate women, immersed in vice, would all too easily return to their old habits. Ignatius replied that even if his efforts brought nothing more than one of these women's refraining from sin for one sole night, he would consider all this work well employed.[4]

As in other works of this kind, when he saw this one firmly established, Ignatius entrusted its direction to other hands. This seemingly occurred about the year 1548.

3. *The House for Endangered Young Women*

There was another work in Rome, related to that of St.

---

1 *RibVita*, III, ix, in *FN*, IV, 411.

Martha, which Ignatius efficaciously furthered. It often happened that this shameful occupation was passed on from mothers to daughters. In any case, there were many girls who found themselves in great danger. To help them a "Confraternity of Unfortunate Single Women" (*Compagnia delle vergini miserabili*) was founded, in a building adjacent to the church of St. Catherine of the Rope-makers (Funari), not far from that of Our Lady of the Way. Pope Paul III orally approved this institution, which must have started in 1545, and Pius IV officially erected it on January 6, 1560.

The part which Ignatius played in this work is known to us from a letter which Father Bartolomé Ferrão, secretary of the Society, addressed to Simão Rodrigues in Lisbon, on April 12, 1546: "In all these things which often occur here Father has taken no little work upon himself, to say nothing of the much he does in getting young girls to abandon their houses, those of the prostitutes, to prevent these girls from being seduced by the enemy through this bad example, and to place them in dwellings of piety, established by His Holiness here in Rome, in such a way that they may live without danger."[5]

4. Spiritual Care of the Sick

Ignatius' zeal to promote good works in Rome had another manifestation in the measures he took to make sure that no sick person died without receiving the last sacraments, something which was often happening. The causes were the usual ones: the spiritual assistance to the sick was so long delayed that the patient was not in a state to make a good confession; or no word was said to him about receiving the sacrametns for fear of aggravating his condition.

To counteract this danger there existed from days long past a decretal of Innocent III, confirmed by the Fourth Lateran Council in 1215. It prescribed that physicians should cease from attending those patients who refused to receive the sacraments. This decree, however, had practically fallen into disuse. On the other hand, it is easy to imagine the objections

5 *EppIgn*, I, 375.

raised against its restoration by the doctors and also by the sick or their relatives.

Ignatius resolved to work for the revival of that law, but in a mitigated form. The physician would cease from offering his services to a sick person, not after his or her first or second refusal of the sacraments, but only after the third. Before proposing his project to the ecclesiastical authorities, Ignatius arranged for a consultation of expert persons, competent both because of their office and also their doctrine and piety. When the consultants met on May 30, 1543, all the votes were positive. The same measure was taken by the general chapter of the Augustinians, held in the spring of the same year under the presidency of their general, Girolamo Seripando. A written document of Ignatius is preserved in which he replies to the difficulties, above all to the one which held that the precept would be against Christian charity.[6]

It was not easy to get the pope's approval, one reason being his absence from Rome. On February 26, 1543, Paul III had moved to Bologna for talks with Emperor Charles V about peace with the King of France, Francis I, and also about convoking the council. He did not return to Rome until August 19. Ignatius approached the protector of the Society, Cardinal Rodolfo Pio de Carpi, who promulgated the decree in his own diocese of Faenza. That the decree was being observed in Rome we know from a letter of Ignatius to Francis Xavier, dated January 30, 1544, in which he tells him: "The matter of the physicians has already been observed for the past twenty days and more."[7] Though Ignatius had hoped to have a general decree published, it appears that at the time all that was obtained was an ordinance of the governor of Rome valid only for this city.

5. The Orphans

War, plague, and famine had left many children of Rome orphans. The word "orphans" then brought clearly to mind the dirty and ragged young vagabonds of the Roman streets.

6 *EppIgn*, I, 264-265.
7 *EppIgn*, I, 271.

The zealous Cardinal Gian Pietro Caraffa wrote to St. Girolamo Emiliani, founder of the Somaschi, asking him to open a center for those unfortunate poor children, similar to those he had founded in the regions of Venice and Lombardy. But Girolamo died on February 7, 1537, and was thus unable to realize this plan. At the request of Cardinal Caraffa and other zealous persons, Pope Paul III, by the bull *Altitudo* of February 7, 1541, established the Confraternity of St. Mary of the Visitation of the Orphans. It had separate houses for boys and girls, adjoining the church of Our Lady in Aquiro in the Piazza Capranica. The early accounts of Ignatius' life tell of the part he had in this work which, as in other similar cases, consisted in his rendering all the support he could to some enterprise initiated by others. Polanco, speaking precisely about this work for the orphans, tells us that similar works were started in other cities of Italy "with the special help of Master Iñigo in some of them."[8]

7. The Roman Inquisition

Among the works promoted by Ignatius in Rome must be listed the tribunal of the Inquisition. Its clear original purpose was to check the advance of Lutheranism in Italy. The chief promoter of this institution was Cardinal Gian Pietro Caraffa, the future Paul IV, who had the reform of the Church so much at heart. It was he who succeeded in bringing Pope Paul III to establish the Roman Inquisition, by the bull *Licet ab initio* of July 21, 1542. The tribunal consisted of the cardinals Gian Pietro Caraffa, Juan Alvarez de Toledo, Pier Paulo Parisi, Bartolomeo Guidiccioni, Dionsio Laurelio, and Tommaso Badia.

Seven days after its foundation, Ignatius informed Simão Rodrigues about it, giving some details of the part he had had in this work: "Strongly and often I urged the cardinal of Burgos [Alvarez de Toledo] and the Theatine cardinal [Caraffa], the cardinals who had a commission from the pope to look into this matter; and, when the new heretical errors were coming into Lucca, these cardinals spoke to the pope on various occasions. His Holiness has designated six

8 *PolSum*, no. 80, in *FN*, I, 198.

cardinals in order that they here in Rome, formed into a body in the form of an Inquisition, might be able to make provision in some or other parts of Italy in regard to such errors—able in every way."[9] In Ignatius' view, therefore, the establishment of the Inquisition in Rome was expedient as a preventive means to check the spread of heterodox doctrines. On the other hand, he opposed creation of the Inquisition in Germany, because there the situation was different and he counseled against it.[10]

7. The Roman College

One of the more monumental buildings of sixteenth-century Rome is the Collegio Romano, in the very center of the city. Anyone who today contemplates the imposing mass of this building, put up during the years 1582-1584 thanks to the munificence of Pope Gregory XIII, can scarcely even suspect how humble its origins were. Its beginnings go back to February 22, 1551. On that day passers-by could read a poster, displayed on a rented house on the Via d'Aracoeli leading up to the Capitol and containing these words: "School of Grammar, Humanities, and Christian Doctrine, Gratis" (*Schola de Grammatica, d'Humanità e Dottrina cristiana, gratis*).

This was the college desired by Ignatius that young men who had entered the Society, and also other extern students, might in its halls study Latin, Greek, and Hebrew. Fourteen Jesuit scholastics transferred to the new college, along with its rector, the French Father Jean Pelletier. For the lay people of Rome, that adverb "gratis" on the poster was what caused great wonderment. This procedure had been made possible by the generosity of the Duke of Gandía, Francis Borgia, who had stayed in the Jesuit house a few months earlier on the occasion of the Holy Year of 1550. Having understood Ignatius' intentions, he decided to support them with financial resources.

The young boys soon filled up the classrooms of that modest building. As a result, we find that five months later on July 13, 1551 a contract was signed for the rental of a house belonging

9 *EppIgn*, I, 219.
10 See below in ch. 13, page 200.

to the brothers Mario and Fabio Capocci, situated on the present day Via del Gesù, which leads from Santa Maria della Strada to the Piazza of Santa Maria sopra Minerva. The rental was for a five-year period at the annual rate of 180 escudos.[11]

The success of the venture excited, as was natural, the jealousy of the teachers in public schools, who feared a drop in the numbers of pupils in their own classrooms with the consequent financial loss. But this opposition did not impede the favorable development of the new institution. On October 28, 1552, the college celebrated its first academic exhibition open to the public, in a hall of the neighboring church of San Eustachio. The method of teaching was that of Paris (*Modus Parisiensis*). In this system special importance was attached both to the selection of the classical authors commented on and to the method of the teaching, based on alternating lectures and repetitions. The following year, a solemn and public exhibition (*acto*) was held on October 28 and 29 and November 4 at Santa Maria della Strada, in the presence of several cardinals and other invited guests. This time there were disputations in theology, philosophy, and rhetoric. For in fact, the teaching had now been extended to these branches, and competent professors had been assigned to teach them. Among these the Basque Martín de Olabe was lecturing on scholastic theology; the Spanish Baltasar Torres on mathematics and physics; the Italian Fulvio Cardulo on rhetoric; and the French André des Freux (Frusius) on Greek.

Given its location in the center of Christendom, it was natural that the Roman College would attract students from various countries. Ignatius desired it to become a model for all the rest of the Jesuit colleges, and to serve as a bridge with those established in various other cities. The difficulty was that with the increase in the number of students and the expansion of the disciplines studied the expenses also went up. Financial difficulties soon arose in 1555. That year witnessed the death, within a few months, of the two popes from whom most help had been received or was hoped for, Julius III and Marcellus

11 For a summary of the contract, see *AHSJ*, XXV (1956), 57-58.

II. But Ignatius did not lose his confidence in God, and just as little did he cease to make use of human means. At the end of 1555 he sent Jerónimo Nadal to Spain with the express commission of raising funds for the Roman College. Nadal had recourse to the generosity of Francis Borgia, who through his Burgos bankers in Florence sent a sum of 3,000 escudos for the Roman College. Of these, 300 were to be sent to the college each year. In this way the financial difficulties were evaded until 1583. In that year Pope Gregory XIII munificently endowed the Roman College, which after his name later on became known by the title of the "Gregorian University."

8. The Roman Confraternities

In regard to Ignatius' participation in the life of religion and charitable assistance in Rome, his affiliation to two important confraternities of the city deserves special mention: to that of the Hospital of the Holy Spirit and that of the Blessed Sacrament.

The very ancient Ospedale di Santo Spirito in Sassia, near St. Peter's, between the Tiber and the Vatican Hill, founded in 1201 by Innocent III, relied upon a confraternity which had been established for the maintenance and promotion of that pious and charitable work. The members contributed a yearly quota of money, and shared in return in specified spiritual graces and benefits. Ignatius became a member of the confraternity on September 24, 1541. On that date Antonio de Araoz and Martín de Santa Cruz paid into a naccount for Ignatius a sum which was not specified in the document of affiliation but which was to last for twenty years.[12]

Although no date is given in the document we possess, we may affirm that in that same year of 1541 Ignatius was enrolled in the Confraternity of the Blessed Sacrament, popularly known as "della Minerva" from the name of the Roman church in which it was constituted in 1538 by the Dominican Tommaso Stella. We have already indicated in Capter 9 that as soon as this confraternity was founded, Ignatius hastened to send to his native town a copy of the bull of founda-

---

12 The document of affiliation, in *FD*, 642-647.

tion, in order that his fellow Azpeitians might share in all the graces granted to its members.

This time Ignatius himself, along with five other members of the Roman house of the Society, was the one who had his name enrolled with this confraternity. On the list of members belonging to the community of Santa Maria della Strada, in the Piazza degli Altieri, in the city ward of Pigna, we read the names of Egnacio de Loyola, Jacobo Laínez, Alfonso Salmerón, Paschase Broët, Pietro Codacio, and Gian Battista Viola. Along with them we find the names of members of some illustrious families of the district, such as the Altieri, Astalli, Capisucchi, Fabi, Maddaleni. Several of these were later connected with the construction of the residence and church of the Gesù.[13]

13 *FD*, 647-650.

Chapter 13

FOR THE DEFENSE OF THE FAITH

1. *Ignatius and the Counter Reformation*

All of Ignatius' biographers, from his companions Polanco, Nadal, and Ribadeneira until now, have noted the contemporaneity of the following events. In the same year of 1521 in which Ignatius was wounded at Pamplona, Martin Luther broke away definitively from the Catholic Church at Worms. The coincidence appears all the more striking if we recall that on May 4 of that year Luther was escorted by the soldiers of Elector Frederic of Saxony to the castle of Wartburg, where he remained in enforced retirement till March 1, 1522. At about the same time, Iñigo of Loyola, wounded at Pamplona on May 20, 1521, spent the time of his convalescence in the solitude of his ancestral castle, from which he departed as a converted man near the end of February, 1522.

There is a similar comparability between Ignatius and Calvin, which is less often noted although it is perhaps more real. But be that as it may, the parallelism between Ignatius and Luther has been made a topic continually repeated. And from this it has been an easy step to the affirmation that Ignatius had founded the Society to set up a dike against Protestantism. For many persons, Ignatius is the champion of the Counter-Reformation or he is simply the anti-Luther.

Oversimplifications of this kind do not endure when subjected to the critical examination of historical analysis. Ignatius' true purpose in founding the Society of Jesus was to serve God and the Church. His ideal was to promote the glory of God and the good of the neighbor. He saw this ideal of service as something carried into practice, in the concrete, in humble and total availability (*disponibilidad*) to the supreme pontiff, considered as the representative of Christ and as his vicar on earth. For Ignatius, to fulfill the will of the pope was the equivalent of doing the will of God, and of offering his life and that of his followers for the greatest undertaking they could imagine.

It is evident that in the disturbed times in which he lived, the chief preoccupations of the Church were concentrated on the reform of its own institutions and the defense against Protestantism, which was then invading a great part of Europe. In Ignatius' plans, the defense of the faith had to occupy a place of prime importance in those regions where he saw the greater threat to it, that is to say, in Germany and England. The work accomplished in this field during Ignatius' lifetime was only a beginning of that which had to be brought to its culmination in the two following centuries.

2. The Society's Labors and Methods in Central Europe

If we limit ourselves to the lifetime of Ignatius, our topic can be considered under two aspects: first, the Society's labors in central Europe; and second, the methods thought out and promoted by Ignatius to face the Protestant danger.

Three of the first companions were soon assigned to work in German lands. Pierre Favre left Rome in October, 1540, ordered to serve as companion to Doctor Ortiz. We find him at Worms attending the colloquy between the Catholics and Protestants, and in the following year present at the Diet of Ratisbon. Here on July 9, 1541, he made his solemn profession; and a little later, on July 27, he left for Spain, always with Doctor Ortiz. Bobadilla arrived the same year in Germany with Cardinal Giovanni Morone. Jay was sent to relieve Favre, who returned to Germany in 1542. In some explanations he revealed that he felt more inclined to labor in Germany rather than in Spain, no doubt because of the greater need there. But he was committed to obedience, and thus we see that he departed anew in 1544 for Portugal and Spain. He had been fortunate to win for the Society the young Peter Canisius, who was to accomplish in Germany the work which his master had hoped to achieve. While in Spain Favre received the order to move to Trent. With his health already undermined by several infirmities, he took to the road in June, 1546. He reached Rome, and there he died on August 1, a few days after his arrival.

Bobadilla continued his journeys through various cities of Germany and Austria, with varying alternations of fortune. In 1548 he had to quit Germany, expelled by the emperor because of his criticism against the *Interim* of Augsburg which was conceded that very year to the Protestants, and he returned to Italy. Jay worked on in Germany to the end and died in Vienna on August 6, 1552.

The work of these Jesuits was that envisaged in the act of founding the Society: to go, within a plan of complete availability, wherever they were called or where they saw themselves able to gather more fruit. They gave Exercises, they preached, gave missions in cities, took part in the colloquies with Protestants, exercised the apostolate of conversation, which, when united with the Exercises, was seen to be their most effective apostolate. For a time Bobadilla accompanied the imperial army as a chaplain. To provide greater stability for the works they started, they turned their thoughts toward the foundation of some fixed residences of the Society.

This, one of Favre's keenest desires, soon became a reality at Cologne. Already in 1544 a college was inaugurated there with seven Jesuits, one of whom was Millán de Loyola, the nephew of St. Ignatius. They were maintained by the Carthusians, the staunchest friends and benefactors of the Society in that city, and also by the generosity of other well-wishers. However, Favre's stay in the Rhineland capital was not one of tranquillity, partly because of the defection of its bishop to Lutheranism in 1546. In 1550 fourteen Jesuits resided there, seventeen in 1551, and twenty-one in 1556. Their rector was Leonard Kessel.

Late in 1549 thought began about the foundation of a college in Ingolstadt. At the request of the Duke of Bavaria, Wilhelm IV, Ignatius sent there Jay, Canisius, and Salmerón. Before their departure Ignatius gave them one of the instructions for which he is renowned. Unfortunately, the duke's death forced a postponement of the plans, since his successor Albert V did not show himself similarly favorable. It was necessary to wait till 1556 for the inauguration of that college.

In 1551 a college was founded in Vienna. It continued successfully in spite of the opposition of the local University. When Ignatius died this college had 320 pupils. A novitiate was also opened in Vienna.

The providential man for Germany was Peter Canisius. Formed in the atmosphere of the Carthusians of Cologne, he entered the Society in 1543, after making the Spiritual Exercises under the direction of Blessed Pierre Favre. Initiated into religious life in Rome at the side of Ignatius, he was able, after a first assignment to Messina, to realize his dream of working for Germany when the foundation of the college of Ingolstadt was under consideration. When this project was held up for a time, he was sent to Vienna, where he lectured in the University. There his reputation continually grew. In 1553 he was proposed for a bishopric, which he refused. The following year he was named dean of the faculty of theology. His great production was the well known *Catechism,* in three redactions: the major, the minor, and the smallest—adapted to the respective capacities of the students. In 1556 Ignatius established the two Jesuit provinces of Lower Germany and Upper Germany. Peter Canisius was appointed provincial of Upper Germany.

In 1556 Canisius went to Prague, where a college was opened. in the same year. Ignatius assigned twelve of his men. When they were united with other workers their number mounted to nineteen. With this staff it became possible to open the classes on July 7.

3. *Ignatius' Attitude toward the Problem of Protestantism*

What was Ignatius' attitude in face of the problem posed by Protestantism? It is important to ask first of all what his understanding of the problem was. It has been noticed that in his many letters there is almost never a mention of Luther or of any other of the reformers. The death of Luther in 1546 is passed over in silence. Does this mean that Ignatius did not possess an exact knowledge of the persons and their doctrines? Or is it, rather, a sign of a rejection simultaneously instinctive and conscious? There is reason to think that the second alternative is true. To begin with, his knowledge in this field was not one drawn from a prolonged study of Protestants' books. Probably it would not have been as easy for him, as it was for Laínez and Salmerón, to draw up, at the request of Cardinal Marcello Cervini, a list of propositions of the reformers' theses for the use of the Fathers in the Council of Trent, and another of the Scripture passages suitable to refute them. But it is clear that both because of his experience and his fine instinct—or, as Pierre Favre would say, because of his keen scent—he was able to perceive the direction from which that grave threat to the unity of the Church was coming.

Apart from what could have reached his ears in Spain, it is evident that during the seven years of his studies in Paris he was living in close contact with the Protestant movement. In October of 1534 he was a witness of the scandalous lampoons against the sacrifice of the Mass and also of the violent repression which extinguished them. In Venice and in Rome he was perfectly aware of the offshoots of Protestantism that were sprouting in Italy. We have already seen how the persecution which he experienced in 1538, and which jeopardized the very foundation of the Society, had its origin in the heterodox preaching of Agostino Mainardi. In his theological studies, even though they were not altogether completed, he had occasion to compare the theses of the Catholics with those of the reformers. Finally, the Rules for Thinking with the Church, whether they were composed in Paris or in Italy, and whether we consider them as a key attitude against Erasmianism or one against Lutheranism, reveal a keen observer of the controversies of his time.

In these Rules we perceive his attitude with clarity. For Ignatius, the drama of his era was above all a drama of consciences. The task on which he focused his attention was the renewal of the interior life of individual persons. But this renewal had to be carried out on an ecclesial plane. To the attitudes of Luther and Calvin Ignatius opposed his fidelity and submission to the hierarchical Church, because he was fully convinced that the spirit of Christ and that of the Church are one and the same. But the Church is not only a community of predestined persons but also a body organized under the authority of the pope. That is the reason why he states in his First Rule "We must put aside all judgement of our own, and keep the mind ever ready and prompt to obey in all things the true Spouse of Christ our Lord, our holy Mother, the hierarchical Church."[1] The distinguishing adjective "hierarchical" explains the entire Rule. In his Latin version of the Exercises he had added another adjective, "Roman."[2] A Catholic ought to search for reasons to defend the precepts of the Church rather than to fight against them; to praise—this verb is repeated at least nine times in those Rules—rather than to criticize; to build up rather than to tear down. The reform of the Church has to be attained principally through the sanctification of its members.

It is important for us to discover Ignatius' plans for the defense of the Catholic faith. We have already seen that he sent to Germany some of his best collaborators. He composed for them a series of seven instructions which reveal his whole strategy to us.

Above all is the reliance on the supernatural means. "Let them with great magnanimity put their trust in God," he wrote.[3] Their chief weapon was to be prayer. Thus he ordered that all the priests of the Society should offer one Mass every month for the needs of Germany and England. What he aimed at in his activity was "to help all Germany in what pertains to the purity of the faith, obedience to the Church, and, finally, sound doctrine and good morals." The second means had to be the example of a good life, deeds more than words.

Next came preaching in its various forms. This is perhaps the most characteristic point. He was convinced that it was much more effective to preach the truth "in a spirit of gentleness"(*in spiritu lenitatis*) than to confront the dissident openly

---

1 *SpEx*, [353].
2 "Quae romana est," in the Versio prima. See in MI, *Sti. Ignatii de Loyola Exercitia Spiritualia. Textuum antiquissimorum nova editio* (Rome, 1969), p. 405.
3 *EppIgn*, XII, 240.

in order to refute their doctrines. In this area private conversations and the Exercises held a primacy of importance. Favre attributed to these Exercises the greatest part of the fruit which he reaped in Germany.[4] "This will be a more peaceful manner of preaching, and lecturing, and teaching the Catholic doctrine, and of providing and confirming it, better than that of raising a disturbance by persecuting heretics, who would become more obstinate if they were preached against openly."[5] Everything ought to be done "with modesty and Christian charity. Therefore, no injurious statement should be made against them, nor any kind of disdain shown toward them, but compassion instead. Nor is it expedient to proceed against their errors openly; rather, through expositions of the Catholic dogmas the hearers would gather which ones of their own are false."[6]

It is noteworthy that this manner of proceeding was completely similar to that employed by Pierre Favre, which he put into writing in eight points meant for Laínez in 1546.[7] The first counsel was to have great charity for those in heresy and to love them genuinely. The second, to bring them to love us: and this is done by conversing familiarly with them about things common to them and ourselves, and by avoiding controversies. In the third place, with heretics it is better to influence the will than to instruct the intellect. Still other counsels follow: to induce them to good moral practices, for it has often been noticed that the doctrinal deviations have had their origin in a bad life in the past; to exhort them to love of good works, for often from their neglect of these has come the loss of their faith. As they often make the precepts impossible for themselves, "spiritual exhortation is necessary to fortify and animate them, for thus they recover their hope to be able to do and to suffer what is commanded, with the grace of the Lord."[8]

In résumé, what was needed was to exhort, to animate them to the fear and love of God and to the practice of good works.

4 *Memoriale Fabri*, no. 22, in *Fabri Monumenta*, p. 500; also in *FN*, I, 46.
5 *EppIgn*, XI, 363.
6 Ibid, 538.
7 Text in *Fabri Monumenta*, pp. 399-402.
8 Ibid., p. 401.

He concluded that often the evils were not so much in the intellect, but "in the feet and hands of the soul and body."[9] For him, that which was most needed in Germany was holiness of life and the spirit of sacrifice. Things, according to him, had reached such a point too that "they [the Jesuits] could not do much through only their learning; for the world has already come to such a state of unbelief that what is needed is arguments of deeds and of blood"; otherwise, the evil will spread and the errors increase.[10]

To these pastoral means another two had to be added: the teaching, by word of mouth and by writing, of sound doctrine, and the foundation of colleges. Ignatius entrusted to Laínez the composition of a compendium of theology which would be of service to both Catholics and Protestants. Because of Laínez' many occupations, this compendium was not completed. On the other hand, the *Catechism* of Peter Canisius in its three redactions (major, minor, and smallest—adapted to the different classes of readers) gained enormous diffusion. As to the colleges, all historians are agreed in recognizing the enormous influence they exerted in stemming the advance of Protestantism in all Europe, but particularly in Germany. Although the greater perception of this impact came after the death of Ignatius, it should be noted that colleges such as those in Cologne, Vienna, Prague, and Ingolstadt were opened during his lifetime.

A work of the utmost importance was the foundation in 1552 of the German College in Rome. Developing the idea received from Cardinal Giovanni Morone, Ignatius started this work and carried it forward with great constancy, overcoming the difficulties, especially in the area of finances. The plan was to unite together in one college, in the center of Christendom, a group of select youths hailing from the various German-speaking regions. From here would go forth the future pastors and bishops who were to work in Germany. For the setting up of this German College, Ignatius mobilized all his negotiating

9 Ibid., p. 402.
10 Letter of Favre to the scholastics of Paris, May 12, 1541, in *Fabri Monumenta*, p. 105.

skill and all his influence with persons in high places, above all with the pope himself.

4. *Ignatius and the Leaders in the Countries Largely Protestant*

Such were the counsels and orientations which Ignatius gave to his men. When there was question of manifesting his opinion to the ecclesiastical and civil authorities, who were in control of coercive means to repress heresy, his words took on a tone more severe. He recommended to Zaccaria Delfino, appointed in 1553 nuncio in the court of the King of the Romans Ferdinand I, to promote above all the giving of good example by churchmen, and their avoiding every kind of avarice, "since this has already done so much damage and is giving occasion for so much bad opinion about this Apostolic See." Care must be taken in the choice of Catholic masters for the schools, excluding Lutherans from them. Heretical books ought to be banned from the schools and Catholic books substituted for them. In his instruction he devotes ample space to the Catholic education of youth. Finally, in addition to private conversations, on which he had insisted so much when speaking to his Jesuits, he recommends to the nuncio public disputations in the diets and other assemblies.[11]

On August 13, 1554, Ignatius sent two instructions to Peter Canisius. One was in Italian and gave him norms about what he himself was to do.[12] The other, in Latin, was meant, at least indirectly, for the King of the Romans.[13] In this second document, which seems to be the result of a consultation held by Ignatius with some of his most intimate collaborators, he puts forward his viewpoints about the means which the king ought to put into practice toward extirpating heresy wherever it has taken root and toward preventing its spread into regions still Catholic. In a preamble, he left to Canisius in his prudence the discernment pertaining to the measures which he was about to propose to him. His purpose was that Canisius, in accordance with what he would judge to be better,

11 Text of the memorial to the nuncio, in *EppIgn*, XII, 254-256.
12 Text in *EppIgn*, VII, 395-397.
13 Text ibid., 398-404.

would somehow cause them to reach the ears of Ferdinand I. These measures can be summarized as follows.

The king ought to declare himself personally hostile to every form of heresy. An efficacious means to avert this danger is to keep persons infected with the error away from posts of government and of teaching. Heretical books ought to be burnt, and those of authors tainted by heresy should be set aside, even though they do not contain errors. This is Ignatius' well-known principle, affirmed by him on other occasions: The reading of heretical authors should be avoided even though they are not in themselves bad, because the reader begins to develop a liking for the author, and from this he easily passes into feeling an attraction to his doctrines.[14] Another help will be the convocation of synods in which the error can be unmasked. It should be forbidden, under penalty of a fine, to call a heretic "evangelical."

For the prevention of heresy in the regions still Catholic, Ignatius proposes the choice of persons clearly orthodox for the posts of responsibility; the appointment of bishops, priests, and preachers and their distribution to various regions to proclaim the Gospel worthily: the removal of ignorant priests from their parishes; care in the selection of directors in the schools; the composition and explanation of a good catechism of Christian doctrine. In conclusion, he suggests the creation of four types of seminaries for the formation of candidates to the priesthood. One of these is the German College in Rome.

This instruction has drawn attention from both Catholics and Protestants for its character certainly severe, particularly because in it the possibility of imposing capital punishment is twice proposed as a remedy against heresy. Methods such as this, which contrast with the conception we have today of religious freedom, must be placed in the context of the times for which they were proposed. Account should be taken, too, of the attitudes characteristic of the era, which were then current among Catholics as well as Protestants.

14 See, e.g., *Cons*, [465].

For the sake of truth it should be noticed that in the first passage capital punishment is suggested, not in absolute terms, but along with alternatives, "forfeit of life, confiscation of one's goods, or exile."[15] In the second passage, Ignatius' statement is that, for those found guilty, "perhaps it would be prudent counsel to punish them with exile or prison or even on some occasion with death. But about this extreme punishment," Ignatius adds, "and about setting up the Inquisition, I do not speak, for this seems to be beyond what the present situation in Germany can bear."[16] The attenuating adverbs "perhaps" and "on some occasion" take much of the force out of this hypothesis of the employment of capital punishment. In this second passage, too, Ignatius draws back from both the imposition of capital punishment and the establishment of the Inquisition in Germany. He who had counseled the introduction of the Inquisition in Rome and Portugal advised against it for Germany, because there it did not seem suitable for the situation of that country.

Ignatius' attitude may well be compared with that of Thomas More, the Chancellor of England. In his *Utopia*, published in 1516, he had shown himself irenic. But in 1528, in face of the Lutheran rebellion, he adopted a radical position. Treating about a danger jointly to the faith and the civil order, he wrote: "The fear of these outrages and mischiefs to follow upon such sects and heresies, with the proof that men have had in some countries thereof, have been the cause that princes and people have been constrained to punish heresies by terrible death, whereas else more easy ways had been taken with them."[17]

We do not know whether or not Canisius succeeded in getting Ignatius' counsels to Ferdinand I. What cannot be denied is that some remedies like those suggested by Ignatius functioned efficaciously in maintaining Catholicism in Austria, Bavaria, and other regions of Germany. In regard to the labors of the Jesuits in this country, the historian of the Reformation in

15 *EppIgn*, VII, 399.
16 Ibid., 401.
17 From *A Dialogue concerning heresies and matters of religion made in 1528 by Sir Thomas More...reproduced in black letter facsimile...with a modern version...by* W. E. Campbell (London, 1927), pp. 274 and 301.

Germany, Josef Lortz, writes as follows: "Beyond doubt, it is to the Jesuits that the chief merit for the renewed Catholic structural features of Catholicism is to be credited—also in Germany. But the manner in which this was realized was not that the Society of Jesus, coming from outside, here laid all the foundations anew. Rather, what happened was that the new vigor of the sons of Ignatius found its most favorable aids in the medieval elements of German piety and in the men who represented it." And this historian next asks himself: "What, precisely speaking, was the new element which the Jesuits brought to Germany? What was it that equipped them to undertake in all its amplitude, even though little by little, the reform which was said to be necessary?" Gerhard Kalkbrenner, prior of the Carthusian monastery in Cologne, gave a specific answer and went to the core of the question, when he said: "They are men full of the Spirit of God, with a fresh enthusiasm and a new vigor. Their words fly like sparks of fire and inflame hearts."[18]

5. *Mission to Ireland, Britain, and Poland*

The work which the Jesuits were able to achieve in England and Ireland was, because of the adverse circumstances, less efficacious than that in Germany. In 1541 Ignatius gladly accepted the designation by Paul III of Salmerón and Broët as apostolic nuncios to Ireland, which was threatened by the contagious schism. For them too he composed one of his instructions.[19] The two papal nuncios passed through Scotland and arrived in Ireland in February of 1542, but within thirty-four days their mission was thwarted because of the opposition they encountered. After crossing to Scotland and holding conversations with King James V, they had to undertake their return journey to Rome.

Some years later, Ignatius greeted with joy the marriage between Philip II and Mary Tudor, celebrated in 1554, and he wrote a letter of congratulations to the king. It seemed that the obedience of England to the pope would be definitively restored. But this illusion lasted only a short while. With the

18 J. Lortz, *Geschichte der Reformation in Deutschland*, 3(1949), II, 131, 140.
19 *EppIgn*, I, 174-181; 727-733.

accession of Elizabeth I to the throne in 1558, England relapsed into schism. The Jesuits could not enter England until 1562, and only secretly then.

Similarly in Poland, a kingdom still Catholic but threatened by the danger of Protestantism, the Society could not get a stable footing during the lifetime of Ignatius. In 1555, Bobadilla was sent there as a companion to the Nuncio Luigi Lippomani. With him he arrived in Warsaw in October of the same year, and from there he passed on to Vilna. A little later he returned to Rome to inform the pope about the affairs in that country.

6. In the Council of Trent

The first two sessions (1545-1547 and 1551-1552) of the Council of Trent were held during the lifetime of Ignatius. The work of some Jesuits in them is worthy of special treatment among the activities carried on by the Society in defense of the faith.

From the beginning of the Council Claude Jay was present at Trent as representative of the Bishop of Augsburg, Cardinal Otto von Truchsess. In February, 1546, Paul III ordered that three more Jesuits should go to the city of the Council. The choice fell on Laínez, Salmerón, and Favre. The first two reached their destination on May 18. Favre received the news of his assignment while he was in Spain. He took to the road immediately and reached Rome in the middle of July. But as a result of fatigue from the long journey and of illness, he died there on August 1, at the early age of forty years.

The Jesuits sent to Trent did not have, for the moment, any other charge than to attend to the spiritual care of the prelates and their retinue. There were, however, various apostolic works which they were able to carry out in the city. About the way of proceeding in this activity they had received an instruction from Ignatius, written about the middle of 1546.[20] But a week after their arrival, they were already admitted to the number of theologians entrusted with the task of preparing the matter for the council sessions. At first those young priests (Laínez

20 *Epplgn*, 1, 386-389.

was thirty-four and Salmerón thirty-one), poorly dressed and unimpressive in appearance, were not well received, particularly by the Spanish prelates. But little by little their reputation grew as observers became aware that their modest appearance hid a vast theological preparation. The Legate of the Council, Cardinal Marcello Cervini, chose Laínez as his confessor.

During the plenary sessions of the Council, Laínez and Salmerón addressed the assembly on original sin, justification, and the sacraments. Special attention was attracted, in particular, by the learned intervention in which Diego Laínez opposed the theory of double justification—the one inherent, and the other imputed—defended by Girolamo Seripando. But apart from their activities during the plenary sessions, the two Jesuits were intensely active in the preparatory sessions of the theologians. Many council fathers consulted them, and the task was entrusted to them of drawing up a list of the errors defended by the Lutherans.

When the decision was taken to transfer the Council to Bologna, Laínez and Salmerón left Trent on March 14, 1547. In Bologna they attended the ninth session, in which they expressed their opinions on the sacraments of penance, extreme unction, and matrimony. In Bologna Peter Canisius joined them. He had been sent by Cardinal von Truchsess to work in company with Jay.

The Council was suspended for four years, 1547-1551. It reopened at Trent on May 1, 1551. This time Laínez and Salmerón were present in the capacity of papal theologians. In the sessions held during this period of the Council, they made interventions when the decrees on the Eucharist, penance, and sacred orders were being discussed. Laínez distinguished himself in the fourteenth session, when on December 7, 1551, he spoke at length and with much erudition, about the Mass as a sacrifice.

During this second session of the Council there was a hope that Protestant theologians would be present, but this plan failed. To complicate the situation came the armed revolt as a result of the treason of Prince Maurice of Saxony, who passed to the Lutheran camp. Matters went from worse to worst for Charles V, for the Protestants occupied the city of Augsburg in the middle of April, 1552. The threat posed by the proximity of the warring armies to the peaceful progress of the Council moved Pope Julius III to decree its suspension on April 15, 1552. With the fall of Innsbruck on May 19, all hope of continuing the sessions was lost.

The Jesuits departed to take up other works. Meanwhile, even if we prescind from their activities during the Council, another result of their presence there became apparent. Many bishops gained their first knowledge of the recently founded Society. Through this the first measures were taken for the foundation of colleges in Germany and Austria. Still another development was the acquisition of Martín de Olabe (Olave), a theologian from Alava sent to the council by Cardinal von Truchsess. There Martín came to know the Society, and after making the Exercises he decided to enter it in 1552.

Chapter 14

"GO TO THE WHOLE WORLD": EUROPE

1. Spain

The first Jesuits to set foot in Spain were Fathers Antonio de Araoz and Pierre Favre. The former was son of a brother of Iñigo's sister-in-law, Magdalena de Araoz. Already in 1539 he joined the group of the first companions in Rome. In the course of his three journeys from 1539 to 1543 he worked in several cities of Spain and thus made the Society known there. Because of the importance and duration of the offices he held, Araoz was a person of the first rank of the Society in Spain, serving as the first provincial of Spain in 1547 and as the provincial of Castile in 1554. He was the Jesuit in closest relationship with the Spanish court until his death in 1573.

Pierre Favre had gone to Spain in 1541 when he was charged to accompany Doctor Pedro Ortiz. He returned there in 1545 and with Araoz made the Society known to the court. In all the places through which he passed he gave edification by his good example, gentleness in dealing with others, and fervent preaching. While in Spain he received the papal summons to help in the council of Trent.

The vocation of Francis Borgia to the Society must be attributed to his contact with Favre and Araoz. Francis was the viceroy of Catalonia when the two Jesuits passed through Barcelona. Borgia took a liking to them and the new religious order which they represented. He soon asked them that a college be founded at Valencia, and this became the first Jesuit college in Spain. It was inaugurated in 1544 and maintained through the material support procured by the first Valencian Jesuit, Jerónimo Domènech. This college was followed one year later by the foundation of the college of Gandía, for

205

which the duke obtained from Pope Paul III in 1547 the title of university. After the death of his wife, Leonor de Castro, on March 27, 1546, Francis' admiration of the Society led him to request his admission into it from Ignatius. It is easy to imagine the impression made on Ignatius by the entrance into the Society of a man of the caliber of the Duke of Gandía. He went so far as to say that the world would not have ears able to stand such an explosion.[1]

Borgia's admission was kept secret, even after he made his solemn profession on February 1, 1548. Only after a journey to Rome on the occasion of the Holy Year 1550 did he request from Charles V authorization to resign his dukedom in favor of his firstborn son, Carlos. This was in 1551, and Francis Borgia, ordained a priest at Oñate on May 23, chose to celebrate his first Mass in the house of Loyola. Borgia's entrance into the Society gave a strong impulse to the new order not only in Spain but also in Italy, because of the good relations of his family with that of Paul III, the Farnese pope, and with the Duke of Ferrara, Ercole II d'Este. We have already mentioned that Francis obtained from the pope the title of university for the college of his native Gandía. In 1548, to counteract the criticism leveled against the book of the *Exercises*, especially in Spain, he obtained from Paul III the official approval of Ignatius' book by the brief *Pastoralis officii cura*, dated July 31, 1548. It is a rare case in the Church, as Nadal wrote, that a book is approved by a papal brief.[2]

The Society kept on spreading gradually in Spain. Erected into a province already in 1547, it was divided in 1554 into three provinces: Castile, Aragón, and Andalucía, which had as provincials respectively Antonio de Araoz, Francisco de Estrada, and Miguel de Torres.

The foundations of colleges[3] made in Spain during Ignatius' lifetime were the following. After Valencia (1544) and

---

1 *EppIgn*, I, 442, which gives Oct. 9, 1546 as the date.
2 *MonNad*, V, 787.
3 From 1540 onward there was an evolution in the institutions designated as "colleges" in the early documents of the Society. Four types can be distinguished.

Gandía (1545) came those of Barcelona and Valladolid (1545), Alcalá (1546), Salamanca (1548), Burgos (1550), Medina del Campo and Oñate (1551), Córdoba (1553), Avila, Cuenca, Plasencia, Granada, and Seville (1554), Murcia and Zaragoza (1555), and Monterrey (1556). Some of these colleges had very modest beginnings indeed. Founded primarily for the formation of young Jesuits, they were gradually opened to extern students. In 1556, at the death of Ignatius, for example, the colleges of Medina and Plasencia had 170 extern students each, and that of Córdoba, the most numerous, 300.

In and after 1554 the province of Castile could boast of a very flourishing novitiate at Simancas, ten kilometers from Valladolid.

During the life of Ignatius, the Society in Spain did not win from the Spanish court the strong support which it received in Portugal from King John III. In the religious field it had to face more than a few difficulties. The novel type of religious life introduced by the Society gave occasion to the attacks of the Dominican Melchor Cano and of Archbishop Siliceo of Toledo. The Exercises came under the attack of another Dominican, Fray Tomás de Pedroche. With patience and tact these obstacles were overcome. On the other hand, there was no lack of strong support like that which came from the saintly Master Juan de Avila, who saw that the Society was the realization of the ideals of renewal which he himself had formed. Several of the best men whom the Society had in Spain came from the circle of this great preacher, St. Juan de Avila.

The first colleges were the houses or dwellings in which the Jesuit students (*scholastici*) merely resided, while following for their studies the courses in the universities or other centers of the city (e.g., at Paris in 1540, or Padua in 1542). A second type arose when lectures for Jesuit students only were introduced, and a third when extern students too were admitted among these Jesuits. The fourth type consisted of those colleges in which the lay students outnumbered the Jesuit scholastics, some of whom however were usually among these externs (e.g., at Messina in 1548). There was, therefore, a gradual transition from colleges intended exclusively for Jesuits to those destined principally for extern students. This was the case in the colleges of Goa, Gandía, and Messina. See in MHSJ Monumenta Paedagogica Societatis Iesu, I (1540-1556), ed. L. Lukacs (Rome, 1965) 6*-8*; George E. Ganss, *Saint Ignatius' Idea of a Jesuit University* (Milwaukee, 1956), pp. 20-23.

When Ignatius died, the Society had in Spain eighteen colleges and about 293 men.

2. *Portugal*

In Portugal, the Society had beginnings which were very promising, more so perhaps than in any other country. Two determining factors contributed to this: the strong support of King John III and his whole court, and the enormous influence wielded by Simão Rodrigues. He was responsible for many activities, starting first in Lisbon with the college of Santo Antão-o-Velho, which was opened as early as 1542. But the chief center was that of Coimbra, where in 1542 was a college with 103 students. In 1555 John III entrusted to the Society the College of Arts there. Also in Coimbra a novitiate was founded in 1553. In the same year the professed house at Lisbon was opened. In 1551 another college was inaugurated at Evora, which in 1559 was raised to the status of a university by Paul IV.

The Province of Portugal was the first such juridical region formed in the Society. It was founded in 1546 with Simão Rodrigues as provincial. Portugal was the point of departure of the first missionaries sent to India (1541) and Brazil (1549). Others went out, with lesser success, to northern Africa and the Congo. Lisbon was the port of embarkation for the Jesuits missioned to Ethiopia, with João Nunes Barreto as patriarch. They arrived in Goa but could not pursue their voyage to their final destination until 1557, when Andrés de Oviedo alone was able to set foot in Ethiopia.

Fervor in religious life accompanied the expansion of the apostolic works. In 1545-1546 Rodrigues composed a set of rules which, though valid only for Portugal, were the first ones the Society had.[4] In 1553 the mission of Jerónimo Nadal, who had been appointed commissary for Spain and Portugal, served to provide a complement and solidity to this legislative work.

Unfortunately, the magnificent development of the Portuguese province was disturbed by a serious and profound crisis,

---

4 *Cons*MHSJ, IV (*Regulae*), 15-134.

the causes of which are not easy to specify. Perhaps candidates were too easily admitted, or there were shortcomings in the religious formation. It seems certain that precise direction was lacking as the province developed. The fact is that before long symptoms appeared of a deviation from the principles of that type of religious life which had been drawn up for the Society. The phenomenon became evident with particular gravity among the scholastics of the college of Coimbra. Deviations arose toward two opposite extremes: on the one hand severity characterized by "holy follies" and spectacular external penances, and on the other a tendency to softness and the comforts of life. The principle of obedience failed, a principle so fundamental in the Ignatian concept of religious life.

To provide a remedy for that developing situation, Ignatius wrote two of his most admirable letters. On May 7, 1547, he addressed to the scholastics of Coimbra what is commonly called his letter on perfection. In it he set down highly prudent norms about the golden mean, a rule of great value for keeping a middle course between severity and laxity. The criterion was to be sought in spiritual discretion enlightened by obedience.[5] The second directive was the well known Letter on Obedience, addressed to the Fathers and Brothers of Portugal on March 26, 1553.[6] By then the crisis had burst into the open in an evident and preoccupying manner.

In the events of those years, the determining action came from the provincial, Simão Rodrigues. Even when we search for all the excuses possible for him, his behavior appears plainly disconcerting. We find ourselves forced to consider, not so much his intentions (which we must think were good), but rather the facts. Near the end of 1551 Ignatius decided to remove him from his office, in which he had remained much longer than the three year term prescribed by the Constitutions, and appointed him in 1552 provincial of Aragón. But Simão did not even take up this new charge. More than that, of his own volition he presented himself in Portugal. The general summoned him to Rome and submitted his case to the judg-

5 *EppIgn*, I, 495-510; *LettersIgn* pp. 120-130.
6 *EppIgn*, IV, 669-681; *LettersIgn*, pp. 287-295.

ment of four fathers: Miona, Olabe, Polanco, and Cogordan—
a Portuguese, a Basque, a Castilian, and a Frenchman. All of
them thought that Rodrigues should not return to Portugal,
and they imposed on him a series of penances, from which
Ignatius dispensed him. The accused accepted that sentence
for the moment with the signs of submission, but he soon rebel-
led against it, deeming it unjust. In this case, as well as in all
those that preceded and accompanied it, we have indications
of weakness of a psychological type; and these make the case
of Rodrigues one more proper for the study of a psychologist
than for the analysis of a historian. We observe his ready
changeability of his state of mind and his decisions. There were
moments when he desired to retire into eremitical life. At
other times he thought of undertaking a pilgrimage to Jerusalem. Neither plan materialized. In contrast, we see that he
had recourse to the intervention of Cardinal Carpi, the protector
of the Society, to ask for an exemption from his obedience to
his superiors.

It is easy to imagine the grief experienced by the Founder
over this sad case of one of his first companions, whom he
sincerely loved and was now in danger of being obliged to
dismiss from the Society. Fortunately, Ignatius did not have
to come to that extreme. Rodrigues worked for some years in
Italy and Spain. Finally he was able to return to his beloved
Portugal, where he ended his days in 1579.

As generally happens in such cases, at least part of the responsibility must be portioned out to some of those who were
called to serve as mediators in the affair. In any case, the
result was extremely painful. For a time the province remained
divided into two groups, those who desired rigorous measures
and those who wanted softness. Many did not stand the trial
and abandoned the Society. But once the crisis was overcome,
the Portuguese province enjoyed a prosperous life and a remarkable missionary expansion.

3. *Italy*

The activity of the first Jesuits in the whole of Italy was
intense, from Venice down to Sicily. It was, above all, an
itinerant apostolate, in keeping with the orienting principle

in the founding of the Society: to go wherever the pope sent the members or where they were called to exercise works of apostolic zeal, such as to preach, administer the sacraments, reform convents, give the Exercises, counsel, or educate youth in a Christian manner. In many cities a desire was soon expressed to rely on a stable presence of the Jesuits. The foundation of colleges took its origin from these requests.

From among the first companions of Ignatius, five spent long years of their lives working in Italy, apart from Jean Codure, who ended his mortal career prematurely in Rome in 1541. Laínez and Salmerón lived habitually in Italy. Broët, after traversing various cities, became the first provincial of Italy, appointed in 1551. When he was sent in the following year to organize the Society's affairs in France, he was replaced in this office by Laínez. We see Claude Jay in Ferrara, Faenza, and Bologna before he moved to Germany. Bobadilla, since 1548, when he had to leave Germany, lived habitually in Italy. There, among other works, he laid the foundations of the college of Naples. What he sowed, as he remarked, was harvested by Salmerón, who was the member most representative of the Society in that kingdom. Among the earliest Jesuits, it is important to point out the Valencian Jerónimo Domènech, who through three appointments governed the province of Sicily for a period of more than twenty years.

The Jesuit college of Padua deserves some space here, because it was the earliest in Italy. In 1542, the doge of Venice, Pietro Lando, through his ambassador in Rome, Francisco Venier, requested the help of two Jesuits. One was sent to him, Laínez, who spent the greater part of the years 1542 to 1545 in the territory of that republic. There he preached, heard confessions, and acted as a counselor. He also established contacts with Andrea Lippomano, the head of the priory of the Trinity. Already in 1537, this prior had granted hospitality in his own home to the early companions while they were waiting for the pilgrimage to Jerusalem. Lippomano conceived the idea of ceding to the Society, as a college for its own students, the priory of Santa Maria Maddalena at Padua, of which he was the administrator. As a matter of fact in 1542 the first students sent by Ignatius went there. In 1545, Lippomano placed the priory in the hands of the pope that he might hand it over to the Society. In September of the same year Ignatius traveled to Montefiascone, where the pope was, to deal among other matters also about this. The pope gave his consent. But this did not resolve all the difficulties. For papal letters, to obtain legal effect in Venice, had to be countersigned by the senate of that republic. This step was opposed by Giovanni Lippomano, Andrea's brother, who was striving to prevent the priory of Padua from going out of the control of his family. The campaign of resistance which he carried on was long and tenacious, but no less so was Ignatius' insistence. In the end, the affair was submitted to the vote of the senate, and the result was positive. Of the 157 members voting, 143 cast their ballots in favor of the Society and only 2 against, while twelve abstained.[7] Thus the implantation of the Jesuits in Padua came to a happy ending. This was in 1548, but the college of the Society had already been functioning in Padua since 1542.

At about this same time a project of founding a college in the city of Venice was under consideration, but this was not carried into effect until 1550.

After Rome and Padua, the third Italian city in which the Jesuits established themselves was Bologna. Francis Xavier had exercised the priestly ministries there from the autumn of 1537 until Easter of 1538. Among the persons who availed themselves of his apostolic activities, one stood out prominently, Violante Casali, the widow of the senator Camillo Gozzadini. She and the young priest Francisco Palmio, pastor of Santa Lucia, asked Ignatius in 1545 to send some Jesuits to Bologna. Alfonso Salmerón preached there during the lent of 1546. In May of this same year Jerónimo Domènech was sent there with two young Jesuits. He was replaced in 1547 by Paschase Broët, who remained in Bologna for three years. In 1551 a college was opened there, with classes in Latin and Greek, attended by about 100 students.

In February of 1551 the classes began in the Roman College. The origin and importance of this college, which Ignatius

---

7 The result of the Venetian Senate's voting can be seen in *FN*, II, 353-355.

desired to be the model for all the other colleges of the Society, have already been treated in chapter 12 above. To its pages 186-188 above we here refer the reader, and to pages 197-198 above in chapter 13 for the German College.

In 1550 a college was opened in Tivoli. In 1551 one was founded in Ferrara. For some time before this, Francis Borgia had shown particular interest in this college and he had requested it from his relative, Duke Ercole II d'Este. In 1552 four more colleges were opened, in Florence, Naples, Perusa, and Modena. In 1553 came the one in Monreale, Sicily, and in 1554 those of Argenta (Ferrara) and Genoa. In 1555 those of Loreto and Syracuse were begun and finally, in 1556 those of Bivona, Catania, and Siena.

All these colleges had a nucleus of Jesuit students varying in number and also a body of extern students. At the death of Ignatius in 1556 these externs numbered between the 50 at Argenta and the 280 at Palermo. The total number of colleges opened in Italy during the lifetime of the founder was nineteen besides the Roman College and the German College.

This proliferation of colleges was possible because of the high number of vocations, which were ever on the increase. From the 85 youths admitted in the whole Society during the years 1540-1545, the number rose to 137 in 1546-1550, and again to 513 in 1551-1556. Many of these vocations came from the colleges. The statistical data just given refer to all the Jesuit provinces taken together. But a large number of those admitted, although coming from various countries, entered the Society in Italy, especially in Rome.

Novitiates were opened for the religious formation of these candidates to the Society. Already in 1547, Ignatius expressed his intention of having separate houses opened for the formation of the novices. But the plan could not be realized at this early stage. In Rome Ignatius himself exercised the office of master of novices for many years. The first separate novitiate in Italy was that of Messina, opened in 1550. In the following year there was a second at Palermo.

The rapid expansion of the Society in Italy brought about the formation of a province, which was created in 1551. From it were excluded the houses in Rome and Naples, which remained dependent directly on the general. The first provincial of Italy was Paschase Broët. As was mentioned above, he was succeeded in 1552 by Diego Laínez. Laínez held this office until 1556 when, after the Founder's death, he was elected vicar general of the Society. Sicily became a province in 1553, with Jerónimo Domènech as provincial, an office which he held for three terms until 1576.

4. *France*

Ignatius always remembered with gratitude the courses of lectures he had attended during his studies at the University of Paris. In 1532, he wrote to his brother Martín García, highly recommending him to send his son Millán to that university, because "I believe that in no other region of Christendom will you find facilities as great as in this university."[8] He repeated similar advice in 1539 in a letter to his nephew Beltrán. This was after Martín's death, and Ignatius was still concerned about Millán's studies.[9]

When the Society began to found colleges in various cities, Ignatius decided that in them the "method of Paris" (*modus Parisiensis*) should be adopted as the plan of studies.

In the spring of 1540, some young Jesuits were sent to Paris to complete their studies, under the direction of Diego de Eguía. They were joined by others in 1541 and 1542. This year they had to take refuge in Louvain because, on the occasion of the hostilities between Francis I and Charles V, the emperor's subjects were expelled from Paris. The students were able to return in 1543, but a little later they again received an order to depart. They succeeded, however, in remaining clandestinely, mingled among other students in the college of the Lombards.

The Society had two good protectors in France: the Cardinal of Lorraine, Charles de Guise, and the Bishop of Clermont,

8 *EppIgn* I, 78.
9 *EppIgn*, I, 148.

Guillaume du Prat. At Trent the latter had established good relations with the Jesuits attending the Council. He possessed a house in Paris which he placed at the disposition of the Jesuit scholastics. He also desired the establishment of another college in Auvergne, within the territory of his diocese.

However, a serious disappointment obstructed the happy and normal realization of these projects. If the Society was to be installed in France with full legal rights, the juridical recognition called "naturalization" had to be obtained. King Henri III granted this recognition orally in 1550, and in writing in 1551. But this royal document, to obtain validity in law, had to be authenticated by the French parliament. This body refused its approval. Moreover, in 1553 it made the difficulty still more complicated by handing the matter over to the University's faculty of theology, which was even more hostile to the Society than the parliament. On December 1, 1554, the faculty issued a decree altogether unfavorable to the Society. This was a great obstacle. But Ignatius did not loose courage; he even said that the matter would never make him lose any sleep.[10] In keeping with his habitual tactics, he put human means into play. He took care to have a letter written to the princes, governors, and universities of the cities where Jesuits were working, to bring them to recommend the Society's cause. It was important, above all, to stress the favor granted to the Order by the popes.[11]

The manner on which he insisted in the drafting of this letter reveals the procedure he employed in matters of moment. The letter had to be composed in such terms that it could be read with satisfaction and edification by the authorities of the University of Paris, in case it should fall into their hands. When Ignatius saw the first draft, he was displeased and ordered a second. He personally corrected the second attempt, "and he had others read and re-read it so many times, that more than two hours and a half, and almost three, were spent in the process. The Father displayed an admirable attention; for though he uses great attention in all he does, in this

10 *Memoriale* of Da Câmara, no. 131, in *FN*, I, 606.
11 Ibid., nos. 131-132, in *FN*, I, 607.

case he showed still more of it."[12] Against the opinion of those who were inclining toward sharpness and said that it was proper to write against the decree of the University, he chose peaceful means and quoted the words of Jesus: "Peace I leave with you; my peace I give to you" (John 14: 27).[13] He did not want in any way to take a step that might irreparably cause estrangement between the Society and the University.

Fortunately, a good opportunity arose to bring clarity and to discuss the points of conflict between both parties. In August, 1555, there arrived in Rome four doctors of the University of Paris who were accompanying the Cardinal of Lorraine on a diplomatic mission to Pope Paul IV. One of the doctors was the Dominican Jean Benoit, the very person who had drafted the University's decree. Ignatius was informed of this and did not let the opportunity slip away. He brought about the holding of a conference between the four doctors and four Jesuits, Laínez, Polanco, de Freux, and Olabe. Two reports written on that occasion have come down to us, one by Olabe and the other by Polanco.[14] The outcome was that the four doctors were satisfied. But this did not suffice to bring the University to retrace its steps. The affair was not finally settled until after the death of Ignatius.

In spite of all these difficulties, the Society became established in France. Ignatius freed Paschase Broët from the offices he had held in Italy and in 1552 sent him to France to conduct the affairs of the Society in his country. In 1555 the province of France was created, with Broët as provincial. In 1554 the number of Jesuits residing in Paris came up to twelve. In 1556 it became possible to fulfill the desire of Guillaume du Prat, through the inauguration of the college in the city of Billom, close to Clermont-Ferand and located within the territory of his diocese. In 1556 this college had ten Jesuits, and the students reached the number of 800. The entire college was maintained through the support of the benefactor bishop.

12 Ibid., no. 145, in *FN*, I, 615-616.
13 Ibid., no. 149, in *FN*, I, 617.
14 Olabe's report was published by Orlandini, *Historiae Societatis Iesu pars prima*, Liber XV, nos. 46-61; that of Polanco is in *EppIgn*, XII, 614-629.

Chapter 15

"GO TO THE WHOLE WORLD": THE MISSIONS

1. The Society a Missionary Order

By its origin and its *Constitutions*, the Society of Jesus is an Order eminently missionary. Its end, as enunciated already in the first bull of its confirmation in 1540, is the propagation of the faith. The professed members make a special vow of obedience to the supreme pontiff to go, without subterfuge or excuses, to any part of the world His Holiness will order, "either to the Turks or any other infidels, even those who live in the parts called the Indies, or among any heretics or schismatics, or any of the faithful."[1] Availability to go anywhere "among the faithful or infidels" is the way of life proposed to the candidate to the Society.

The origin of this missionary vocation is to be sought in the personal vocation of Ignatius. If the pilgrimage to the Holy Land could be for the convert of Loyola a passing act of devotion, for the exercitant of Manresa it developed into a stable plan of life. When Ignatius was embarking for Jerusalem in 1523, he had a firm intention to remain there for the rest of his life, in order to dedicate himself to the search for devotion, to visiting the holy places, and to "helping souls," who in this concrete case were the Mohammedans. We already know that it became impossible for him to carry out this plan which he had cherished so long.

The vow of Montmartre, made in 1534 by Ignatius and his first companions and renewed in the two successive years, was a missionary vow. As Polanco writes, what they wanted to do was "to go to Jerusalem, and then preach, if opportunity allowed, to the infidels or die for the faith of Jesus Christ among

---

[1] The Formula of the Institute, *Regimini*, in *ConsMHSJ*, I, 27.

them."[2] This plan too could not be accomplished. But for those men this seeming failure served to broaden their horizons until they took in the entire world. On their part there will be no special preference. They will go wherever the pope will wish to send them.

Once Ignatius was elected general of the Society, he could not be a missionary; but throughout his whole life he maintained his desire to be one. The missions of which he dreamed and where he desired to end his days, were the most difficult: that of North Africa and that of Ethiopia. As he could not abandon his post, he had to content himself with being a missionary from Rome, by sending many of his sons to the missions, giving them wise instructions on how they ought to act, reading avidly the reports they sent him, and comforting and encouraging them with his letters.

In the founder's lifetime, the missions which became most firmly established, in regard to the number of missionaries and foundations, were those of India and Brazil. Both of them were declared independent provinces of the order, India in 1549 and Brazil in 1553. Attempts were made to establish other missions, such as that of Spanish America and that of Ethiopia, but the results did not succeed in becoming established there until after Ignatius' death. Some other foundations, such as that of Congo, did not go beyond an attempt destined not to endure at that time.

2. *India and the Far East*

The great missionary of the infant Society was St. Francis Xavier. Ribadeneira discovered an inkling of Xavier's missionary vocation in a story told him by Laínez. While the companions were journeying through Northern Italy, and probably while in Venice, Xavier and Laínez used to sleep in the same room. On many occasions Xavier, vividly influenced by a dream, awakened his companion; and once he said: "Jesus, how exhausted I am! Do you know what? I dreamed that I was carrying an Indian on my shoulders, and he weighed so much that I couldn't bear him."[3] Jerónimo Domè-

2 *PolSum*, no. 57, in *FN*, I, 185.
3 *FN*, II, 381-382.

nech adds that while he and Xavier were together in Bologna, Francis manifested his great desires of going to India.[4]

In spite of all these indications of his future destiny, Xavier's departure for India was due to a fortuitous event. Ignatius, acceding to a desire of King John III of Portugal, destined Simão Rodrigues and Nicolás Bobadilla to India. Rodrigues left Rome immediately for Portugal. Bobadilla had to travel in the company of the Portuguese ambassador Pedro de Mascarenhas. But at the time appointed for his departure he fell ill. Then, as Ribadeneira tells us, Ignatius, who was at that time sick in bed, called Francis and told him: "Master Francis, you already know that at the order of His Holiness two of ours must go to India, and that we have chosen Master Bobadilla as one of these. He cannot travel because of his illness, and the ambassador cannot wait until he is well. This is an enterprise for you.' With great joy and readiness Xavier replied: 'Surely, right away! Here I am' (*Pues, sus! Héme aquí*). Thus, on that day or the one after, after repairing some old pants and a worn cassock, he departed."[5] This was on March 16, 1540. It should be noted that at the time the Society was not yet officially approved and Ignatius was not yet general. But for Xavier that commission counted as a clear sign of God's will.

The work accomplished by Rodrigues and Xavier at Lisbon during the time of their preparations to sail was so highly appreciated by the king and the entire court, that John III wished to keep them there. The solution finally reached was that Rodrigues was to remain and Xavier to depart. He set sail from Lisbon on April 7, 1541, and after thirteen long months of navigation, he landed in the harbor of Goa on May 6, 1542.

This is not the place to recount Francis Xavier's evangelical achievements. But it is opportune to follow his footsteps in a systematic way, in order to see how the Society expanded into the regions of the Far East during Ignatius' lifetime.

4 Ibid.
5 Ibid. See also *RibVita*, II, xvi, in *FN*, IV, 303.

The first field of his apostolate was the region of Cape Comorin, where he labored in the conversion of the Paravas, a cast of pearl fishers. In Travancore he baptized, as he himself wrote, 10,000 persons in one month. On February 1, 1546, he embarked on a cruise of 1,740 miles in order to work on the Moluccan islands. A fortnight later he disembarked on the island of Amboina. He tarried for a time in the islands of Ternate and Moro. On his return to Malacca, he met a Japanese named Anjirô, who had been in search of a spiritual guide who would help him to bring back peace to his troubled conscience. He found one in Xavier and returned with him to Goa. After the proper preparation, Anjirô received baptism and the Christian name Paul, in the cathedral of Goa, March 20, 1548.

From his talks with this Japanese Xavier inferred that there were great possibilities for the introduction of Christianity into Japan. The method had to be one of persuasion and example of a good life, for the Japanese were led entirely by the law of reason. Animated by these hopes, Xavier embarked anew for Malacca on April 15, 1549, and from there on June 24 for Japan. He carried with him a good supply of gifts for the "king of Japan" and of letters of recommendation from the governor of India and from the bishop of Goa.

On Assumption day, August 15 of that year of 1549, he entered the port of Kagoshima, the native city of his friend Anjirô. His stay in Japan lasted until November, 1551. We see him at Yamaguchi, Miyako (the present Kyoto), again at Yamaguchi, and at the court of the king of Bungo. His greatest success, perhaps, was that achieved at Yamaguchi, where he made some 500 converts. But the Japan mission had to be one, above all, of an exploratory character. Other missionaries would, by their preaching and blood, complete the implantation of Christianity in the empire of the Rising Sun.

During his stay in Japan, Xavier came to the conclusion that to achieve an efficacious ministry there, it would be better to make a beginning through China. For in Japan this difficulty was put to him: How can the Christian religion be true if it is not known in China? Hence he decided to travel to the

Celestial Empire, though not before fulfilling his obligations in India. Thus in December 1551 we see him again at Malacca, where he found a letter of Ignatius appointing him provincial of India and of all the lands in the Orient.[6] Once back in Goa, he endeavored to solve the many pending problems which confronted him. But his mind was firmly set on the journey to China. He was not deterred either by the hazards of the voyage or the threat of capital punishment which faced those who dared enter China without an authorization. One pretext which occurred to him for overcoming this obstacle was to present himself as a member of an embassy of the king of Portugal. But this way did not turn out to be possible. Then he was content to have someone take him to the coast of Canton. He secured passage in a small boat. But he could not set foot on the continent. Soon after disenbarking on the island of Changchuen (Shan Chuan), ten kilometers from the shore, he fell seriously ill. During the night between December 2 and 3, 1552, he peacefully died. He was only forty-six years of age, of which he had spent about eleven and a half in the East.

In a biography of Ignatius it is of special interest to bring out in relief the intimate friendship which united these two great men, Ignatius and Xavier. Ignatius concluded one of his letters to his former companion of Paris with these revealing words: "Entirely yours, without my being able to forget you, ever at any time, Ignatius." Xavier quoted the words in his reply and continued: "Just as I read these words with tears, so do I write them now with tears, while remembering past times and the great love you have always had for me and still have."[7] On another occasion, when he was informing Ignatius about his project of going to Japan, he concluded with phrases which show him as a disciple formed in the school of the Exercises: "Thus, dear father of my soul and most revered, I come to my conclusion, by asking your charity—while kneeling on the ground as I write this, as if I had you present before me—by asking you to commend me earnestly to our Lord in your holy sacrifices and prayers, that he may grant me to know

6 The letters patent of appointment are dated October 10, 1549. The text is in *EppIgn*, II, 557-558.
7 Letter of Jan. 29, 1552, in *EppXav*, II, 287.

his holy will in this present life, and grace to fulfill it perfectly.
...Your least profitable son, Francis."[8]

Of the esteem in which Ignatius held Xavier we have,
among many others, these two revealing indications: one, the
freedom he allowed him in his movements as in the case of
the projected voyage to Japan; the other, his recall to Rome
expressed in Ignatius' letter of June 28, 1553. The purpose of
the recall was to report to the king of Portugal and the Holy
See on the affairs of the Indies, "in order to make the provision
of spiritual matters which is necessary or very important for
these new Christian peoples and for the old Christians living
in those regions."[9] Some have thought that Ignatius' desire
in recalling Xavier was to prepare him to be his successor as
general of the Society. But the plans of God were different.
When Ignatius was writing his letter, he was unaware that
his intimate companion had surrendered his soul to God
half a year earlier. The news of Xavier's death did not reach
Rome until the beginning of 1555, and even then it was considered as something not yet certain.

The state of the Jesuit missions in the Orient at the time
of Ignatius' death becomes clear from some precise data
recorded in a catalog which was published in Goa in late
1555.[10] The Jesuits working in those distant lands numbered
78, of whom 28 were priests. Of the sum total of these missionaries, 7 were assigned to the mission of Ethiopia. Apart
from those working in India, there were 3 priests and 7
scholastics in the Molucca Islands; 4 priests and 8 brothers in
Japan; 1 priest and 1 brother at Ormuz. There were colleges
of the Society, some of them very small, in Goa, Bassein,
Cochin, Quilon, and Ormuz. In this island, situated at the
entrance of the Persian Gulf, Gaspar Berze, sent there by
Xavier, had labored selflessly. There too in 1555 were Father
Antonio de Heredia and Brother Simón de Vera. There were
other mission stations in India, at Thana, Comorin, and
São Tomé (Madras).

8 Letter of Jan. 12, 1549, in *EppXav*, II, 16.
9 *EppIgn*, V, 150.
10 In MHSJ, *Documenta Indica*, III, 409-412.

3. The Americas

The remote origins of the Jesuit missions in the Americas can be found in an offer which Ignatius thought he ought not to accept. He himself gives us the information in his *Autobiography*. In 1540, Juan de Arteaga, his former companion in Barcelona and Alcalá, was nominated bishop of Chiapas in Mexico. He then wrote to Ignatius, offering that miter to some member of the new Society. Ignatius refused the offer, surely because already then he foresaw the renunciation by the Society, on its part, of ecclesiastical dignities.[11]

Other frustrated attempts came from Juan Bernal Díaz de Luco, the bishop of Calahorra and a member of the Council of the Indies, and from Vasco de Quiroga, bishop of Michoacán, who wrote asking for some members of the Society.

The only mention of Spanish America which we find in Ignatius' letters is in one dated January 12, 1549. Writing to the provincials Francisco de Estrada and Miguel de Torres, he tells them verbatim: "You may send some to Mexico, if it seems good, if someone requests them, or without such a request."[12] But this mission was not carried into effect during the founder's lifetime. It had to wait for his second successor, Francis Borgia, who was the first to send Jesuits to Florida, Mexico, and Peru.

The mission which was inaugurated, amid favorable signs, within the lifetime of St. Ignatius was that of Brazil. Simão Rodrigues had thought of going there personally. In the end he appointed Manuel de Nóbrega, who together with five other Jesuits sailed from Lisbon on February 1, 1549, in the fleet of the Governor General Tomé de Sousa. They disembarked at Bahía on March 29 of that year. Among the members of this pioneering party was a scholastic named Juan de Azpilcueta, a nephew of the famous Navarrese doctor Martín de Azpilcueta and a relative of Francis Xavier.

The mission entrusted to these missionaries was threefold:

11 *Autobiog*, no. 80.
12 *EppIgn*, II, 302.

the preaching of the faith to the gentiles, the pastoral care of the Portuguese, and the Christian education of the children.

A second expedition of four priests followed in 1550. The third, in 1553, was made up of three priests and four brothers, among them the future apostle of Brazil José de Anchieta, then a young scholastic of nineteen. He had been born at La Laguna, on the island of Tenerife, the son of Juan de Anchieta, of the house of this name situated at Urrestilla, Guipúzcoa, an ancient family that intermarried with that of the Loyolas.

On July 9, 1553, Ignatius nominated Manuel de Nóbrega provincial of the new Jesuit province of Brazil, made up of some thirty priests and brothers, including scholastics. These were distributed in Ilheus, Porto Seguro, Espirito Santo, San Vicente, and the village of Piratininga. In this village of Piratininga was founded, in 1554, the college of São Paulo, and there its name was later taken over by the imposing Brazilian metropolis which arose there, and which is still called São Paulo.

Chapter 16

SAINT IGNATIUS AND THE ORIENTALS

When Ignatius set out from Loyola and Manresa for Jerusalem, he had a double objective in view: to dedicate himself to the pursuit of devotion by visiting the holy places, and "to help souls." By "souls" he then understood those of the Mohammedans of Palestine and those of the Christian pilgrims who came to visit the Holy Sepulchre. In the vow of Montmartre, according to the formulation given by Laínez, the ideal of the companions was to work "among the faithful and the infidels."[1] The word infidels was then understood to mean both the pagans and also the heretics and schismatics. In the bull of confirmation of the Society, granted by Paul III in 1540, the end of the Society was specified more precisely in this point by the statement that those who desire to enter it will have to be indifferent to go wherever the pope will wish to send them, "whether it be to the Turks, or to any other unbelievers, even in the parts which they call the Indies, or to any heretics or schismatics, or even to any of the faithful."[2] The Society, therefore, was explicitly opening itself to the ministry among the orientals.

Apart from other sporadic attempts such as the plan of calling to Rome ten or twelve Greek students, or that of sending some Jesuits to the communities of Nestorian Christians, Ignatius' activity on behalf of the Eastern Christians was polarized around two projects. He cherished these with the greatest interest for long years, but they did not come to any effective realization within his lifetime. One was the foundation of three colleges, respectively in Jerusalem, Cyprus, and Constantinople; the other was the mission of Ethiopia.

1 *FN*, I, 110.
2 *Regimini militantis Ecclesiae* [4], repeated in *Exposcit* debitum, [4], in *Cons*MHSJ, I, 27, 378).

1. *Jerusalem, Cyprus, and Constantinople*

A gentleman from Bermeo in Biscay, attached to the imperial embassy in Rome and preoccupied with the Turkish menace in the Mediterranean, conceived the idea of founding a Confraternity of the Holy Sepulchre, which would be based in Rome but would have branches in other cities. Its end was to be to provide the material means for the preservation of churches threatened with destruction, and also to protect the spiritual interests of Christianity in the Middle East. One of these means was to be the foundation of three Jesuit colleges in the cities mentioned above. The Basque gentleman communicated his plans to the pope and Ignatius. Julius III gave his approval through the bull *Pastoralis officii cura*[3] of October 6, 1553, thus founding the Confraternity of the Holy Sepulchre. On March 8 of the following year the confraternity was erected in the Roman church of Santa Maria sopra Minerva. The name of the promotor of this initiative was Pedro de Zárate.

Ignatius received with favor the project of the foundation of the three colleges, for which the pope offered sufficient endowment. Father Simão Rodrigues, who after his departure from Portugal was then planning a journey to the Holy Land, was one who could be put in charge of the initial steps toward that foundation. But Simão had to abandon his journey, and other external circumstances also prevented the realization of that plan. With the death of Julius III in 1555 the chief patron of the project ceased to be present. After the fleeting pontificate of Marcellus II, his successor, Paul IV soon became entangled in another enterprise, the war against Spain. As far as the Jerusalem project was concerned, fresh difficulties arose on the part of the Franciscans, who did not look with favorable eyes upon a foundation that seemed to pose a threat to their privileges in the Holy Land. Ignatius, however, continued to nurse the idea, and even on July 20, 1556, eleven days before his death, he directed his secretary to write to Pedro de Zárate about this matter. But, realist

3 The bull was published by H. Lammens, in *Etudes* (Paris), 1897, tome 10, pp. 72-86. A summary of it is in I. Ortiz de Urbina, *San Ignacio y los Orientales*, Madrid (1950) pp. 19-22.

that he was, he acknowledged: "But this is still very far away, and there is no need to deal with it in detail for the present."[4] In 1563, Pedro de Zárate also died, and the project was forogotten.

2. *Ethiopia*

Perhaps no apostolic project was undertaken by Ignatius with so much warmth and tenacity as the mission to Ethiopia. From the information that reached him, he must have conceived a firm hope that the moment had come to effect the union of the Coptic Church of that country with the Roman Church.

How did it come about that so many hopes were placed in a mission which the facts have shown to be extremely difficult, and which in fact did not succeed? The knot of the problem lay in the real dispositions of the two kings who intervened in the matter: Lebna Dengel and his son and successor, Galâwdêwos. Did these two sovereigns have a sincere disposition and will to bring about the union with Rome? If some doubt exists in the case of the first, the matter becomes far more problematical still in respect to the second, with whom the negotiations had to be carried on in the time of Ignatius. For the negus of Ethiopia an alliance with the Portuguese was a matter of absolute necessity, in order to put up a strong resistance to the repeated attacks of the Mussulmans. Beyond any doubt, this alliance and friendship with Portugal were factors abetting the tendency toward improved relations of Ethiopia with the Catholic Church. But whether this disposition was firm and sincere remains still to be seen. When the moment of truth arrived, Galâwdêwos refused to submit. Manuel Fernandes, the companion of the patriarch Andrés de Oviedo, called the negus' gesture "perfidy." There is no doubt that Fernandes understood this term as a synonym for the failure on the part of the negus to stand by his word. But it is highly probable that in reality the king had never had a sincere determination to submit to Rome.

The events pertaining to the mission of the Society evolved in the following manner. Lebna Dengel, known in Europe as

4 *EppIgn*, XII, 155.

David, died in 1540. He was succeeded by his son Galâwdêwos (1540-1559), called Claude by the Europeans. He was then a youth of eighteen years. When he took charge of the King-dom, the situation of his country seemed desperate because of the repeated defeats inflicted by the Mussulmans. Almost the entire Ethiopian territory was in the hands of the invaders. Through successive warlike activities the situation grew better.

About the year 1546 many in Portugal believed that the moment for the submission of Ethiopia had come. King John III placed his hope in the Society for undertaking this impor-tant mission. On August 26 of that year he wrote a letter to Ignatius. In it he recommended to him to take in good part the proposals which his ambassador in Rome, Baltasar de Faria, was about to make to him. The first thing to be done was to designate a father who could be promoted to the office of patriarch of Ethiopia. The king proposed Pierre Favre, unaware of his death in Rome on the first of that very month.[5]

From the start, Ignatius accepted enthusiastically the mis-sion of Ethiopia and offered to participate in it personally. Replying to the king of Portugal, he stated: "I have reflected in the Lord about the writing of this letter in my own hand. If my companions who have this same ideal or profession, to which (as far as we can persuade ourselves) his Divine Majesty has called us, do not forbid me—and I would avoid opposing them all, just as I think they will not forbid me—I offer myself to you, in case another of our members does not wish to undertake this enterprise to Ethiopia, to take it myself most willingly, if I am commanded to do so."[6]

Such promising auspices were followed by seven years of apathy. Only in 1553 did discussion about that mission begin again. It must be noted that one of the reasons why Ignatius recalled Francis Xavier to Rome that year (without knowing that the apostle of the Indies had died already half a year earlier) was that he might be the one to coordinate the affairs of Ethiopia: "Notwithstanding these reasons, which are all

5 *EppIgn*, I, 428.
6 Ibid. 429.

in favour of the good of India, I think that your visit would stir up the king's enthusiasm about the matter of Ethiopia, which he has now kept pending for so many years, and no action about it is seen."[7]

From that time on Ignatius put his hands to the task. For five days, all the Masses and prayers of the Jesuits in the house and college of Rome were to be offered for this intention. Ignatius invited all the fathers and brothers to manifest their availability to go to the new mission. "The whole house and college are full of persons who wish to join this enterprise,"[8] Ignatius wrote to Salmerón on June 24, 1554.

The most pressing and delicate problem was the choice of the patriarch and his two auxiliary bishops. Ignatius, who had so strongly resisted the appointment of Jay to the bishopric of Trieste and of Laínez to the cardinalate, did not have any special difficulty about accepting these bishoprics in a mission land. For the post of patriarch, since Favre had died, he proposed Paschase Broët, but King John III preferred that the choice should fall on a Portuguese. For a short while Simão Rodrigues was under consideration. But after he was dropped, the one chosen was João Nunes Barreto, who had worked effectively in the African city of Tetuan, engaged in the ransom of captives. As coadjutor bishops and successors Andrés de Oviedo and Melchor Carneiro were chosen. Another twelve Jesuits were to accompany them.[9]

Oviedo and his Jesuit missionaries who were to accompany him set out from Rome for Portugal and Ethiopia in September, 1554.

João Nunes Barreto and Andrés de Oviedo received episcopal ordination at Lisbon, May 4, 1555. The other members of the expedition, under the direction of Melchor Carneiro, had sailed for India one month earlier. Nunes and Oviedo followed them, taking ship on March 28, 1556. Goa was intended to be one stage and the point of departure for Ethiopia. But it

7 *EppIgn*, V, 150.
8 *EppIgn*, VII, 169.
9 *EppIgn*, VI, 101-102; *EppMixt*, IV, 105-106; *FN*, I, 599.

turned out to be impossible for the patriarch designate Nunes Barreto to reach his goal, and he died in Goa in 1562.

For the guidance of these bishops and missionaries, Ignatius addressed to the patriarch João Nunes in February, 1555, a series of "Points Which Can Help toward the Reduction of the Kingdom of Prester John to Union with the Church and the Catholic Religion." In these he expounded the tactics which they were to adopt on reaching Ethiopia.[10] The first step should be that of winning the good will of the negus, in confidence that if he should come to favor the plans which were being proposed, the entire population would follow his example. It was proper, too, to win over the persons most influential in the court. It would be better to use methods of suavity and persuasion, rather than those of violence such as the theological disputations. The activities of those sent should be exclusively of a spiritual character, for example, preaching, direction of Exercises, and administration of the sacraments. Attention should also be given to the education of children by the foundation of colleges. In the administration of the sacraments and other rites, accommodation to the Latin usage was counseled. But this was only a recommendation, not an imposition. To pursue these objectives more easily, it was fitting that some promising youths of the country should enter the Society.

On February 23, 1555, Ignatius wrote a lengthy letter to the negus Claude, in which he pondered the importance of the unity of the Church: "The Catholic Church is only one throughout the whole world, and it is impossible that there should be one under the bishop of Rome and another under the bishop of Alexandria."[11] He praised the qualities of the patriarch designate and those of his auxiliaries and successors, as well as those of the other Jesuits who were being sent. To them he recommended that they in turn should be respectful and obedient to the sovereign.

To prepare the ground for a mission so much desired and so full of expectation, the viceroy of India, Pedro Mascarenhas—

10 *EppIgn*, VIII, 680-690.
11 Ibid. 462.

the man who fifteen years earlier had interceded for the sending of the first Jesuits to India—was of the opinion that, before the departure of the patriarch, a precursor ought to go to Ethiopia to prepare the way. The one designated was Gonçalo Rodrigues, who left Goa on February 7, 1555. On reaching Ethiopia he was received by Galâwdêwos; but when the negus came to know of the plans which were being proposed, he rejected the envoy. Though Gonçalo had prepared a written exposition of his projects, the negus was not open to persuasion, and Gonçalo had to return to India in February, 1556, with nothing achieved.

Within the lifetime of Ignatius, therefore, the dream which he had cherished so long was not carried into effect. In 1557, the year following the founder's death, Andrés de Oviedo was able to set foot on Ethiopian soil, but what he could achieve was very little. Forced to retire to Fremona in the Tigré province of Ethiopia, to exercise his episcopal ministry from there in the measure he could, he lived a life of poverty so great that it became necessary for him to cultivate a garden for his own sustenance. He died there on July 9, 1577.

Chapter 17

THE CONSTITUTIONS OF THE SOCIETY OF JESUS

1. *The Formula of the Institute*

The plan of giving a juridical structure to the Society was set in motion as soon as the foundation of the new religious order was decided upon in the deliberations of 1539. It was evident that this new organism required some norms to regulate its life and activities.

The first stage consisted in the drafting of the "Formula of the Institute." According to Nadal, Ignatius was the one charged to prepare it, but manifestly in collaboration with the other companions.[1] This Formula, of which we have spoken when dealing with the approbation of the Society, became a document of papal law when it was incorporated into the bull *Regimini militantis Ecclesiae*, dated September 27, 1540, by which the Society was approved. From that time it has been considered as the "fundamental Rule" of the order, containing the whole substance of its legislation.

This does not mean, however, that the Formula could never receive changes. In fact, in March of 1541, only a few months after the approval by the pope, the fathers already began to think that some of its points could be expressed with greater clarity and precision or adapted to what experience was teaching them. As the years passed, corrections which might be introduced were noted down and finally, in 1550, a new draft of the Formula was submitted for the approval of Pope Julius III. He approved it by the bull *Exposcit debitum* of July 21, 1550.

The reasons in favor of elaborating this new bull are enumerated in its introduction. They may be reduced to these three:

---

1 *FN*, II, 95; *EppNad*, V, 247, 640.

1. A new confirmation of whatever had been granted by Paul III.

2. Inclusion in the bull of the privileges conceded by the pope after 1540, of which the chief ones were: the suppression of the restrictive clause limiting the professed members to the number of sixty (1544); the institution of the grades of both spiritual and temporal coadjutors (1546); the confirmation of the privileges granted by Paul III in his bull *Licet debitum* of October 18, 1549, which was called a great sea (*mare magnum*) of privileges.

3. Expression with greater precision and clarity in regard to some points which might raise doubts or scruples.

All this was obtained by the bull of 1550, after which the Formula of the Institute has received no further change. It has remained the Magna Charta of the Society.

2. The Book of the "General Examen"

At the same time while Ignatius was working on the *Constitutions,* he elaborated a text called the *General Examen,* which was to serve as a preamble to them.[2] Its first redaction was completed in 1546 or 1547.

This book, as its title suggests, contains the points which a candidate who desires to enter the Society should ponder and also, in turn, the matters on which he ought to be examined in order that a correct judgment can be made in regard to his suitability for admission.

It is necessary to propose to the candidate, above all, the end of the Society. This is "not only to attend with God's grace to the salvation and perfection of the members' own souls, but also with that same grace to labor strenuously in giving aid toward the salvation and perfection of the souls of their fellowmen"([3])[3]

2 On the genesis of the *Constitutions,* see A. de Aldama, "La composición de las Constituciones de la Compañía de Jesús, "*AHSJ,* XLII (1973), 201-245.
3 The English translations used throughout this chapter are taken from St. Ignatius,

After the end come the various means to attain it. These are, especially, the three religious vows as understood by the Society. Other points proposed to the candidate are: the vow of special obedience to the pope to go anywhere His Holiness will order; the exterior manner of living in the Society, which is ordinary, without penances or other austerities imposed by rule ([8]); the grades of persons in the Society—professed, spiritual coadjutors (priests), temporal coadjutors (brothers, canonically termed laymen), scholastics preparing for the priesthood, and novices ([10-15]); the simple vows to be taken by the scholastics before their definitive incorporation into the Society ([16]).

The fourth chapter of the *Examen* is of particular importance because it presents to the candidate the ideal of spiritual life to which he should aspire. In the Society must be received only "those persons...already detached from the world and determined to serve God totally" ([53]). This means, above all, that "they must distribute all the temporal goods they might possess and renounce and dispose of those they might expect to receive" [53], according to the evangelical counsel, "Give to the poor and...follow me" (Matt. 19:21). A candidate should "endeavor to put aside all merely natural affection for his relatives and convert it into spiritual, by loving them only with that love which rightly ordered charity requires, as one who is dead to the world and to self-love and who lives only for Christ our Lord, while having Him in place of parents, brothers, and all things" ([61]).

The Constitutions of the Society of Jesus. Translated, with an Introduction and a Commentary, by George E. Ganss (St. Louis, 1960), (abbreviated *ConsSJComm*). The reference numbers in square brackets refer to the paragraph numbers, now standard, which modern editors have added to Ignatius' text to facilitate reference, as explained ibid., pp. 356-357.

As a matter of editorial policy, throughout this present book *Constitutions* (in italics) refers to Ignatius' published book, *The Constitutions of the Society of Jesus*, a collection of some 827 constitutions, each an ordinance, rule, or directive of perhaps five to fifty words. Hence the word Constitutions (in roman but capitalized) is used to refer to his book while still in manuscript before publication, or to one, or a few, or a portion of these constitutions either before or after publication (*ConsSJComm*, pp. 356-357). On the similar policy in regard to *Spiritual Exercises* (italics) and Spiritual Exercises (roman), see fn. 24 of ch. 4, above on pp. 64-65.

He who joins the Society should be willing to have all his errors and defects manifested to his superiors, and he in turn to collaborate in this fraternal correction, "with due love and charity, in order to help one another in the spiritual life" ([63]).

"His food, drink, clothing, shoes, and lodging...will be what is characteristic of the poor." At this stage the example of the first Fathers is proposed to the candidate: "For where the Society's first members have passed through these necessities and greater bodily wants, the others who come to it should endeavor, as far as they can, to reach the same point as the earlier ones or to go farther in the Lord" ([81]).

After this ideal of poverty, humility is shown to the candidate, in accordance with the example of Christ. Just as men who follow the world love and seek with such great diligence honors, fame, and esteem for a great name on earth, so those who are progressing in the spiritual life and truly following Christ our Lord love and intensely desire everything opposite, that is to say, "to clothe themselves with the same clothing and uniform of their Lord because of the love and reverence which He deserves," to such an extent that they would wish to suffer injuries, false accusations, and affronts, in order "to resemble and imitate in some manner our Creator and Lord Jesus Christ, by putting on His clothing and uniform, since it was for our spiritual profit that He clothed Himself as He did" ([101]).

It is obvious that so lofty a degree of perfection, and in particular so total a following of Christ poor and humiliated, could be proposed only to one who has already made Ignatius' Exercises well. For in them is proposed to him, as a supreme goal, enlistment under the banner of Christ poor and humble, and thereby his making himself like his divine Master in a manner as total as that which is proposed in the third kind of humility. Ignatius is perfectly aware that this cannot be asked of one who has just left the world. He therefore adds that the newcomer be asked whether, in case he does not experience in himself such ardent desires in our Lord, he has at least any desires to experience them ([102]).

In a further step, the candidate is told that, the better to arrive at this degree of perfection, "his chief and most earnest endeavor should be to seek in our Lord his greater abnegation and continual mortification in all things possible" ([103]).

3. The Constitutions: Their History

It can be said that Ignatius worked at the composition of the Constitutions throughout the whole time of his generalate.[4] As long as it was possible, he developed all the points in collaboration with the other companions then present at Rome. As we have already stated in chapter 11 above, in 1541, before a general had been elected, a sketch of Constitutions was composed, containing forty-nine points which touched the most important topics. The document was signed by Ignatius, Laínez, Salmerón, Codure, Broẽt, and Jay. Never again afterwards were they able to meet together again. On Codure's death, August 29, 1541, the whole task of drafting the Constitutions fell upon Ignatius.

From 1541 into 1547 he worked on some topics pertaining to the "missions," the refusal of ecclesiastical dignities, the teaching of catechism to children, the foundation of colleges, and the poverty of the houses of the Society. In this period belong the pages which have come down to us from his *Spiritual Diary*, February 2, 1544—February 27, 1545. They were written while he was pondering the topic of the poverty of the churches of the Society. But because of the general's delicate health and his occupations in governing, he had little time left for the redaction of the Constitutions.

In 1547, with the appointment of Juan de Polanco to the office of secretary of the Society, the composition of the Constitutions began to move forward with long steps. Nadal observed that from early 1547 onward Ignatius began to devote himself "seriously" to the Constitutions. The allusion to the arrival of the new secretary is clear.[5]

Polanco had been born at Burgos in 1517. After his study of

4 See fn. 2 above.
5 *FN*, II, 207.

philosophy in Paris, he moved to Rome where he obtained the occupation of an amanuensis to the Holy See (*scriptor apostolicus*). In 1544 he entered the Society, and afterwards was sent to complete his theological studies at Padua. Shortly later he was called to Rome to take up the office of secretary of the Society. That was indeed a happy choice, for Polanco seemed to combine all the qualities of the ideal secretary: great capacity for work, identification with his superior and interpretative undertstanding of his mind, and clarity as well as precision in executing the tasks entrusted to him. He made himself "the memory and the hands of the general," as the secretary depicted in the Constitutions is expected to be ([800]).

Doubts have arisen as to what was the contribution of Polanco in the composition of the Constitutions. Although attainment of an absolute certainty on this matter is impossible, it can be said that a series of indications confirms the statement of Ignatius, recorded by Nadal, "that with respect to the substance of the content, there is nothing of Polanco's in the Constitutions, unless something concerning the colleges and universities; and even that is according to his own thought."[6] What Polanco did is indeed much; but even when he worked with a certain measure of autonomy, he did it always while interpreting the mind of the founder and consulting with him about all his doubts.

Polanco made an intelligent start by collecting all the pertinent material he found on his arrival in Rome. As this left him some difficulties, he gathered four "Lists of Problems" (*dubiorum series*) to present them to Ignatius for solution. Other important work was that of reading the rules and constitutions of the older religious orders. We have his autograph excerpts from the same.

In a further step, he composed in 1548 a series of twelve "Resources" (*Industriae*) "to aid the Society to proceed better toward its end."[7] These *Industriae* may be considered as a

6 *Cons*MHSJ, II, clxiv; *FN*, III, 637, no. 3.
7 In MHSJ, *Polanci complementa*, II, 725-775.

preliminary plan of the Constitutions. In 1549 he compiled some "Constitutions of the Colleges."[8]

With this and other materials it was possible to proceed toward preparation of an organic text. About the middle of 1550 the first text which we possess of the Constitutions (text *a*) could already be considered completed. It contained ten parts, those which the definitive book was to have. But this text was not more than an advance draft of another more elaborate one. This, text A, followed a little after the former, text *a*, and was ready in September of the same year 1550. Ignatius corrected it in his own hand. His alterations appear no less than 230 times. They consist of corrections of words or phrases, or cancellation of entire paragraphs, or indications of various kinds.

The time had now come to submit the work thus far done to the examination and approval of the fathers who could come to Rome. Ignatius summoned them and the meeting took place during the very late part of the holy year 1550 and in early 1551. The fathers made various observations. Ignatius took that opportunity to offer his resignation as general. All of them refused it, except Andrés de Oviedo. He ingenuously remarked that if Ignatius recognized himself to be unfit, credence ought to be given to him since he is a saint.

In 1552 a further text was complete, text B, which came to be known as the autograph text because it contained corrections and marginal insertions in Ignatius' own hand. This text was promulgated by Nadal in 1553 and 1554 in the provinces of Spain and Portugal. But Ignatius continued to work on the Constitutions until the end of his life. Five months before he died, as Polanco wrote, he was still introducing corrections.

At the time of Ignatius' death, however, the Constitutions could be regarded as finished in every way, as Laínez and Nadal recognized. If the author did not wish to declare them

8 *Cons*MHSJ, IV (*Regulae*), 213-245. The second part has also been published in *Monumenta Paedagogica Societatis Iesu*, I (1540-1556), ed. L. Lukács (Rome, 1965), 37-45.

closed, we should, with Polanco, attribute this to his humility.[9] When he died he left on his table that work which had cost him so many prayers and such great fatigue, in order that the Society might be the one to say the last word. The approbation of the Constitutions was decreed by the First General Congregation, assembled in 1558 to name a successor to Ignatius.

This is, in broad outline, the external history of the composition of the Constitutions. We know that they are the result not only of his work as writer but also of his prayers and the illuminations which he received from God during the whole long period of their elaboration. The saint himself acknowledged this. When Gonçalves da Câmara asked him about the method he had followed in composing them, he replied: "His method of procedure when he was composing the Constitutions was to say Mass every day, and to lay the point he was treating before God, and to pray over it. He always made the prayer and said the Mass with tears."[10] A little before, while speaking about the divine visions, he had said: "When he was composing the Constitutions, he had them very frequently. This he could now affirm the more easily because every day he wrote what passed through his mind, and he then found this written material."

Câmara fortunately took occasion from this lofty vein of thought to ask him to show him those jottings. Ignatius showed him a fairly large bundle of his writings, from which he read one part to him. The larger portion consisted of visions which he saw in confirmation of one or another of the Constitutions," seeing now the Father, now all three persons of the Trinity, now our Lady who was interceding for him or sometimes confirming what he had written. Câmara asked him to let him have those writings for a short time, but Ignatius did not wish to do it.[11] This was a pity, for the author later tore them up. The only portion preserved is what he wrote in 1544 and 1545, while he was deliberating on the poverty to be observed by the churches of the Society. It is only a little, but

9 *FN*, I, 768.
10 *Autobiog*, no. 101.
11 *Autobiog*, no. 100.

it has been sufficient to enable us to discover the lofty gifts of infused contemplation which God had granted him.

4. The Constitutions: Their Content

The *Constitutions* are divided into ten parts. The treatment of the matter does not follow a topical or logical order but rather one which we might call evolutional or an order of execution. It follows one by one the several stages of the life of a Jesuit from his admission into the Society to his apostolic mission (Parts I-VII); next it treats of the members' relations among themselves and their head or superior general (Part VIII); then of the general himself (Part IX); and lastly of the body of the Society as a whole and of its preservation and development (Part X).

Part I deals with the admission of candidates to the Society, the qualities required in them, and the impediments to admission.

The problem of dismissal is treated with prudence and charity in Part II. In this delicate matter two principles are set down. The first is that "just as excessive readiness should not be had in admitting candidates, so ought it to be used even less in dismissing them; instead, one ought to proceed with much consideration and weighing in our Lord" ([204]). The second principle is that the more serious ought the reasons to be, the more fully one has been incorporated into the Society ([204]). The dismissal should be carried out more in a fatherly manner than as a judicial process. The superior should pray much over the matter and consult others before making a decision.

Part III contains the marrow of the Ignatian spirituality. It deals with the spiritual life of the candidate after his admission to the novitiate. The title of its first chapter is significant: "The preservation of what pertains to the soul and to progress in the virtues." Points treated are: guard over the senses ([250]), temperance ([250]), activity, contrary to idleness ([253]), poverty [254-257, 287]), obedience ([258-259, 284-286]), devotional practices, openness of conscience and docility to the director ([263]), the manner of anticipating temptations

([265]), the correction of defects ([269-271]), obedience to physicians and infirmarians ([272]), uniformity in doctrine ([273]), and a right intention ([287]). After attending to the spiritual part, in the second chapter the care of the body is taken up, including what refers to diet, sleep, clothing, preservation of one's bodily health and strength ([296-306]).

Part IV is dedicated to the intellectual formation of the Jesuit and the apostolate of schools and universities. This part has been considered as an anticipation of the future Plan of Studies (*Ratio studiorum*) of the Society. It deals with the foundation of colleges, gratitude to the founders, the program of studies to be introduced, the spiritual formation of the students, the government of the educational institutions.

Once the spiritual and cultural formation period of the Jesuit is completed, the next step is to proceed to his full incorporation into the Society. This is the subject of Part V, dedicated to the topics raised by such incorporation: the qualities of those admitted, the manner of making the final profession, the admission to it of the spiritual and temporal coadjutors.

Part VI treats of the personal life of those admitted. The central theme focuses on the three religious vows as they are understood and practiced in the Society. Here Ignatius develops in his particular way the topic of obedience, completing what he expounded in Part III. He desires that his men should distinguish themselves in this virtue, by being obedient not only to the expressed command of the superior but also to a simple indication of his will. This will be possible, if they "keep in view God our Creator and Lord for whom such obedience is practiced, and [if] they... endeavor to proceed in a spirit of love and not as men troubled by fear" ([547]). The obedience should extend not only to the execution of what is commanded but also to the will and understanding. Here occur the references to blind obedience, a lifeless body and an old man's staff, metaphors which Ignatius did not invent but borrowed from the tradition of religious institutes and made his own. The religious ought to allow himself to be carried and directed by Divine Providence, who makes use of the superior for His own purpose. The treatment of the vows is followed by an explanation of the religious life of formed Jesuits.

By the time a Jesuit has been fully incorporated into the Society and has committed himself to live according to the norms of his state, he is a trained man ready to be sent wherever his activity may be of greater usefulness. Part VII is devoted to such "missions"— a term derived from the Latin and meaning basically any sending or being sent, and derivatively any task for which or place to which one is sent. This part of the Constitutions treats the manner of distributing the Society's members in the vineyard of the Lord. This touches an essential aspect of the Society. The Jesuit is one who is sent (an apostle), a worker or laborer (*operario*) in the vineyard who must go to the field allotted to him. What should this field of action be? Here the typically Ignatian criteria for the choice of ministries are expounded. The supreme norm is always to be the greater glory of God and the greater good of our fellowmen. That field of service is to be preferred where the need is greater; where the hope of wider diffusion of the fruit is greater, as happens in work with influential persons; where the work is considered to be of greater importance. Thus, other considerations being equal, spiritual ministries ought to be preferred to those benefiting the body, and those more universal to those particular. This is the passage which enuntiates a rule of gold ([622, d]): "The more universal the good is, the more it is divine" (*bonum, quo universalius, eo divinius est*). Other criteria too should be used: preference should be given to a field where the enemy of Christ has sown cockle; to more urgent needs rather than those less pressing; to works which no one else undertakes, rather than those already cared for; to works of an enduring value rather than those ephemeral. In brief, we see how Ignatius, in a matter of so much moment as the choice of ministries, applies the rule of "the greater" (*magis*), which stems from the Principle and Foundation of the *Exercises* ([23]). As is but natural, account must be taken of the qualities of the persons, by sending to the more difficult missions persons in good health, and to those of greater importance men properly qualified and prepared. And so in all other things.

242

The fact that Jesuits are intended to be dispersed throughout the world (*societas ad dispersionem*) may carry with it a danger of disunion. Part VIII is the preventive against this danger: "Helps toward uniting the distant members with their head and among themselves." Above all, the union of hearts must be assured. "The more difficult it is for the members of this congregation to be united with the head and among themselves, since they are scattered among the faithful and among the unbelievers in diverse regions of the world, the more ought means to be sought for that union.... Therefore the present treatise will deal first with what can aid this union of hearts ([655]). The bond of obedience, spreading its desired effects into subjects and superiors, will be a great help to this union. But the principal bond ought to be that of charity. "The chief bond to cement the union of the members among themselves and with their head is, on both sides, the love of God our Lord. For when the superior and the subjects are closely united to His Divine and Supreme Goodness, they will very easily be united among themselves" ([671]). Ignatius' aspiration was that in the Society there should reign "uniformity, both interior uniformity of doctrine, judgments, and wills, as far as this is possible, and exterior uniformity in respect to clothing, ceremonies of the Mass, and other such matters, to the extent that the different qualities of persons, places, and the like, permit" ([671]). One help especially apt for furthering this union will be frequent communication by letters. Every four months, a man appointed for the purpose in each house, should write a letter to the provincial, relating the most noteworthy events of that period. And these letters will be distributed among the various provinces ([675]). These are the "Quadrimestrial Letters" (*Litterae quadrimestres*) of great interest for the history of the Society, which were made annual from the late sixteenth century onward. These are the "Annual Letters" (*Litterae annuae*), especially important for matters pertaining to the history of mission lands. Those for the years 1581-1654, arranged year by year, have been published and comprise a total of thirty-six volumes.

All that pertains to the general congregation is treated in this Eighth Part—a clear indication that in the mind of Ignatius this assembly, not periodical, of the highest legislative organ of the Society was to be considered as a potent factor of unity. Points treated are: the cases in which this meeting is to be held, persons who ought to participate in it, who has the authority to convoke it, and its place, time, and procedure. There are separate treatments for the cases in which a new general is to be elected, and for those in which other business is to be transacted.

The whole of Part IX is dedicated to the superior general, an office which in the Society was to last for life, for the reasons which the founder gave. All Ignatius' biographers are in agreement that when he enumerated the qualities which the general should have, he unwittingly drew his own self-portrait. The first quality he must possess is that he be a person closely united with God and intimate with Him in prayer ([723]). Second, he should be a man of much virtue, endowed especially with charity and genuine humility, in which he should be a model for his subjects. He should have all his passions under control. He should blend rectitude and necessary severity with kindness and gentleness. Magnanimity and fortitude of soul are highly necessary for him to bear the weaknesses of many, to initiate great undertakings in the service of God, and to persevere in them without losing courage in the face of contradictions. He ought to be endowed with great understanding and good judgment. Although learning is highly necessary, still more necessary is prudence and experience in spiritual matters, that he may be able to discern the various spirits and to converse befittingly with such various persons from within and without the Society. He should be vigilant in undertaking projects as well as energetic in carrying them through to their completion. Among the external qualities to be considered are: good physical health, good presence, a proper age. Among extrinsic endowments, other things being equal, some help can come from nobility and wealth which was possessed in the world, offices previously held, and other similar factors. Such are the qualities desirable in the general. It is difficult to find them all in one same person. If this ideal is unattainable, "there should at least be no lack of great probity and of love for the Society, nor of good judgment accompanied by sound learning" ([735]).

The crown of the *Constitutions* is Part X, the last, which propounds the means whereby "this whole body of the Society can be preserved and developed in its well-being," as its title states. The first means can be none other than the hope which is placed in God alone. For the Society "which was not instituted by human means, cannot be preserved and developed through them but through the omnipotent hand of Christ, God and our Lord" ([812]). For the preservation and development of the Society, "the means which unite the human instrument with God and dispose it that it may be wielded dexterously by His divine hand are more effective than those which equip it in relation to men" ([813]). When based upon this foundation, the natural means must also be employed, "not that we may put our confidence in them but that we may cooperate with the divine grace according to the arrangement of the sovereign providence of God our Lord" ([814]). Great help will be derived from maintaining the colleges in their good state and discipline....For [their students] will be a seedbed (*seminario*) for the professed Society and its coadjutors ([815]). Poverty must be preserved in all its vigor, as it is "like a bulwark of religious institutes which preserves them in their existence and discipline" ([816]). Therefore every appearance of avarice is to be shunned. Similarly to be precluded from the Society is ambition, "the mother of all evils in any community or congregation" ([817]). Therefore the door must be closed against the seeking of dignities within or without the Society. The criteria on the selection of those who ask to enter the Society should be maintained firm by avoiding the admission of a crowd, or of persons unsuitable for our Institute ([819]). Other means for this preservation are: the union of hearts; temperate restraint in spiritual and bodily labors; a similar moderation (or proper midpoint, *mediocritas*) in relation to the Constitutions which do not lean toward an extreme of rigor or toward excessive laxity ([822]); an effort to retain the good will and charity of all, even of those outside the Society; discretion and moderation in the use of the favors granted by the Apostolic See; and attention to the preservation of the health of the individual members for the divine service ([825-826]).

5. The Constitutions: Their Spirit

Anyone who casts even a cursory glance at the *Constitutions* of the Society can easily discover some characteristic features which reveal their striking originality, excellence, and far-reaching vision. These *Constitutions* are not merely a body of laws. In them the juridical element is intertwined with the spiritual and the institutional with the ascetical. It has been said that they are a law which is not law, a legal document which is not legal, precisely because of that wise blending of juridical and spiritual elements.

The *Constitutions* have as a foundation the *Exercises,* which the candidate of the Society must make for a full month at the beginning of the novitiate. The ideal proposed to him is that of the *Exercises:* to seek in all things what is most conducive to the end of man, to aim at reproducing in himself the image of Jesus Christ in its essential traits of poverty and humility. When the candidate is offered, as the supreme goal, the imitation of Christ poor and humiliated in the terribly austere passage which constituted Rules 11 and 12 of the former Summary of the Constitutions, what he is asked to do is nothing else than to put into practice the oblation "of greater worth" which he made in the meditation on the Kingdom of Christ, to enroll under the Banner of Christ and to aspire to the third kind of humility.

In the Society one's own sanctification and the apostolate do not comprise two separate ends. The Jesuit should sanctify himself by means of exercising the apostolate, and the apostolate in turn should produce an effective repercussion in his interior life. Poverty and obedience themselves should be considered in an apostolic perspective. The Jesuit must live in a poor manner, renouncing even fixed stipends for Masses or other ministries, that he may act with greater freedom. Obedience is viewed as a factor of cohesion and efficiency without neglecting its spiritual aspect. Prayer itself should help the Jesuit not to shut himself within himself, but to live united with God and receive from this union a greater impulse to work for the neighbor. The apostolate in its turn should lead the Jesuit to seek God in his personal prayer, through a close interaction between the work and the prayer.

One of the fundamental concepts in the *Constitutions* is that of "mission," described in detail in the seventh part. A Jesuit should be a man who lives ready to go wherever the pope or a superior of the Society sends him. This is the import of the vow of Montmartre, institutionalized in the fourth vow of obedience to the pope in regard to the missions which the professed of the Society take.

"Mission" demands mobility. The *Constitutions* state repeatedly that "our profession and manner of proceeding" are "to be ready to travel about in various regions of the world" ([92]). The need for this mobility is what excludes conventual life, the use of choir, the practice of corporal penances prescribed by rule indiscriminately for all, and ministerial assignments which permanently bind one to a fixed place.

The security afforded by conventual life and the unifying norms of devotional practices are compensated for by a long formation. The novitiate lasts for two years, instead of the one year prescribed by the earlier religious orders. Then follows a long period of cultural formation, and a year in the "school of the heart" ([516]) or "third probation" at the end of the studies. Various elements supply cohesion, more than exterior rules. One is obedience, a virtue in which Ignatius desired his sons to excell. Through openness of conscience and apostolic availability, this obedience establishes between superior and subject a relationship of father to son and of director to the one being directed. Thus it is pointed toward yielding beneficial results and toward avoiding the dangers which might occur along the way. Another help is the union of minds and hearts, a virtue through which Francis Xavier, even when he was traveling in the remotest parts of the world, felt himself united to his brothers in what he called a "Society of love."[12]

Through this the image of the itinerant Jesuit has emerged. We have an example of it in another of Ignatius' companions, Blessed Pierre Favre. While Ignatius remained anchored in Rome, although he too longed for the most arduous missions

12 *EppXav*, II, 8.

such as that of Ethiopia, we see his companions dispersed throughout various nations, each carrying out the mission he had received.

Two characteristic notes of the Constitutions are "moderation" (*mediocridad* as middle point) and "discretion" (*discreción* as right jugdment). The term moderation should be understood as the correct mean between excessive rigor of legislation and excessive leniency. For a Jesuit, the fundamental rule set down in the preamble of the *Constitutions* should always hold true: "the interior law of charity and love which the Holy Spirit writes and engraves upon hearts" will be more helpful than any exterior constitution ([134]). A sign of this is that in the Society the rules, as such, do not bind under pain of sin ([602]).

The "discreet charity" or love directed by the spiritual discernment learned in the Exercises, is an expression signifying that the Jesuit ought always to proceed under the impulse of charity, but a charity that is guided by the norms of discretion, to guard against falling into any extreme. In the concrete in regard to what concerns prayer and penances, Ignatius desires, instead of obligatory norms applicable to all alike, that the formed Jesuit should follow the dictates of discreet charity. Guided by this, he will neither neglect to attend to his ministries in order to devote himself to prayer and penances, nor will he let himself be so absorbed by exterior activity that it suffocates his familiar dealing with God. Once his duty has been fulfilled, the formed Jesuit has no other norm for his prayer and penances than that of discretion.

Original elements in the Society are the simple vows— public and perpetual but not solemn—which are taken at the end of the novitiate; the differentiated forms of poverty for houses and colleges, the latter being permitted to have fixed revenues; the government of the Society centralized in the general, holding a life-long office but assisted and helped by his counselors. Many of the innovations introduced into religious life by the Society have become common patrimony of modern religious congregations.

Ch. 17: The Constitutions of the Society of Jesus

The Society has always held in highest esteem the *Constitutions* which its founder bequeathed to it. But increased attention to study of them has been a characteristic of our recent decades. This manifests a desire to return directly to Ignatius' thought. As the centuries passed after his death, the Society continually adapted its legislation to the requirements of the times and to the norms of the Church, but it has sought to maintain his *Constitutions* intact. It has never felt a need to change their text.

Chapter 18

SPIRITUAL AND FATHERLY GOVERNMENT

For fifteen years (1541-1556) Ignatius exercised the office of superior general of the Society. Before his election, the companions had been taking their turn, one week each, in governing the group. Favre was considered as the eldest brother. But beyond any doubt, all of them recognized that Ignatius, who had brought them together, was their true head. This was proved by the unanimity of the ballot papers bearing his name at the moment of the election.

Ignatius accepted his election to the office of general on April 19, 1541, after eleven days of resistance.

This aversion to office contrasted with his undeniable talents of government: knowledge of men, winning manners, a clear vision of problems and situations, prudence in making decisions, constancy in pursuing them to the end, flexibility, and adaptability to circumstances. He himself possessed the qualities which he wrote down, in an unintended self-portrait, as the traits desirable in a general of the Society. This is found in Part IX of the *Constitutions*.

Father Luis de la Palma found, among the papers left by Ribadeneira, a brief treatise on Ignatius' manner of governing.[1] It was intended for the superiors of the Society, to inspire them in their manner of governing, by the example which the first general of the Society had left them. The observations made by this first biographer of the saint, who had lived with him in the Society for sixteen years and had used special care to note down the most significant data, coincide with those which we have from the other contemporaries.

---

1 "De ratione quam in gubernando tenebat Ignatius." It is published in *FN*, III, 610-634.

By collecting some of these testimonies, it is not difficult to reconstruct a portrait of Ignatius in regard to this important aspect of his life. It is not our intention here to sketch a complete picture of Ignatius as a superior, but only to select some data and present them as examples.

1. Admission and Dismissal

For the Society he wanted men truly capable. The qualities which candidates should possess are those described in the book of the *Examen* and in the First Part of the *Constitutions*. A general norm laid down by Ignatius is: "The greater the number of natural and infused gifts someone has from God our Lord which are useful for what the Society aims at in His divine service, and the more experience the candidate has in the use of these gifts, the more suitable will he be for reception into the Society" ([147]).

Ignatius speaks of "natural" gifts. Ribadeneira expresses this concept by commenting that Ignatius "looked much at each one's mettle and temperament." He used to say that the person who was not good for the world was just as little good for the Society. Acting on this principle, he admitted a skilful and industrious candidate with greater pleasure than another who was tame and listless (*mortecino y quieto*). He made great account of the health and the bodily strength necessary for study and work. As to age, he wanted—Ribadeneira tells us —those admitted to be "fairly mature and not just out of their childhood" (*grandecillos y salidos de muchachos*). He had an eye too for physical appearance, excluding those who had some physical defect which might prove repulsive. He once complained of the admission of one who had a crooked nose. The dictum was sometimes attributed to him: "A bad face, mischief afoot" (*Mala facies, malum faciens.*)[2]

As it is natural, he attached greater importance to the moral qualities of the candidate which, in doubtful cases, might compensate for the lack of some natural gifts.

When he saw that someone possessed the requisite quali-

2 *FN*, III, 611, no. 5; see also ibid., 572, no. 449.

fications and a genuine vocation, he admitted him and showed at the time no great concern about financial straights in which the Society might then be. He placed his trust in God who would not fail to send him the means to maintain those to whom He had given a vocation.

He was not obsessed with numbers. He used to say that his greatest fear was that a crowd of men might enter the Society. Though in the early years he was not difficult in admitting persons to the Society, he was later on. He went so far as to declare that if there was one reason why he would like to live longer, it would be in order to be severe in admitting men into the Society.[3]

He took great care that those admitted would remain faithful to their vocation. If they were tempted, he helped them with his prayers and advice and suggested that they consult about their cases with prudent persons. On occasions he would ask them to wait for a period of time. To a novice who was bent on leaving he said that, since the Society had retained him at his own request for four months, he ought now to stay on for another fortnight at the superior's request, without his having to obey anyone during this period.[4] Once, suspecting that the cause of a temptation was some sins committed in the world, he told the troubled novice part of the story of his own life, including some of the misdeeds he had done. The remedy was effective. The poor fellow manifested his case, and it turned out to be a matter of no importance.[5] After all the means possible had been taken, if the tempted person insisted on going, Ignatius always took care to send him away with love. A clear case was that of Ottaviano Cesari, a Neapolitan youth, the son of the secretary of the duke of Monteleone. This young novice resisted for a long time the pleadings and tears of his mother. Ignatius aided him, even by interceding with cardinals and Pope Paul IV himself. In the end, Ottaviano succumbed and, much to Ignatius's regret, he left the Society.

These cases concerned novices. More delicate was the matter

3 *FN*, II, 475, no. 23.
4 *Memoriale*, no. 43, in *FN*, I, 553; see also *FN*, II, 482, no. 3.
5 Memoriale, no. 78, in *FN*, I, 576.

of those who left after pronouncing their vows. We can state that Igntius made his own the norm which he had dictated in the *Constitutions:* "The discreet charity of the superior... ought to ponder before God our Lord the causes that suffice for dismissal" ([209]). If candidates should not be admitted too easily, still greater caution should be exercised in dismissing those admitted: "The more fully one has been incorporated into the Society, the more serious ought the reasons to be" ([204]).

In regard to concrete cases, it is often difficult to form a precise judgment. The data we have may be insufficient. In so delicate a matter factors of conscience enter which often are not recorded on paper. We know that Ignatius dismissed some members without revealing the reason to anyone, in order to save the reputation of the person concerned. Other norms to which he adhered were that the reason for dismissal should be a just one, and that before reaching a decision all the means to avoid the departure should be tried. Such means could be to induce the subject to make the Exercises or to consult about his case with prudent persons. If Ignatius saw that someone ought not to continue in the Society, he put the reasons before him in such a manner that he himself would ask for the dismissal. The founder took special care that those who left remained well disposed toward the Society.

2. The case of Isabel Roser

Connected with the topic of dismissal from the Society there is an altogether unique case, that of Isabel Roser and her two companions. It merits attention for two reasons: first, it deals with a great benefactress of Ignatius thoughout the whole course of his studies from Barcelona to Venice; and second, her exclusion in the end represented a decisive step toward the total elimination of a feminine branch in the Society.[6]

In brief, the facts evolved as follows. In 1542, Isabel Roser, after her husband's death, decided to move from Barcelona to Rome with the firm purpose of placing herself under obe-

6 The documents about the case of Isabel Roser are published in *FD*, pp. 696-713.

dience to Ignatius. She had two companions who shared her plan: a lady of the Barcelona nobility, Isabel de Josa, and a maidservant, Francisca Cruillas. The three set out for Rome in April, 1543.

Once in Rome, they expressed their desires to Ignatius, but he firmly refused to accept them. For this reason, perhaps, Isabel de Josa gave up her intention. On the other hand, in Rome, another Italian lady, Lucrezia da Biadene, associated herself with Roser. Biadene is a village in the present province of Treviso.

Isabel Roser did not consider herself vanquished and had recourse to the pope. In an autograph letter written in 1545 she earnestly petitioned the Holy Father, for herself and her maidservant, for permission to make their profession in the Society of Jesus, and to command Ignatius to accept such vows.[7] Although it seems strange to us today, the fact is that the pope gave a rescript granting the request. On Christmas Day, 1545, the three women knelt before the altar in the little church of Santa Maria della Strada in the presence of their revered Master Ignatius and pronounced their solemn profession in the Society of Jesus.[8] Through it the Society had dependent on it, in fact, a branch of feminine Jesuits, which was something not foreseen at the time of its foundation.

But this unusual situation did not proceed well. Ignatius arranged that Isabel Roser should live in the House of St. Martha, attended by the Brother Esteban de Eguía. Very soon difficulties arose there. Isabel, who had always shown herself so generous to Ignatius, in Rome began to give signs of being mercenary, by making the accusation that the Society was appropriating her goods to itself. In this she was supported by one of her nephews, recently come from Barcelona, by name Francisco Ferrer. It was necessary to review the accounts. It became clear that the Society had spent more on the lady of Barcelona than she had given to the Society, by a difference of 150 ducats.

7 *FD*, pp. 698-699.
8 For the text of her profession, see *FD*, p. 701.

In circumstances like these, the situation clearly could not continue. There followed a series of deliberations and consultations. Finally, on September 30, 1546, a meeting was held in the mansion of Doña Leonor de Osorio, wife of Juan de Vega, the Spanish Ambassador to the Holy See. Present were, on the one side, Ignatius, Nadal, and Codacio (the administrator of the Roman house) and Brother Juan de la Cruz (the buyer). On the other side were Isabel Roser, Lucrezia da Biadene, Francisca Cruillas, and the Barcelona priest Juan Bosch. That meeting was decisive. On the following day, October 1, Ignatius—who had explained the situation to the pope in a letter of May, 1547 and had received beforehand from him the necessary authorization—dispensed the three women from their vows.

Isabel Roser returned to Barcelona, where she retired in the Franciscan convent of Our Lady of Jerusalem. There she died a holy death late in 1554. In her heart she did not keep any sentiments of bitterness toward Ignatius. This is evident from two letters of 1547 and 1554, full of gratitude for the good she had received, and profuse apologies for all the trouble she had caused.

The painful experience had been useful. Soon after, on May 20, 1547, Paul IV acceded favorably to a request, in virtue of which the Society remained free for all times from the care of women subject to its obedience.[9] The experiment of feminine Jesuits did not proceed successfully.

Yet new attempts were not lacking. Two other women from Barcelona—Teresa Rajadell (Rejadell) and Jerónima Oluja—nuns of the Benedictine convent of St. Clare, desired to place themselves under obedience to Ignatius, as the best remedy for a distressing situation created in their convent community which was in urgent need of reform. Ignatius promoted this reform by all the means at his disposal; but he did not yield to these entreaties of Sister Rajadell and Prioress Oluja, in spite of his sincere desire of their spiritual good. This is very clear in the letters of spiritual direction which he wrote to Teresa Rajadell.

9 *Cons*MHSJ, I, 181-185.

3. Spiritual Principles

For his subjects Ignatius was not only their superior but also a true spiritual father. He had marvelous ability for the formation of men. In this, the great prestige which he enjoyed with all and his towering moral stature were great aids to him. Laínez used to say that when Favre, one truly skilful in directing souls, was compared with Ignatius, he seemed like a child beside a very wise man."[10]

He had a gift of coming to know quickly and in depth anyone whom he met and, as Father Emond Auger stated, he knew how "to analyze the living structure of a soul" (*faire l'anatomie toute vive d'une âme*).[11]

He knew how to bring peace to disturbed and afflicted consciences. Even when the one who was talking to him could not explain what was going on within himself, Ignatius dealt with him as one who had grasped the whole situation. And the advice he offered brought serenity of mind as if he were dissipating the clouds by a sweep of the hand.

When someone disclosed his innermost feelings to him, he captured Ignatius' heart.

Some principles, among others, by which he guided himself in giving spiritual direction were these. He judged progress in virtue by the effort which each one put in, rather than by one's good disposition and exterior modesty. To the minister of the house who brought some complaints about a young brother, he replied: "I believe that he has made more progress during these six months than this one or that one have made in a year." He mentioned the names of two who had sweet dispositions and gave great edification.[12]

He considered mortification of the passions even more important than the exercise of prayer, and said: "Mortification of honor is better than that of the flesh, and mortification of

10 *FN*, II, 379, no. 86.
11 *FN*, III, 268; see also *Memoriale*, no. 199, in *FN*, I, 647.
12 *FN*, II, 493, no. 81.

the affections than prayer."[13] Once, when someone strongly praised a certain religious by saying that he was a man of great prayer, Ignatius replied to him, "He is a man of great mortification."[14]

With regard to the length of time that scholastics had to devote to prayer, he used to say that studies require the whole man, and therefore he did not permit long hours of prayers, except in cases of special spiritual need. And he gave the reason: For a man who has his passions mortified, a quarter of an hour ought to be enough for him to find God.[15]

He was a person of great flexibility, and adjusted himself to each one's character. One of his sayings was that in spiritual matters there is no error more pernicious than that of wishing to rule others as one rules oneself, and of thinking that what is good for one is good for all.[16]

He used to test more severely those who were of greater worth.[17] If he demanded something difficult from a person, he knew how to sweeten the trial. It was said of him that he possessed a great charism of knowing how to inflict and how to relieve pain. "Whoever desires to direct others ought to lead the way by his example; and if he wishes to set others on fire, he should be aglow with charity himself."[18]

He suggested these means to those who wished to correct their defects: constant prayer, frequent self-examination, giving an account to someone else of the progress made.[19]

The points we have listed here are merely a few indications on a topic which could be made into a lengthy chapter.

4. Love for His Subjects

Ignatius' manner of governing was based on the fatherly

---

13 *FN*, II, 419, no. 24.
14 *Memoriale*, no. 195, in *FN*, I, 644.
15 Ibid., no. 196; see also *Cons*, [340, 361].
16 *Memoriale*, no. 256, in *FN*, I, 677; Ribadeneira in *FN*, III, 635, no. 12.
17 *FN*, III, 620.
18 *FN*, II, 420, no. 31.
19 *FN*, III, 621.

love which he had for his sons. He made no distinctions, to such a point that each one felt himself to be the object of "the Father's" strong liking.

He knew how to blend strictness with gentleness. Câmara says that Ignatius inclined more to the side of love and that was why he was so much loved by all. Câmara added that he did not know anyone in the Society who did not have a great love for him and did not feel himself loved by the Father.[20]

He tended to put a good interpretation on the actions of others, so much so that "the Father's interpretations" became a proverbial phrase.[21]

He promoted every means helpful to the union that ought to reign among all. One of those was the community recreations. He was once asked whether the recreation ought not to be dropped on fast days, since there was no supper. He answered that the recreation was held not only to avoid injury to health by study right after the meal, but also that the brothers might deal with one another and thus come to that mutual knowledge and esteem and to foster charity.[22]

5. Care of the sick

One of the clearest proofs of his love for his subjects was the special and minute concern which he showed for the sick. Manifestations of it, among others, were these: his asking the house buyer to inform him twice each day if he had bought all that the infirmarian had requested; his imposing penances for incidents of negligence in attending to the sick; and his ordering the rector of a college to inform him when anyone fell sick.[23]

When the needs of the sick were concerned, he did not look closely at expenses. He once sold some pewter plates which the house possessed, to be able to buy the prescribed medicines. He said that, if necessary, even the sacred vessels would

20 *Memoriale*, no. 86, in *FN*, I, 579.
21 *Memoriale*, no. 92, in *FN*, I, 581.
22 *FN*, II, 488, no. 18.
23 *Memoriale*, no. 31, in *FN*, I, 545; see also *FN*, III, 617.

have to be sold. At one time the blankets available in the house were precisely the same in number as those living there. He ordered lots to be drawn to see who should surrender one if it was necessary to sell it for the good of the sick.[24]

He took care of the sick personally and served them with great humility and charity, as though he had nothing else to do. He made no distinctions and wanted even those who were in the first probation to receive the same attention as the others.[25]

On one occasion, he delegated the functions of superior of the house to Nadal, but he reserved to himself what pertained to the care of the sick.[26] He used to say that what was given to the sick was not a singularity or fault against the norm of common life.

To supply relaxation for the students of the Roman College, he bought a vineyard at the foot of the Aventine hill, near the church of St. Balbina and the Baths of Caracalla. He did this in a time of great economic difficulties.[27] He built a house there or remodeled one already existent. Some days before his death Ignatius himself retired to this house, but as this remedy did not help, he returned to the house of Santa Maria della Strada, where he died.

6. His Skill in Dealing with Others

The manner in which Ignatius dealt with those under him was admirable, as a few random facts will make clear.

He knew how to accommodate himself to each one's disposition. Those who were spiritually weak he treated with acquiescence as long as they could profit from this, but he used rigor in dealing with the strong.[28] It was commonly said that to the former he gave milk, as to children, but to the rest he gave bread with crust, as to men. In dealing with

24 *Memoriale*, nos. 31-33, in *FN*, I, 546-547.
25 *Memoriale*, no. 144, in *FN*, I, 614.
26 *Memoriale*, no. 37, in *FN*, I, 548; *FN*, II, 366.
27 *Memoriale*, no. 135, in *FN*, I, 608.
28 *FN*, II, 487, no. 15; see also ibid., 386, no. 97.

normal cases he was not accustomed to give many external manifestations, although in his heart he loved them all.[29]

He treated with a certain severity those in whom he had greater trust—for example, Laínez, Nadal, or Polanco.[30] He spoke with great simplicity and was not given to the use of superlatives.[31]

He had great skill in winning shared feelings (*simpatías*) from those with whom he dealt. He was spoken of as a very courteous and polite man.[32]

In the matter of domestic discipline he used to say that the Father Minister had to supply the vinegar, and he himself the oil.[33]

He welcomed all with affection; and when he wanted to give someone special delight, he seemed to be trying to take him into his very heart. Once when he wished to give an embrace of welcome to a Flemish youth who had just arrived and who was very tall, Ignatius, who was small in stature, leaped up to reach the young man's neck.[34]

When he had to treat about some important business with someone, he invited him to his table. He did this also with guests.

He possessed the gift of spiritual conversation. He would never interrupt his interlocutor. He had great patience while listening to useless words.[35]

When something important was asked of him, he wanted it put down in writing, in order to reflect about it. If his reply was negative, he gave it in such a way that the petitioner was satisfied and convinced that this was what was best.[36]

29 *FN*, III, 620.
30 *Memoriale*, nos. 103-104, in *FN*, I, 587; *FN*, III, 620.
31 *FN*, II, 412.
32 *Memoriale*, no. 290, in *FN*, I, 697.
33 *Memoriale*, nos. 83, 296, in *FN*, I, 578, 700; *FN*, III, 649.
34 *Memoriale*, nos. 46, 47, in *FN*, I, 554-555.
35 *FN*, II, 412.
36 *Memoriale*, no. 281b, in *FN*, I, 692; *FN*, III, 616.

He took great care to protect the reputation of all. When, therefore, he had to consult about something in regard to another person, if one consultor was enough he did not ask two; if two were required, he would not call three. And even to the consultors he would explain the case plainly and without amplifications. He once imposed a penance on another because he had repeated what a sick person had said in his delirium.[37]

When someone spoke with exaggeration, Ignatius tried to find extenuating reasons, without saying anything that might supply the offender with a weapon against him, until this offender gave in or recognized that he had no excuse.[38]

When he had to converse with a person of the house or an outsider who might take from what was said a pretext to accuse him, he arranged to have witnesses present who could testify to what was said on both sides.

When something occurred which was poorly done—the sort of thing which usually upsets men—Ignatius was accustomed, before saying anything, to act as if he were recollecting himself or speaking to God, thinking and weighing what he should say.[39]

He was not guided by feelings, but by reason.[40]

He imposed commands in virtue of obedience only in very serious cases.[41]

Sebastiano Romei, rector of the Roman College, said that in his time great joy was prevalent among all the members of the community, because Ignatius by his presence and conversation brought life to them all.[42]

7. His Employment of His Subjects

Ignatius knew how to draw profit from the qualities of his subjects, by assigning each one to the offices for which he saw

37 *Memoriale*, no. 249, in *FN*, I, 672-673; *FN*, III, 616.
38 *FN*, III, 617, no: 8.
39 *FN*, II, 412, 413, 478.
40 *Memoriale*, no. 300, in *FN*, I, 702; see also 697, in *FN*, III, 648, no. 81.
41 *Memoriale*, no. 263, in *FN*, I, 681.
42 *FN*, III, 572, no. 7.

him to be most suited. This is the criterion he laid down in the *Constitutions* ([624]).

He, who so highly esteemed that religious indifference which is freedom from bias, tried to concur with each one's inclinations; and before making an assignment he used to ask him to what he was inclined. However, he praised one person because, upon being asked, he replied that he was inclined not to be inclined[43].

He did not impose on any one charges heavier than those he could bear.[44]

When he entrusted some important task to someone, he showed him his confidence in him. He explained to him the nature of the mission and the means which he thought fitting to bring it to a successful outcome. But then he allowed him complete freedom to proceed according to his own initiative. Câmara says that this was what had occurred in his own case, and that when he returned home after completing some charge, Ignatius used to ask him: "Do you come back satisfied with yourself?"[45]

When he wished to give someone an assignment outside Rome, he used to train and test him there. If there was question of a post of government, he asked him to render a daily account of his experiences to a father whose prudence was well known to the founder.[46]

He who is not good for himself, he used to say, cannot be good for others.

He gave more attention to the good of the person than to the work. Therefore, if he saw that someone was fit for an office but the office did not fit him, he did not give it to him, or he removed him from it if he already had it.[47]

43 *Memoriale*, nos. 114-117, in *FN*, I, 593-597.
44 *FN*, II, 413.
45 *Memoriale*, no. 269, in *FN*, I, 684.
46 *Memoriale*, no. 112, in *FN*, I, 592; *FN*, II, 486, no. 3.
47 *FN*, III, 684, no. 8.

His habit was to leave the execution of his orders in the hands of the superiors who were on the scene. He left the provincials a free hand in matters pertaining to their office, and he recommended them to act likewise with local superiors.[48]

8. His Manner of Handling Affairs

The manner of making decisions which Ignatius usually employed was the following. He first tried to gather all the information possible about the matter. Then came a period of deliberation in which he applied the criteria of spiritual discernment. Next he consulted with others about the matter and prayed over it. Finally, he made his decision.

Once he had taken a decision, he pursued the matter with much tenacity. Referring to this, Cardinal Carpi once remarked of Ignatius: "He has already driven in the nail", meaning to say that Ignatius would not be moved from his decision.[49] When people saw the result, they usually recognized that Ignatius' decision had hit the target.

He availed himself of the human means available, but above all he placed his confidence in God. Much has been said and written about the exact meaning of this Ignatian principle. Ribadeneira formulated it in these clear words: "In matters which he took up pertaining to the service of our Lord, he made use of all the human means to succeed in them, with a care and efficiency as great as if the success depended on these means; and he confided in God and depended on His providence as greatly as if all the other human means which he was using were of no effect."[50]

The occasion for the formulation of this saying was probably given by a case of which we learn from the same Ribadeneira. On one occasion Ignatius paid a visit to the Spanish Ambassador in Rome, the Marquis of Sarria. The ambassador did not give him a very good welcome, possibly because he thought that the Society was not making sufficient use of his possible

48 *Memoriale*, no. 270, in *FN*, I, 685.
49 *Memoriale*, no. 20, in *FN*, I, 539; see also no 282b, in *FN*, I, 693.
50 *FN*, III, 631, and the references in fn. 14 there; also *Cons*, [812-814].

services as its principal protector. In view of this, Ignatius told Ribadeneira, he thought of saying to the ambassador that "there were thirty years through which our Lord had given him to understand that in the things pertaining to His holy service he ought to use all good (*honestos*) means possible, but after that he had to place his trust in God and not in the means; and that if His Excellency chose to be one of these means, the Society would give an embrace of welcome to him in that capacity, but in such a way that he would know that the Society's hope would rest not on the means but on God, on whom it was leaning."[51]

In November 1525, Ignatius went from Rome to Alvito, a village in today's province of Frosinone, to try to bring about the reconciliation of Doña Juana de Aragón with her husband, Don Ascanio Colonna, parents of the renowned Marcantonio Colonna, the hero of the battle of Lepanto. It so happened that on the morning appointed for the departure, it was raining in torrents. Polanco, his fellow traveler, suggested that it would perhaps be advisable to put off the journey. Ignatius replied that for the past thirty years he had not postponed the doing of anything at the hour he had set because of rain, or wind, or any other atmospheric storm.[52]

Another of his sayings was that we ought to be convinced that an apostle does not always deal with perfect men, but often finds himself amid those who are perverse. A Jesuit ought not to let himself be upset by this. What he ought to do is to combine the simplicity of the dove with the prudence of the serpent.[53]

51 *FN*, II, 391, no. 108.
52 *FN*, II, 414.
53 *FN*, II, 421, no. 35.

Chapter 19

DAILY LIFE AT SANTA MARIA DELLA STRADA

From the day of his election as general in 1541 until his death in 1556, Ignatius did not leave Rome, except for a few very rare occasions. In September of 1545 he went to Montefiasconc to meet Pope Paul III, who was there on his way to Perusa. In 1548 and in 1549 he undertook two short trips to Tivoli. The purpose of the first was to try to bring peace between the citizens of that town and those of Castel Madama; and that of the second to attend the inauguration of the college of the Society. In November of 1552 he went to Alvito, as we have just said at the end of the preceding chapter. During the season of Easter 1555, Ignatius had planned a journey to Loreto, in order both to satisfy his devotion to that Marian shrine and to carry forward the plans for the foundation of a house or college of the Society there. But the death of Pope Julius III in March that year and the consequent vacancy in the papacy obliged Ignatius to drop that journey.

1. The House of Santa Maria della Strada

From February of 1541 to September of 1544 Ignatius and his companions, after leaving the house of Antonio Frangipani, lived in another, rented from Camillo Astalli on the street which still bears this name today. In September of 1544 they occupied the unfinished house they were building for themselves, joined to the church of Santa Maria della Strada. This church had been handed over to the Society by Paul III on June 24, 1541, and the Society took official possession of it on May 15, 1542. Both the church and the house faced what is now the Piazza di Gesù, at the corner of the via d'Aracoeli. In this house was the suite of small rooms (*camerette*) which St. Ignatius occupied until the day of his death, and in which also lived and died his first two successors, Diego Laínez (d. 1565) and St. Francis Borgia (d. 1572). These are the only rooms of the old house which were saved from demolition, thanks to Father General Claudio Acquaviva in 1602, during the construction of the present Collegio del Gesù, which was destined to be the Society's generalate until the suppression of the Society in 1773, and again from 1820 until 1873.

Persons devout to St. Ignatius who come to Rome love to visit this very modest apartment, consisting of four narrow rooms only eight and a half feet high, with walls of which the longest is a trifle over twenty feet and the shortest eleven and a half feet.[1] Among the precious remains are the original roof beams, the wooden doors, two plain and small cabinets, and part of the fireplace and chimney. Two of these rooms are now transformed into chapels. In the larger one an altar has been placed, above which there is a framed picture representing the Holy Family before which Ignatius used to celebrate Mass. The other chapel is the room in which Ignatius lived. It opens onto a tiny balcony from which, according to tradition, Ignatius often contemplated the starry sky and exclaimed: How trivial the earth appears when I look up to the heavens! (*Quam sordet tellus cum coelum aspicio*). The later constructions now obstruct the view of the sky which he had. Another little room, converted today into a sacristy, was that of Ignatius' "companion" Brother Juan Pablo Borrell. A faded yellow parchment placed above the door informs us that, "when Father Ignatius called to his companion, Brother Juan Pablo Borrell, who lived in this adjacent room, he would open this door."

Here is where Ignatius passed his last twelve years. From here he conducted the affairs of the Society, wrote his letters, composed the *Constitutions*, received visitors, (among them saints Philip Neri and Charles Borromeo), and here he peacefully died.

The household furniture of his room was the simplest imaginable. A bed, a table, a footstool, writing equipment, a washbowl and lamp, two or three books. Everything was neat and without any show. Oliverius Manaraeus (Mannaerts) related to Nicolaus Lancicius (Lenczycky) that Ignatius had

1 That is, respectively 2.5 meters high, 8 metres long, and 3.5 meters wide.

nothing else on his table but a copy of the New Testament and the book of the *Imitation of Christ,* which he called the partridge among spiritual books.[2] Câmara adds that this book was so familiar to him that "to deal with the Father seemed to be nothing else than to read Gerson put into practice."[3] He kept also the *Missal,* with which he prepared the Mass for the following day.

2.   The Daily Order

Although it is not possible to discuss a fixed time table, we can conjecture how Ignatius passed the hours of the day and night. He used to say that the time devoted to sleep should vary between six and seven hours, account being taken of the need of each individual. In fact, the time assigned for sleep in the Roman College was seven hours. Ignatius slept little, though this varied with the state of his health. He usually retired late, after pacing up and down in his room for a considerable time while reflecting. We may suppose that he was putting into practice what he advised to others who were dealing with affairs of importance—that for the morning they should plan what they had to do, and that during the course of the day they should twice reflect back over what they had thought, said, and done. He also wanted those to whom he had given some task to give him an account in the evening about what they had done, and then he allotted the work for the following day.

He exercised this checking on himself still more in what concerned the spiritual life. Each hour, at the stroke of the clock, he made a brief examination of conscience, unless he was occupied or conversing with someone. Even at night, if he was awake, he made this examination. He compared the progress of one day with that of another, of one week with another, and of one month with another, as he recommended in the book of the *Spiritual Exercises* ([27-30]) in regard to the particular examination.

Dinner, the main meal, used to be at ten in the morning,

2 *FN,* III, 431.
3 *Memoriale,* no. 226; see also nos. 97-98, in *FN,* I, 659, 584.

and supper at six in the evening,[4] so that eight hours would separate the two meals. We shall speak later of Ignatius' diet.

Apart from the time devoted to prayer and the Mass, Ignatius spent his day transacting business with his collaborators, receiving visitors, and writing letters. We have seen the long hours he spent in the composition of the *Constitutions of the Society*. He went out of the house seldom, unless it was to visit some cardinal or person of importance.

One such visit worthy of mention occurred on August 27, 1545 when he was urgently summoned to the Palazzo Madama to render spiritual assistance to Margaret of Austria in a difficult delivery. The daughter of the Emperor Charles V made her confession to Ignatius, heard Mass, and received Communion with great devotion. She gave birth to twin boys. The first, who was hurriedly baptized by the midwife and given the name of Juan Carlos, died a few months later. The second, at the request of those present, was baptized by Ignatius, who gave him the name of Juan Pablo. In the solemn supplying of the ceremonies which took place on November 30 at the church of San Eustachio, the boy was given the name Alessandro, that by which he has been known in history, Alessandro Farnese, Duke of Parma and Piacenza, and Governor of the Low Countries.

Only occasionally was Ignatius seen walking in the garden of the house. The physician attributed Ignatius' ailments partially to this lack of physical exercise.

3. *Ignatius' Prayer*

Three general observations can be made with regard to St. Ignatius' prayer. First, he devoted much time to formal prayer. Second, his prayer had the celebration of holy Mass as its center. Third, in addition to the time dedicated to prayer, he lived in intimate and constant communication with God.

---

4 These were the hours of meals in summer. In winter the main meal (*comida*) was at 11:00 A.M. and the lighter meal (*cena*) at 7:00 P.M. (see *Cons*MHSJ, IV (*Regulae*), 44-45, no. 3. Surprising as it seems to us today, breakfast for all was not customary, but some received permission from the minister to take it (see ibid., p. 186, no. 16, fn. 4).

Undoubtedly there were variations in the different periods of his life. In the years 1544 and 1545, about which we are best informed, Ignatius used to distinguish the sentiments which he experienced "before the Mass, during the Mass, and after the Mass," a formula which is repeated many times in his *Spiritual Diary*. This *Diary* takes in precisely those years.[5]

From this it appears that we have three "times" or stages in the Ignatian prayer. The first was that filled by what he called "the usual" or "customary" or "first" prayer. He began this prayer immediately after awakening and, to judge from the data in the *Diary*, while he was still in bed. On one day he notes that he began it at half past four in the morning. This prayer, preceded at times by an examination, must have been a prolonged one. It was, in its turn, divided into three parts: the beginning, the middle, and the end. Sometimes he records what he experienced from the middle to the end, at other times, from the beginning to the end.

Câmara tells us that during this time he was accustomed to recite the Hail Marys which Paul III had given him in 1539 as a commutation for the recitation of the Breviary.[6]

After rising and dressing, he prepared for the celebration of Mass. At times this preparation began in the room in which he slept. He always continued it in the chapel. In this preparation there are two moments in which he experienced special emotions: while he was preparing the altar and while putting on the vestments.

Next came the celebration of the Mass which, to judge from the mystical phenomena he experienced during it, lasted a long time.

After Mass he recollected himself again in prayer, in the

---

5 The complete Spanish text of the *Spiritual Diary* was published in 1934 by A. Codina in *Cons*MHSJ, I, 86-158, and again in 1963, with marginal numbers in square brackets which greatly facilitate references, by I. Iparraguirre in *Obras completas de san Ignacio* (Madrid, 1963, 1977 and 1982), pp. 318-386. We shall give our references here to this last named edition. There is an English translation by W.J. Young (Woodstock, 1958 and Rome, 1980).

6 Text in *FD*, 623-624; *Memoriale*, no. 179, in *FN*, I, 637.

chapel or in his room. He always adhered to this custom. Referring to the year 1555, Câmara observes that after Mass "he remained in mental prayer for the space of two hours."[7] During this time he desired not to be disturbed. He gave orders that messages arriving during this time should be passed to the father minister, who was Câmara himself. When some matter could not be delayed, he tells us, he went to the chapel and saw Ignatius there with his whole countenance resplendent.[8]

4. His Mass

The celebration of Mass was for Ignatius the occasion most propitious for his intimate communion with God. This is one of the most surprising aspects in the spirituality of this saint. We have already seen how, after his priestly ordination, he postponed his first Mass for eighteen months to prepare himself better for its celebration.[9] It is true that another factor which influenced this postponement was—probably, even though he never mentioned it—his hope of being able to celebrate his first Mass in Bethlehem or some other sacred place in the Holy Land.

Such was his esteem of the priesthood. He said that he ought "to behave or be like an angel for the ministry of saying Mass."[10] His devotion during the holy sacrifice was so great that at times he came near to losing the power of speech. But the phenomenon which recurs most frequently in the *Diary* is that of tears. He mentions them 175 times. The last part of the *Diary* is almost completely reduced to noting whether he had tears or not. At times, the tears produced "pain in the eyes, because they were so abundant."[11] Some twenty-six times they are accompanied by sobs. He speaks also of his hair standing on end and of experiencing "a burning sensation all through his body."[12]

7 *Memoriale*, ibid.
8 *Memoriale*, ibid.
9 See p. 163 above in ch. 11
10 *SpDiar*, [141], March 10, 1544, in *Obras completas*, ed. 4 (1982), p. 379; also in *Cons*MHSJ, I, 122.
11 *SpDiar*, [4], Feb. 5, 1544.
12 Ibid., [7], Feb. 8, 1544.

It is not surprising that such vehement emotions had repercussions upon his poor health. For this reason on many occasions he considered himself obliged to give up the saying of Mass. Some days he fell ill on the day on which he celebrated.

Making use of the freedom allowed in that era for choosing among the Masses in the missal, Ignatius frequently said the Mass in honor of the Blessed Trinity, and also those of the Holy Name of Jesus and that of Our Lady. Sometimes he imposed on himself, as a penance for some fault committed, the foregoing of saying the Mass of the Trinity. He did this, for example, on one day when he had a reaction of impatience on hearing a noise made near him during his time of prayer.[13]

It was during Mass that he reached his most intimate experience of God. There that phenomenon of La Storta was repeated when he felt that "the Father was placing him with the Son"[14] in a mysterious mystical union. There he felt as though the Name of Jesus was being imprinted in his innermost self. He perceived Jesus as his guide to the Father. Jesus and His Mother acted as intermediaries, ever propitious to intercede on his behalf. When he held Jesus in his hands, he beheld him in heaven and on the altar.

To the Mass he carried his intentions and preoccupations, which during all the time embraced by his *Diary* were concentrated on the theme of the type of poverty to be established in the houses of the Society.

All this we know thanks to the publication, in 1934, of the comlete text with all its details, of his *Spiritual Diary*. The dissemination of this exceptional document has transformed the concept commonly held about St. Ignatius. The cold and calculating man, the severe superior and the rigorous ascetic has now come to be seen as the contemplative capable of the most tender sentiments and as the mystic endowed with the highest degrees of union with God.

13 Ibid., [23], Feb. 13, 1544.
14 Ibid., [65], Feb. 23, 1544.

5. Contemplative in Action

Even outside the times expressly dedicated to intercourse with God, Ignatius continued to experience the divine presence. For him "devotion" meant to find God in all things.[15] He said of himself that he had this kind of devotión wherevet and whenever he wished, while conversing with others or transacting business and even when walking through the streets.[16] We have an example of this in what he jotted down in his *Diary* for February 24, 1544: "afterwards, as I was walking along the street, Jesus was showing himself to me, while I had great emotion and tears. Likewise, after I spoke with Carpi [Cardinal Rodolfo Pio de Carpi] and was returning, I felt much devotion. After eating, particularly after I passed through the door of the vicar [Filippo Archinto], in the house of Trana [Cardinal Domenico de Cupis, Bishop of Trani], I experienced or saw Jesus, with many interior motions and many tears."[17]

His mind was constantly active, to such a point that at times it became necessary to turn his attention elsewhere. In a word, he exemplified in himself what Nadal synthetized in a significant expression: to be a contemplative in action (*simul in actione contemplativus*).[18]

The testimonies regarding the degree of contemplation which Ignatius attained are explicit. The saint himself told Laínez that in the things of God he used to proceed more passively than actively; and this, his confidant Laínez adds, is

15 *Autobiog*, no. 99.
16 *FN*, II, 122-123, 315-316; *Mon Nad*, V, 162.
17 *SpDiar*, [74], Feb. 24, 1544.
18 *MonNad*, V, 162 contains the text and context of this formula of Nadal which is so important for Ignatius' concept of apostolic spirituality. A literal translation of Nadal's text is this: "Father Ignatius, through a great privilege given only to a few, conceived that manner of making contemplative prayer [focused on the Trinity]; and then that additional privilege, by which in all things, actions, and conversations he perceived and contemplated the presence of God in all things and an affection for spiritual things, being a contemplative even while in action (which he used to explain by saying that God is to be found in all things)."
For helpful references to discussions about this text as an aphorism reflecting Ignatius' concept of apostolic spirituality, see fn. 19 in *MonNad*, V, 162; fn. 4 in *ConsSJComm*, pp. 183-184; also, *MonNad*, IV, 651-652.

something which Sager (Gaspar Shatzgeyer, O.F.M., d. 1527) and other authors locate in the highest degree of perfection or contemplation.[19] Speaking one day with Nadal, Ignatius told him: "I was now higher than the heavens." As Nadal asked him to explain what he meant by that, Ignatius turned the conversation to another subject.[20]

He even went so far as to say that he was not making his decisions by means of the criterion of consolation or desolation —as recommended in the second time for making an election in the *Exercises*, [176]—because he was finding consolation in all things.[21]

He said that he would not be able to live without these divine consolations.

He had more light, determination, and constancy in the last years of his life than at the beginning.

Many noticed in him an incredible ease in recollecting himself in the midst of business, so much so that he seemed to have at his own command the spirit of devotion and even the gift of tears.

Nature lifted his mind to God. At night he took great delight in contemplating the star-studded sky, and from this he developed a sentiment of regarding earthly things as relatively of little value. He saw God in every creature. Nadal says that he saw the Trinity in a leaf of an orange tree.[22]

Music and sacred chant aided him extraordinarily. When he entered a church during the time of the chanting of the Divine Office, he admitted to feeling an interior transformation in himself. From this we can deduce the magnitude of the sacrifice he had to make when he excluded choir and chant in the Society.

To conclude, we may affirm that Ignatius had an interior experience of God which was genuinely extraordinary. When

19 *FN*, I, 138, no. 59; see also *FN*, II, 415, no. 13.
20 *FN*, II, 125, no. 19.
21 *FN*, II, 415, no. 14.
22 *FN*, II, 123, no. 11.

he wrote in his *Exercises* of "interior knowledge,"[23] he meant by this a cognition which passes from the sphere of knowledge into an experience deeply interior, from the intellectual to that of perceptible emotion, from the mind into the heart. And that was the kind of knowledge which Ignatius himself had of God.

6. His Collaborators: Nadal, Ribadeneira, Polanco, Câmara

From prayer to work. The organization and government of the Society demanded of Ignatius a total dedication. First of all, it was necessary to give to the new-born religious order a set of laws by which it could be ruled. We have already briefly recounted the labor expended by the founder in the composition of the *Constitutions*. To these he added other rules of a type more circumstantial, adapted to the conditions of place, time, and qualities of persons. Such were, among others, the rules of the scholastics, and those for various offices.[24]

In solving the problems of business which arose, he made use of consultations, private conversations, and letters. His correspondence merits the separate treatment which it will receive below. As superior of the house in Rome, Ignatius had to give his attention to the persons in it and to its affairs. He had to think about the novices, and for some time he personally took charge of their formation.

Ignatius knew how to avail himself of assistance from his collaborators. Chief among them were his first companions. Among the others, those deserve a special mention here whose testimony is adduced frequently in the pages of this book.

For the task of acquainting the Jesuits dispersed through Europe with the contents and the spirit of the *Constitutions* and for other matters of moment, Ignatius made use of the services of Jerónimo Nadal, justly considered a faithful interpreter of the founder's mind. This learned Majorcan (1507-

---

23 *SpEx*, [104].
24 Published in *Cons*MHSJ, IV (*Regulae*), passim; see, e.g., pp. 169-191, 481-486. See also *Cons*, [360-362; 455].

1580) had made his university studies at Alcalá, Paris, and Avignon. Ignatius, who knew him in Paris, soon took account of the outstanding talents of this person, well trained in mathematics, languages, theology, and Sacred Scripture. From then on Ignatius, with help from Laínez and Favre, laid a veritable siege around the man to win him over to his cause. But Nadal repulsed all advances, partly because he had some plans of his own, and partly because he mistrusted the orthodoxy of that band of students revolving around Ignatius.

Back in his native island, after seven years of incertitude and anguish about his future, he decided to go to Rome. Just then a letter of Francis Xavier was making the rounds of Europe, challenging the learned in the universities. In Rome he agreed to make the Exercises under the direction of the Valencian Jerónimo Domènech, an expert in the art and his friend from Paris days.

The case of Nadal is typical in regard to the matter of the election of a state of life, made according to the norms of the *Exercises*. After a stubborn resistance, and when it seemed that he had already discarded any thought of decision to enter the Society, Nadal made that decision. He was admitted on November 29, 1545, at the age of 38. Among some other important offices entrusted to him by Ignatius, we should mention his mission to start the college of Messina (1548), and the offices of commissary general for Portugal and Spain (1553), vicar general of the Society (1554), commissary for Italy, Austria, and other countries (1555)—to limit ourselves to the time of Ignatius. Regarding his understanding of Ignatius' thought, it will suffice to adduce Polanco's testimony: "He [Nadal] has great understanding of our Father Master Ignatius, because he has dealt much with him, and he seems to have his tenor of thought (*espíritu*) well understood, and to have penetrated the Institute of the Society, as well as anyone else whom I know among its members."[25]

Pedro de Ribadeneira (1526-1611), from Toledo, was a lad of only thirteen years when he accepted the invitation offered

---

25 *EppIgn*, V, 109.

to him in 1539 at Toledo by Cardinal Alessandro Farnese to accompany him to Rome as his page. While in the service of this cardinal, one day after he had perpetrated a prank and was in fear of a probable punishment, he took refuge in the house of Doctor Pedro Ortiz, his fellow countryman and perhaps a relative—his father was an Ortiz—who in turn introduced him to Ignatius. This was the occasion for the young Pedro to join the Society definitively on September 18, 1540, nine days before the papal confirmation of the order.

Here it is of interest to us, above all, to point out his knowledge of matters concerning Ignatius. It was the result not only of his dealing frequently with him for a long period of sixteen years, but also of his expressed intention to gather and note down anecdotes regarding the holy founder. This explains the fact that when a search was being made in 1566 for a biographer to write the life of the Society's founder, the choice by the general Francis Borgia fell upon Ribadeneira, whose thorough humanistic formation and command of language were recognized by all. Ribadeneira undertook the task with great eagerness. In 1572 he published, in Latin, the first edition of his classic Life of St. Ignatius (*Vita Ignatii Loyolae*). In 1583 he brought out another edition in Spanish. This *Vida*, which created a new type of biographical narrative, has justly been considered one of the most attractive historical works of the sixteenth century, the *Siglo de Oro*.

Something only recently discovered ought now to be incorporated into the life story of Ribadeneira, the fact that he was of Jewish descent. He was the son of Alvaro Husillo Ortiz de Cisneros, a juryman of the municipal government of Toledo. The Husillo family were Jewish converts.[26]

Among the close collaborators of the first Jesuit general, two names stand out: that of his secretary for nine years, Juan de Polanco (1517-1576), and that of the minister of the house of Rome, Luis Goncalves da Câmara (c. 1519-1575).

---

26 José Gómez-Menor, "La progenie hebrea del padre Pedro de Ribadeneira S.I. (hijo del jurado de Toledo Alvaro Husillo Ortiz de Cisneros)," *Sefarad* (Madrid), 36 (1976), pp. 307-332.

We have already mentioned the labor expended by Polanco at the side of Ignatius in the composition of the *Constitutions*. But this activity extended to all the tasks proper to a secretary. As soon as he was appointed to this office in 1547, the first thing he did was to organize it. In that same year he drafted a set of rules on The Office of the Secretary (*Del oficio del secretario*), meant to help the smooth running of the secretariat of the Society.[27] He also put order into the incipient archives of the Society, which were considered to be a prolongation of the secretariat, and were intended to preserve the documents which passed through that office. If the original documents pertaining to the foundation of the Order and the times of its first generals have been preserved to this day, we owe it, in great part, to Polanco.[28]

As happens in the case of every secretary, Polanco's work dealt chiefly with the correspondence. It was his task to receive the letters which came to Rome and to prepare the reply to be given to them. Apart from other letters in which he certainly had a hand, there are some of importance which appear as written by him expressly "by commission" from Father Ignatius.

With an unerring vision of the future, he prepared the materials for the composition of a history of the Society.[29] Soon after his arrival in Rome, he asked Laínez, then at the Council of Trent, to write for him his recollections about the origin of the Society. Thanks to this, we possess the remarkable letter, written by Laínez in 1547, which is justly considered as the earliest life of St. Ignatius, written nine years before his death.[30] Taking this account as a foundation, Polanco built up in 1547 and 1548 his "Summary of the Most Notable Events regarding the Institution and Progress of the Society of Jesus" (*Sumario de las cosas más notables que a la institución y progreso de la Compañía de Jesús tocan*).[31] A sequel of this account

27 Published by M. Scaduto, in *AHSJ*, XXIX (1960), 305-328.
28 See G. Schurhammer, "Die Anfänge des Römischen Archivs der Gesellschaft Jesu (1538-1548)," *AHSJ*, XII (1943), 89-118; also, pp. 160-161 of E. J. Burrus, "Monumenta Historica Societatis Jesu (1894-1954)," *Woodstock Letters*, 83 (1954), 158-168.
29 See *FN*, II, 23*-39*.
30 Published in *FN*, I, 54-145.
31 Published in FN, I, 146-256.

was another, more concise and updated, published in Italian in 1549 and 1551.[32] Thus he was paving the way to the composition of a genuine history. When in 1573 Polanco found himself free from duties of administration and saw himself excluded from the election to the generalate which once appeared imminent, he dedicated his best efforts to the writing of the history of the Society, in the form of Annals which run from the year 1539 to 1556.[33]

For the handling of the current affairs of the house of Rome, Ignatius had an excellent collaborator in the Portuguese Luis Gonçalves da Câmara. From the day he entered the Society in 1545, Câmara desired to see and know Ignatius personally. Two motives impelled him: to learn from the lips of Ignatius himself in what did obedience of judgment consist, which had been recommended to him so much from his novitiate days onward, and second to ascertain for himself the founder's reputation for sanctity which had spread even to Portugal. The desires of this Portuguese were fully satisfied when he was sent to Rome in 1553 by the official visitor of Portugal, Miguel de Torres, to report to the general about the affairs of that province. After this mission had been fulfilled, he remained in Rome, and in September of 1554 he was appointed minister or bursar of the Roman house.

Right from the start, he made it a point to jot down whatever he heard and observed in his daily dealing with Ignatius. Thus came into being his Memoirs of What Our Father Tells Me about the Things of the House (*Memorial de lo que nuestro Padre me responde acerca de las cosas de casa*), generally known as Câmara's *Memorial*.[34] Written in Spanish, it treats the period from January 26, 1555 to the summer of the same year. On October 23, Câmara left Rome, assigned again to Portugal. He carried with him the notes he had taken in Rome. Years later in 1573-1574, going over those jottings he wrote down in Portuguese a commentary about the most important things which came into his memory. Evidently, this commentary

---

32 Published in FN, I, 256-298.
33 *Chronicon*, 6 vols. in MHSJ. A Life of Ignatius in Latin precedes these Annals and is published also in *FN*, II, 506-597.
34 These Memoirs are published in *FN*, I, 508-752.

does not have the same value as his earlier notes taken at the time and on the scene of the actual incidents.

The bequest of his *Memorial* is not Câmara's only merit. He had the knack of insinuating himself into the mind of Ignatius. He obtained from him what other more commendable men had tried in vain to get—that Ignatius would give him an account of his life. This is how the personal memoirs of Ignatius came to be written. They have rightly been given the title of *Autobiography* or, in some modern versions, the Pilgrim's Story, because in this document Ignatius frequently referred to himself as "the pilgrim".[35] Although these memoirs were not written by Ignatius' own hand, Câmara assures us that he took the greatest care to take down, after each conversation, what Ignatius had told him, without adding or changing any word. The account was begun in September of 1553. It was interrupted in 1554, resumed on September 22, 1555, and ended on October 20 or 22 of the same year, that is, on the eve of Câmara's transfer to Portugal. This explains why the narrative does not cover the whole of Ignatius' life but goes only up to the incidents which occurred in 1538, with a few hasty notes at the end on how he had composed the *Exercises* and the *Constitutions*.

A daily witness of the life of Ignatius was also the Navarrese Diego de Eguía, a brother of Miguel de Eguía, the Alcalá printer who published the *Enchiridion* of Erasmus in 1526. Diego had known and helped Iñigo at Alcalá. With another brother of his, Esteban, he joined the band of the first companions in Venice in 1537. In Rome Ignatius chose him as his confessor. A special quality shone in Don Diego, as he was commonly called: he could comfort and retain those tempted about their vocation. In his great simplicity he exceeded himself in his praises of Ignatius, saying that he was a saint and more than a saint, and suchlike things. Ignatius took it ill, so much so that, besides imposing on him a good penance, he ceased going to him for confession, although it is not clear whether he did this definitively. Toward the end of his life Ignatius was accustomed to confess to the Barcelona Jesuit

---

35 The original text is published in *FN*, I, 323-507. Translations exist in many languages.

Pedro Riera.[36] Good Don Diego went to his reward a fortnight before his penitent did.

Among the domestic collaborators special mention should be made of the Italian Brother Gian Battista de Anzola (Travaglino), who was the cook of the house, of uncertain culinary expertise. This good brother, a dealer in spices by profession, had brought with himself when joining the Society an image of Christ crucified, to which he had extraordinary devotion. Ignatius let him keep it for some time, but later he took it away from him, saying that "since he had now implanted and engraved the Crucified One in his heart, he would bear to be dep_ived of his image."[37] There is a story that one day the good cook burnt his hand and Ignatius healed him by his prayers.

About the intimate life of Ignatius his "companions" could tell us interesting anecdotes. These were, besides others who held this post only occasionally, two Catalan coadjutor brothers. Juan Pablo Borrell, a native of Tremp, entered the Society in Rome in 1543. Besides looking after the general's personal things, he used to accompany him when he went out, as on the journey Ignatius made to Alvito in 1552. This Brother usually lived in torment from scruples and anxiety. Ignatius succeeded in restoring peace to his soul, as if with his hand he had dispelled the anxiety.

The Barcelona-born Juan Cors entered the Society in his native city in 1551. In Rome he was made "companion" of the general, probably as a substitute for Juan Pablo Borrell. He was a man of great simplicity. Ignatius regarded him as a model because of the fact that he never contradicted anyone. One day Ignatius ordered him to administer a public rebuke to another, adding that he should do it with anger or choler (*con cólera*). Juan replied that he had no choler, because he had vomited it all during his trip by sea from Barcelona to Italy. He lived in a room next to that of Ignatius, and when he had no other tasks to do, he spent his time knitting woollen

36 *FN*, III, 459, 10°.
37 *Memoriale*, no. 106, in *FN*, I, 88-589.

slippers and socks. With him Father Ignatius recited the litanies daily during the conclave that elected Pope Marcellus II.

7. His Correspondence

Second only to conversation, letter writing was the means of communication employed most by Ignatius. Almost 7,000 of his letters have been published. Few were written in his own hand. At times we have only memoranda which contain the points which were to be developed more fully in the letters actually sent. The fact that Polanco wrote many of the letters "by commission" detracts nothing from their authorship—except for what pertains to the style—because it is clear that the secretary was doing nothing else than putting down in writing what the general committed to him.

The epistolary activity of Ignatius was intense. It is known that on one day alone he despatched some thirty letters, after reading them once or twice. There is still extant, and now published, a very interesting "Roman Memorial" (*Memoriale di Roma*).[38] It contains a dated résumé of the letters received by the general and sent by him from October of 1545 to May of 1547. A quick glance at this document allows us to perceive the rhythm of activity in the secretariat of the Society during this year and a half. This is merely a cross-section example of what went on during the fifteen years of Ignatius' generalship.

More worthy of our attention than the quantity of his letters is the attention and care which he used in writing them, especially when they were dealing with matters of greater moment or addressed to important persons. Ribadeneira tells us that "he spent much time in considering what he was writing, in scrutinizing again and again the letters once written, examining every word, canceling and correcting. Sometimes he ordered the letters to be recopied, considering as well employed all the time and labor necessary for this."[39]

Of this meticulous care we have a good example in the letter which he ordered to be written to all the members of the

38 *FN*, III, 722-743.
39 *FN*, II, 494, no. 83.

Society, requesting them to obtain testimonials in favor of it from princes, governors, and universities. His purpose in this was to use these testimonials in opposition to the University of Paris, which was resisting the recognition of the new order in France. The extreme care with which he wanted that letter to be composed has been treated above in connection with the Society's entrance into France.[40] He desired the other members of his order to imitate in their own letters the same care which he used in his. To one of them he sent a reprimand because the letter he had written contained many blemishes and corrections.

Ignatius sent a lengthy instruction on the manner of writing letters to Favre, on December 10, 1542. In it he formulates the principle on which his care in this matter was based. "What is written should be examined more carefully than what is spoken, for the written word remains and bears perpetual witness, and it cannot be so easily patched up or glossed over, as when we speak."[41]

When his subjects wrote to Rome, he wanted two different letters to be composed. The "principal" letter was to contain the information which could be communicated to others; the other, which he calls the "little daughter" (*hijuela*, a page attached to the principal document), was one in which the more private or reserved matters could be written. The principal letter ought to be carefully corrected.

The collection of his letters, together with the *Autobiography* and the *Spiritual Diary*, are the documents in which we can see the personality of Ignatius best portrayed. In them we find abundant data about his spiritual doctrine, his apostolic orientations, and his manner of governing. His letters reveal to us also the whole gamut of his correspondents, who are not only Jesuits but also persons of every class. The publication, in one separate volume, of his letters to women has met with great success, beyond doubt because it has revealed a hitherto little known and perhaps unsuspected facet of his

40 See above, pp. 214-216, and *Memoriale*, no. 145, in *FN*, I, 615.
41 *EppIgn*, I, 237.

character, his openness to the feminine world.[42] It would not be a difficult task to collect a similar volume of his letters to the important persons of the earth — kings, princes, cardinals, bishops, and the like.

Classified by themes, the letters of Ignatius could come under the following or similar headings: familiar letters, letters of spiritual direction, letters on government. From all of them emerges and comes alive a figure outstanding as a spiritual director, an apostle, a superior, and a saint.

8. His Relations with Four Popes

The generalate of Ignatius coincided with the pontificates of four popes: Paul III, Julius III, Marcellus II, and Paul IV.

Paul III (Alessandro Farnese, pope October 13, 1534-November 10, 1549) gave a benevolent welcome to Ignatius and his companions from their first arrival, and he soon grasped the opportunity of approving the foundation of the Society. His is the phrase "the Spirit of God is here," (*Spiritus Dei est hic*"), pronounced at Tivoli on September 3, 1539, when the "Formula" of the new institute was read to him. One year later, after the bureaucratic difficulties had been solved, he issued the first bull of confirmation of the new order. With four bulls and three papal briefs he granted to the Society its novel juridical configuration and bestowed abundant spiritual favors upon it. He made to it the gift of the church of Santa Maria della Strada. At the request of Francis Borgia, then Duke of Gandía, he approved the book of the *Spiritual Exercises* in a brief of July 31, 1548. This was, as Jerónimo Nadal says, "a great privilege, rare in the church", that a book be approved in such a solemn form.[43] This and the other manifestations of his goodwill toward the Society were in no small part due to the good relations of the Farnese pope and his family with the family of the Duke of Gandía. We have already pointed out how Paul III accepted the offer, made under a

---

42 H. Rahner, *Ignatius von Loyola Briefwechsel mit Frauen* (Freiburg-im-Breisgau: 1956). English translation by Kathleen Pond and S. H. A. Weetman, *Saint Ignatius Loyola: Letters to Women* (New York, 1960).
43 *Mon Nad*, V, 787-788.

special vow, of the first companions. He soon sent some of them on various "missions," even though he had originally intended to keep them in Italy.

Regarding Julius III (Giovanni Ciochi del Monte, pope Feb. 7, 1550-March 23, 1555) two facts, above all, should be mentioned. The first is the bull *Exposcit debitum,* of July 21, 1550, by which he again confirmed the Society, while incorporating into this bull the new Formula of the Institute, which to our own days has never been altered. The other outstanding gesture was the decisive support he offered to the incipient Roman College and German College, securing for them much needed financial help. In favor of the Roman College, just before he died, he took measures for its stable foundation. Besides these two colleges, he had thought that a third might be started in Rome for students from all nations, which he wanted to entrust also to the Society.

Ignatius offered special prayers for the pope every day. When he was informed of the pontiff's serious illness, he prayed for him twice a day and asked all those of the house to join him in this. When Pope Julius died, he ordered that all should offer Masses and prayers for nine days and pray also for the election of his successor.

Marcellus II (Marcello Cervini, pope April 9, 1555-May 1, 1555) could do but little for the Society in the 23 days of his pontificate. His election was hailed as an announcement full of promise for the much longed-for reform of the Church. On this point his ideas coincided with those of Ignatius. The news of the election of the new pope was welcomed with great jubilation by the Society, particularly by Ignatius, as is manifest from the letter which he asked Polanco to write the very day of the election, April 9, 1555.[44] Only a few days later Pope Marcellus asked Ignatius to give him two Jesuit priests who would stay in the papal palace and act as his advisers in matters of the reform. In such a delicate matter Ignatius preferred not to make the choice on his own authority but to leave the designation to the vote of the fathers in Rome. The choice

44 *Epplgn,* VIII, 665-667.

fell on Laínez and Nadal. Nevertheless Ignatius thought of retaining Nadal and proposing other names to the pope. Because of the pope's early death nothing of this could be done.

Orlandini recounts in his history that when Ignatius presented himself to the new pope to offer his obedience and that of the Society, the pontiff told him: "You enroll the soldiers and prepare them for war; We shall make use of them" (*Tu milites collige et bellatores instrue; nos utemur*).[45]

An anecdote, told by Ribadeneira, reveals the high esteem that Marcellus II, when still Cardinal Cervini, had of Ignatius. In a conversation with Martín de Olabe, the cardinal exposed the reasons why, in his opinion, the Society ought not to reject the dignities which were offered to it. All the arguments of the learned Olabe seemed insufficient to him. In the end, Olabe as his last argument stated that for the Society the authority of Ignatius was enough. "Now I give in," the cardinal replied, "for although I believe reason to be on my side, the authority of Ignatius has more weight."[46]

When, some days after his election, the pope became gravely ill, Ignatius sent some of his men on a pilgrimage to Loreto to implore the cure of the pope from whom so much was hoped for the reform of the Church and the good of the Society.

With Pope Paul IV (Gian Pietro Caraffa, pope May 23, 1555-August 18, 1559) the relations of Ignatius were always difficult. These two men were very different in character and outlook. In particular, they had diverse conceptions of religious life, as became manifest already in 1536 in Venice.[47] An additional source increasing the difficulties was the strong anti-Spanish tendency of the Neapolitan pope. They became more patent after the death of Ignatius, when the Caraffa pope got entangled in an unfortunate war against Spain.

Already earlier, when the conclave was searching for the man to succeed Julius III, Ignatius feared that the election

45 *Historiae Societatis Iesu*, Pars I, Lib. XV, no. 3.
46 *FN*, II, 352-353.
47 See pp. 140-142, 144 in ch. 10 above.

might fall on Cardinal Caraffa. In his *Memorial,* Câmara notes down for April 6, 1553: "First, on Father's fondness for music and how he fears the Theatine cardinal [Caraffa] in regard to the matter of chanting. Second, on what the Father said today about offering prayers that, if it be to the equal service of God, there will not be elected a pope who will make changes in what pertains to the Society, for there are some among the candidates (*papabiles*) about whom there is fear that they would make such changes."[48]

This accounts for the initial reaction of Ignatius when, on May 23, 1555, feast of the Ascension, he heard that the election to the supreme pontificate had fallen precisely on Cardinal Caraffa. Câmara relates how, while he was in a room with the Father, they heard the pealing of bells announcing the election of a new pope. A few moments later the news came that the one elected was the Theatine cardinal. "On receiving this news, the Father showed a notable change and disturbance in his countenance and, as I came to know later (whether from his own lips or from the Fathers to whom he told this, I do not know), all his bones were shaken within him." His reaction was the usual one on such great occasions: "He got up without saying a word and went to the chapel to pray. He returned from there after a short while, as joyful and content as if the election had turned out much in conformity with his desires.[49] In the new pope, as he had done even before his election, he paid heed only to the positive points, above all to what was expected from him toward furthering ecclesiastical reform.

Before his election to the papacy, Gian Pietro Caraffa had manifested desires that his Theatine order and the Society should be amalgamated into one sole institute. Ignatius put up a tenacious resistance. As we have indicated, Ignatius' great fear was that the new pope might modify the Institute of the Society in essential characteristics. This fear accompanied him until his death. Fortunately, the fear was not verified during Ignatius' lifetime. But after the founder's death, Paul IV did order two important changes: the introduction into the

48 *Memoriale,* no. 326, in *FN,* I, 712.
49 *Memoriale,* no. 93, in *FN,* I, 581.

Society of the Office in choir, and the reduction of the mandate of the general to a term of three years. But this command, communicated only by word of mouth and not accompanied by an abrogation of the privileges granted by the preceding popes, remained in force only during the lifetime of the pope who had expressed it.

But not everything was negative for the Society during Paul IV's pontificate. On the positive side, apart from indications of friendship and appreciation he showed to some Jesuits, such as Laínez (whom he wished to make a cardinal) and Bobadilla, there is a fact deserving special mention. On January 17, 1556, he granted to the Roman College (the future Gregorian University) the power of conferring academic degrees in philosophy and theology even to students who were from outside the Society.

On the eve of his death, Ignatius did not forget to request the Holy Father's blessing. At daybreak of July 31, 1556, Polanco rushed to the Vatican for this purpose but on returning to Santa Maria della Strada, the secretary found that Ignatius had died. The papal blessing had not reached him in time; but here the matter of chief importance was that last meeting itself, though even at a distance, of those two men who, in spite of their divergences of criteria, had the same common ideals of service to the Church.

9. His Health

His health posed a problem to Ignatius from the time he was wounded at Pamplona. His right leg caused him not only a slight limp but also some pain and discomfort. Laínez informs us that right from Manresa he, who "had been before robust and of a strong constitution (*recio y de buena complexión*), underwent a complete change in his body."[50] Ribadeneira's comment runs in the same vein: "At first he was of great physical strength and robust health, but he wore himself out by his fasts and excessive penance, from which he came to suffer various ailments and very severe pains of the stomach, caused by his great abstinence during the first years."[51]

---

50 *FN*, I, 78.
51 *RibVita*, I, V, in FN, IV, 111; *FN*, I, 78.

The beginning of his bad health, therefore, has to be linked with the austerities he practiced from Manresa onward. Already in that city on the Cardoner he was gravely ill more than once. From that time his health was a continuous alternation of relapses and recoveries. At Barcelona he enjoyed fairly good health. Toward the end of his sojourn in Paris, the physicians found no better remedy than a return to his native climate. Ignatius spent three months at Azpeitia but there too he fell ill. Soon after his arrival at Bologna to continue his studies, he saw himself forced to change the climate and surroundings. Therefore he moved to Venice, where he spent the year 1536.

In Rome he had continual ups and downs. In 1550 he was very gravely ill, and this was one of the reasons why he presented his resignation of the generalship to his companions. In 1552, on the other hand, he fared pretty well. From that time, the spells of ill health alternated with periods of relative improvement, until July, 1556, when death came.

It is of special interest, to us to know what the illness from which he suffered truly was. He always spoke of pain in the stomach, but what he had in reality was discovered only after his death. On the very day of his death the autopsy was conducted by the renowned surgeon from Cremona, Realdo Colombo. This excellent physician was the successor, in the chair of anatomy at Padua, of the Belgian Doctor André Vésal (Vesalius), the physician of Charles V and Philip II, but he was then in Rome in the service of the papal household. He himself published the result of the autopsy which he carried out on Ignatius in his treatise on anatomy (*De re anatomica*), published three years later in Venice, in 1559. In it he wrote: "With my own hands I have extracted almost innumerable gallstones (*cálculos*) of various colours, found in the kidneys, the lungs, the liver, and the portal vein, as you, Giacomo Boni, could see with your eyes in the case of the venerable Egnacio, Founder of the Congregation of Jesus."[52] Harmonizing with this is the testimony of another witness who was present, the Belgian scholastic Theodoric Geeraerts, who wrote that the surgeon found three stones in the liver.[53]

52 *FN*, I, 769, fn. 16.
53 *FN*, I, 776.

Building upon these data, the Roman specialist Alessandro Canezza wrote in 1922: "After these expositions, it is easy to establish that the illness of Ignatius was biliary lithiasis with particular symptoms which caused repercussions in the stomach. The recurring painful attacks presented the singular character of irradiating to the stomach, thus giving the impression of an illness in this organ, as happens precisely in that form of biliary colic, termed precisely gastralgic because of this symptomatology."[54] Canezza adds that the data given by the autopsy prove that Ignatius must have been suffering excruciating pain which he bore with serenity and fortitude. Colombo found the stones in the portal vein, into which they had passed from the gall bladder, in a process which presents always an acutely painful syndrome, accompanied by serious functional disorders.

Faced with this information supplied by medical science, one thing stands out: the marvelous patience of that holy man who, for more than three decades could bear such grave physical infirmities with so much fortitude, without interrupting his normal activities because of them.

10. His Dress

In this brief exposition of what the daily life of Ignatius was, there ought to be some observations about two matters of his external deportment — his manner of dressing and his diet.

Ignatius dressed like the priests of his time. He did not want the members of the Society to have a distinctive habit. According to Araoz, his desire for the members of the Society was, not that the habit should sanctify them, but that they should sanctify it.[55]

His dress consisted of a black cassock of "romanesque" cloth, fastened by a cincture at the waist. The collar of the cassock was high, fastened with a hook. The collar of the shirt was not visible over the cassock. A band of several folds pro-

---

54 *FN*, I, 769. Canezza's diagnosis of "biliary lithiasis and hepatic cirrhosis" is confirmed by Gregorio Marañón, "Notas sobre la muerte de San Ignacio de Loyola," *AHSJ*, XXV (1956), 153.
55 *FN*, III, 790.

tected his weak stomach. In winter he wore an overcoat inside the house. In the house, too, he wore slippers to protect his delicate feet. When he went out, he put on shoes and wore the long cloak or cape. His headgear was the broad brimmed hat of clerics and students, fastened with a ribbon to the neck as a precaution against the wind. As a walking stick he used a cane.

Lancicius, who has preserved these details for us,[56] adds that when Ignatius walked through the streets, he observed a great modesty, without looking this way or that. This is what he recommended in his Rules of Modesty.

11. *His Rosary*

Ignatius used a rosary, formed by a series of beads strung on a cord. It had no medal. He did not wear the rosary on his cincture, but kept it in his room and slept with it on. We can suppose that he made use of this rosary (*corona*) to say the Hail Marys which he substituted for the recitation of the Divine Office from which Paul III dispensed him in 1539 because of his poor health.

12. *His Food*

Usually Ignatius ate his meals in a room next to his sleeping room. He invited fathers with whom he had to transact business to eat with him. He also invited those who had recently arrived in Rome, and those about to depart for various destinations. Sometimes, too, he invited those who were not members of the Society, employing the expression which we read also in Cervantes: "Do stay with us, your honour, if you wish to do some penance."[57] In this case we may suppose that it was not a mere formality.

On the dietetic regime determined for Ignatius by the physicians, two medical prescriptions have come down to us. They belong to two different periods of his life. The second prescription, written about the year 1554, bears the direction:

56 *FN*, III, 718-721.
57 *Memoriale*, no. 185, in *FN*, I, 640.

"Diet for our Father Master Ignatius" (*Regimiento para nuestro Padre Maestro Ignacio*). In it the following dietary menu is prescribed for Ignatius: "The foods which Your Paternity may take are those whose nourishment is dry and lean. Such are young chickens or hens, cockerel, pullet, chicken, partridge, turtle, young pigeons, veal in summer, capon in winter, roasted kid. On days of abstinence it is healthy to take the yoke of fresh eggs, *amigdón*, peeled barley with almond milk. Among the vegetables, borage is safe in all seasons, after it has been boiled and the water removed, and then cooked with almond milk or a soup from meat; also boiled lettuce; and cooked fennel. Fruits suitable at all times are dry figs, raisins, almonds; the others may be taken or not according to the person's disposition. Roasted apples are good; so is nougat candy (*turrón*), especially that made of almonds and small hazel nuts."[58]

---

58 *FD*, 666-667; 686-688; see also *Memoriale*, nos. 186-188, in *FN*, I, 640-641.

Chapter 20

"THE SAINT HAS DIED"

When the rumor about the death of Ignatius began to spread through Rome in the early hours of July 31, 1556, the voice of the people was unanimous: "The Saint has died."[1] The verdict of the people in such opinions is seldom wrong. A man who had full knowledge of the case expressed the same judgment, Diego Laínez, who was seriously ill in a room near that of Ignatius. When some Fathers visited him that morning they tried to conceal the news, to spare him from the grief. But he intuitively grasped the situation and asked: "Is the saint dead, is he dead?"[2] When in the end they told him the fact, he lifted his eyes and hands to heaven and begged the Lord to let him accompany his Father, to enjoy the bliss of heaven with him. But this was not to be. In a short while Laínez recovered and was elected vicar general of the Society.

1. His Last Illness

Ignatius was not afraid of death; further still, he desired it, "that he might see and glorify his Creator and Lord," as Polanco states.[3] Already in 1550, Ignatius passed through a very grave crisis during an illness which both he and others thought could be his last. In that danger, he says in the *Autobiography*, "while thinking about death, he found so much joy and so much spiritual consolation about his having to die that in his whole being he melted into tears; and this became so continuous with him that he often turned his thoughts from death to avoid having so much of this consolation."[4]

---

1 *FN*, III, 584, no. 11.
2 *RibVita*, IV, xvii, in *FN*, IV, 719.
3 In his letter about the death of Ignatius, written on Aug. 6, 1556: *FN*, I, 764. This letter is the principal source for this present chapter. See C. de Dalmases, "La muerte de san Ignacio," *Razón y Fe*, 154 (1956), 9-28; also H. Rahner, "Der Tod des Ignatius," *Stimmen der Zeit*, 158 (1955-1956), 241-253.
4 *Autobiog*, no. 33.

That time he recovered. But during the first months of 1556 he found himself again very ill. On February 8, he noted down that for the past month he had not been celebrating Mass and had to be content with receiving Communion every eight days. Early in June, he seemed to be improving, but already on the eleventh of that month he had a relapse. This continuous succession of ups and downs caused Diego de Eguía to say that "it was through a miracle that he was living," since for a long time "he had a liver so diseased that I do not know how he could be living naturally, unless God our Lord, because of his being necessary for the Society, preserved his life by supplying for the deficiency of the bodily organs."[5]

This miracle could not be prolonged for long. At the end of June, his health deteriorated so much that it was thought that a change of airs and a more tranquil environment would benefit him. Therefore, after a physician had been consulted, he was transferred, on July 2, to the vineyard of the Roman College. Ignatius delegated the government of the Society to Cristóbal de Madrid and Juan de Polanco. At first this remedy seemed to be effective, but the hopes soon faded. Therefore, about July 27, Ignatius was carried back to the house in Rome. A witness of the events says that "his illness was of four days' duration, and did not seem to be dangerous."

This latter statement accounts for what happened during those last days. His spells of illness were so frequent that it was thought that this was just one like the others. No one, not even the physicians, were aware of what was in reality taking place. This impression was increased by the fact that in the house there were also others seriously ill — among them, as we have mentioned, Laínez.

The fact even is that the doctors were not visiting Ignatius. The only one to realize that the end was approaching was the sick man himself. On July 29, he summoned Polanco to tell him to request Father Baltasar Torres, who was a physician, to visit him too as he did the other patients. From that day both Father Torres and the physician Alessandro Petroni visited him.

5 *FN*, I, 769.

On Thursday, July 30, after four o'clock in the afternoon, Ignatius directed that Polanco should be summoned. After sending the infirmarian out of the room, he told Polanco it would be fitting for him to go to the Vatican to inform His Holiness that "he was near the end and almost without hope of temporal life, and that he humbly begged from His Holiness his blessing for himself and for Master Laínez, who also was in danger." Polanco replied to him that the physicians saw no particularly alarming symptoms in his illness and that he himself hoped that God would preserve him for some years more. He asked Ignatius: "Do you really feel as ill as that?" Ignatius' answer was: "I am so ill that nothing remains for me except to expire." Polanco then promised the Father that he would fulfill his desire, but he asked him if it would suffice to do it on the next day. The reason was that on Thursdays the mail went out for Spain, via Genoa, and he had still some letters to dispatch. Ignatius replied: "I would be pleased more today than tomorrow, or, the sooner the better. But do what you think best in the matter. I leave myself entirely in your hands."

For his own greater peace, Polanco consulted Doctor Petroni, and asked him whether he thought that the Father was in danger. Petroni answered: "Today I cannot say anything to you about his danger; I will tell you tomorrow." With this answer Polanco believed he could wait till the following morning, and continued his work on the correspondence.

Toward nine o'clock in the evening Ignatius ate a good supper, one ordinary for him. Polanco and Madrid were present. The three conversed for some time. We know what the last business was which occupied Ignatius' mind: the purchase of a house from Giulia Colonna for the Roman College. It was situated on the Piazza Morgana. Without any special anxiety, Polanco and Madrid retired for the night.

The infirmarian, Brother Tommaso Cannicari kept watch over the patient. Later he related what he observed during that last night.[6] For some time Ignatius moved in restlessness and

---

6 This Brother was replying to the questions, published in *FN*, III, 457-460 and 582-584, which were addressed to him by Nicolaus Lancicius and Luigi Maselli about the death of Ignatius.

occasionally he pronounced some words. About midnight he became calm and only repeated from time to time the exclamation: "Ah, my God!" (*Ay, Dios!*) The name of God was the last word he pronounced, that name which he bore so deeply engraved in his heart.

2. An Ordinary Death

At dawn, Polanco tells us, the fathers found Ignatius failing and near to death. They quickly sent Brother Cannicari to fetch Pedro Riera, who was Ignatius' confessor in the last years. But he could not be found. It is evident that what was hoped for from Riera — who, besides being the Saint's confessor, was also the prefect of the church — was the administration of the sacrament of the sick to the dying man. Polanco hurried to the Vatican. In spite of the early hour he was received by Pope Paul IV, who "showed great sorrow, gave his blessing and everything he could give, in an affectionate manner." But when Polanco reached the house, he learned that Ignatius had already peacefully died, "without any struggle."

Only two fathers were present at the time he expired, Madrid and Des Freux, rector of the German College. The time was "earlier than two hours of sunlight," as Polanco states. If we take into account that on July 31 the sun rises in Rome at three minutes after five o'clock, we may infer that Ignatius expired a little before seven in the morning, solar time, on that July 31, 1556, which was a Friday.

Judged by outer appearances, the death of Ignatius was an ordinary one. Polanco recognized this when he wrote: "He passed from this world in the common manner." No one was aware of his serious condition. Physicians attended other patients in the house more than him. He died without the last sacraments, but he had received communion two days before his death. The pope's blessing, which he so much desired, reached him too late. But these circumstances, disconcerting from the human viewpoint, detract nothing from the greatness of that closing act of the saint's life. If a man's worth is measured by the manner in which he dies, and if the virtues of a person are appreciated more after death, we cannot do less than admire all the sublimity of a death like this, even within its apparent ordinariness.

Polanco viewed all this under the aspect of the humility of Ignatius, "who, although he was sure that he was about to die...he did not wish to summon us in order to give us his blessing, or to name a successor, or even a vicar, or to close the Constitutions, or to give any other such manifestation, such as some servants of God often do in such circumstances. Rather, just as he thought so humbly of himself and did not desire the Society's confidence to be placed in any being other than God our Lord, he passed from this world in the common manner and perhaps he had in a fitting way obtained this favor from God, whose glory alone he desired, that there should not be any striking signs in his death."[7]

A death accompanied by such clear indications of genuine humility bore evident signs of the Spirit. Fruit of the Spirit also was the reaction of peace and serenity which spread to the minds of all his sons, which well deserve to be compared with the peaceful serenity experienced by the Apostles after the Lord's ascension. "In this house and in the colleges"— writes Polanco—"although we cannot escape missing keenly the loving presence of such a Father, of which we have been deprived, our sense of bereavement is without sorrow, the tears are those of devotion, and the longing for him is less because of an increase of grace and spiritual joy. In regard to him, it seems to us that it was now time for his continuous labors to come to true repose, his infirmities to genuine health, his tears and uninterrupted sufferings to perpetual bliss and happiness."[8]

3. *Preserving His Memory*

We now take up again the thread of our narrative. After the first moments of bewilderment had passed and they had recommended his soul to God, the sons of Ignatius took all the means to preserve, as far as was possible, the image of their father. About two in the afternoon, the renowned surgeon,

7 *FN*, I, 767-768.
8 *FN*, I, 764; *MonNad*, I, 345.

Realdo Colombo performed the autopsy, the result of which we already gave while treating of Ignatius' health.[9] The body was then embalmed. That very day efforts were made to obtain a portrait of him, since all attempts to get one during his lifetime had proved fruitless. The artist chosen was the Florentine painter Jacopino del Conte, a pupil of Andrea del Sarto. Jacopino had been a penitent of Ignatius, and the portrait which he made is preserved today in the consultation room of the father general of the Society of Jesus and has been reproduced many times. It faithfully reflects the characteristic features of Ignatius' physiognomy. The historian Daniello Bartoli says that, although the portrait was drawn from the countenance of Ignatius after death, it was retouched by the artist, according to the image which he had in his mind because he had visited him so often. Bartoli adds that this was considered as the best portrait of Ignatius. But this opinion is not shared by all, as some prefer the portrait made in Madrid by Alonso Sánchez Coello, and others the one that was kept by the Jesuits residing in Flanders.[10]

Means were taken to have an expert make a death mask (*mascarilla*) of plaster, from which others were later produced in wax and gypsum. One of these made in wax was kept in Madrid by Ribadeneira. Another made by brother Domingo Beltrán in clay removed the traces of death and served as the model for the portrait made by Alonso Sánchez Coello, who also followed the oral directions given him during the process by the same Ribadeneira.[11]

The holy body was kept until the following day, Saturday, August 1. After Vespers, about five o'clock in the evening, the obsequies were celebrated with a great concourse of the faithful. Some kissed his hands, others his feet, and they touched his body with their rosaries. Labor was necessary to ward off those who tried to take away some relic. Benedetto Palmio pronounced the funeral oration, a memorial "both

9 See pp. 287-289 above.
10 About the portraits of Ignatius, see *FN*, III, 236-239; 440-457.
11 *FN*, III, 243-244, no. [4]. This original, preserved in the Jesuit professed house in Madrid, went up in flames together with priceless manuscripts, during the civil disturbances in 1931 (*FN*, III, 238).

modest and full of piety." The body, dressed in priestly vestments and enclosed in a wooden coffin, was interred in a grave dug in the ground at the Gospel side of the main altar in the church of Santa Maria della Strada. This was a provisional tomb "until another is seen to be more appropriate."[12] As a matter of fact, the remains were transferred several times while the modern church of the Gesù was being constructed, where they are venerated today in the splendid altar dedicated to St. Ignatius.

Over the grave a tombstone was placed, with a Latin epitaph which is worthy of notice, above all because it contains the precise statement that Ignatius died at the age of 65 years. This is equivalent to saying that he was born in the year 1491.[13] This was not a date placed there lightly, but after mature deliberation on the part of the fathers. As is well known, there was from the beginning a discrepancy of opinions about the year of Iñigo's birth; and writers as close to the facts as Polanco and Ribadeneira changed their opinion more than once. Today expert critics consider as the most probable opinion that expressed by the fathers who composed the inscription on the tomb of the saint.

4. *Mission Accomplished*

"He died when he had accomplished his mission."[14] Nadal wrote this succinct statement, and the facts confirm it. Ignatius used to say that there were three things he wished to see accomplished before he died: the first, the approval and confirmation of the Society; the second, the approbation likewise of the *Exercises;* and the third, the completion of the *Constitutions.*[15] When these three wishes of his had been fulfilled, the Fathers nearer to him began to fear that the end was near at hand.

Enlarging on these points, Polanco in his *Chronicon* enumerates the following seven graces which were bestowed on Ignatius before he died.[16]

12 *FN*, I, 770.
13 The text of the epitaph is in *FN*, I, 776.
14 *FN*, II, 8.
15 *FN*, I, 354-355, in Nadal's prologue to the *Autobiography*.
16 Polanco, *Chronicon*, VI, 39-41.

The first was that he saw the Society not only approved but also confirmed by several supreme pontiffs.

The second consisted of the ample privileges, graces, and faculties granted to the Society by the same pontiffs.

The third was the writing of the *Constitutions* and Rules of the Society, and his seeing that they were being spread and put into practice, although he left to the general congregation the authority to give them the definitive approval.

The fourth was his leaving behind so many followers of his vocation and Institute. According to the calculations which have been made, the number of Jesuits at the time of the death of Ignatius oscillated around the figure of one thousand. The Spaniards, including those outside Spain, would be not less than 300. The question at issue is not whether the members were many or few. It is known that the founder did not preoccupy himself as much with the numbers as with the quality of his followers. It is good to recall his saying which confirms this attitude: that if there something which could make him desire to live longer, it was to be more rigorous in admitting recruits to the Society.[17] We have data to confirm this principle, at least regarding those admitted to the definitive incorporation into the Society. The calculations give no more than about 38 professed of four vows, 11 of three vows, 5 spiritual coadjutors and 13 temporal coadjutors.[18]

The fifth was the fruit harvested by the Society in its apostolic ministries, not only among Catholics but also among those separated from this faith.

The sixth was the prestige which the new order enjoyed, not only with the supreme pontiffs and high ecclesiastical authorities, but also in the eyes of secular princes and various peoples and nations, after more than a few persecutions and much opposition had been overcome.

17 *FN*, II, 475, no. 23.
18 List in *FN*, I, 63*-68*.

The seventh was to see the Society established in various regions. The Society numbered more than a hundred houses or colleges, distributed in eleven provinces.[19]

19 Polanco states in his letter (*FN*, I, 771) that the provinces of the Society numbered 12, and that they would be 13 if that of Ethiopia were included. These numbers, however, must be reduced respectively to 11 and 12, as will become clear from the list which we shall give a few pages below, and as Polanco himself recognized in *Chronicon*, VI, 41.

Chapter 21

THE STATE OF THE SOCIETY AT THE DEATH OF SAINT IGNATIUS

We have just spoken about the number of Jesuits at the time of the founder's death.

1. Houses and Colleges in 1556

Here we append a list of houses and colleges of the Society founded up to 1556. Where no other specification is given there is question of a college. Numbers within parentheses indicate the year of foundation. Several of these colleges were modest institutions. Some had only an ephemeral existence.[1]

ITALY

Rome, professed house (1540)
Padua (1542)
Bologna (1546)
Messina (1548),
      novitiate (1550)
Palermo (1549)
      novitiate (1551)
Tivoli (1550)
Venice (1551)
Roman College (1551)
Ferrara (1551)
Florence (1552)
German College, in Rome
      (1552)

Naples (1552)
Perugia (1552)
Modena (1552)
Monreale (1553)

Argenta (1554)

Genoa (1554)
Loreto (1555)
Siracusa (1555)
Bivona (1556)
Catania (1556)
Siena (1556).

SPAIN

Valencia (1544)

Córdoba (1553),
      novitiate (1555)
      moved to Granada(1556)

1 See Polanco, *Chronicon*, VI, 42-43.

Gandía (1545; raised to a
   university in 1547)
Barcelona (1545)
Valladolid (1545)
Alcalá de Henares (1546)
Salamanca (1548)
Burgos (1550)
Medina del Campo (1551)
Oñate (1551)

Avila (1554)
Cuenca (1554)
Plasencia (1554)
Granada (1554)
Sevilla (1554)
Simancas, novitiate (1554)
Murcia (1555)
Zaragoza (1555)
Monterrey (1556)

PORTUGAL

Lisbon, college (1542)
   professed house (1553)
Coimbra (1542), with a noviti-
   ate (1553), College of
   Arts (1555)
Evora (1551)

FRANCE

Paris (1540)
Billom (1556)

LOWER GERMANY

Louvain (1542)
Tournai, house (1554)
Cologne (1544)

UPPER GERMANY

Vienna (1551), with a
   novitiate (1554) later
   separated from the
   college.
Prague (1556)
Ingolstadt (1556)

INDIA

Goa, college for Jesuits (1543)
   another for Indian boys(1543)
   a novitiate (1552)

Basein (1548)
Cochin (1549)
Quilon (1549)

BRAZIL

São Vicente (1553) ˙
Piratininga, now São Paulo
   (1554)
Salvador de Bahía (1555)

JAPAN

Bungo (Oita), a house
Yamaguchi, a house
   (till May, 1556)

In other parts of the Orient Jesuits labored without having

302

a fixed residence: Malacca, Ormuz, the Moluccan Islands (Ternate, Amboina, Moro Island).

2. Jesuit Provinces in 1556

These houses and colleges were grouped into eleven provinces of the order, and these would be twelve if they could include that of Ethiopia, where the Society did not succeed in establishing itself during the lifetime of Ignatius.

Here we give these provinces in the order of their foundation, indicating the year and the name of the first provincial.

1. Portugal, October 26, 1546. Provincial: Simão Rodrigues
2. Spain, September 1, 1547. Provincial: Antonio de Araoz.
3. India, October 10, 1549. Provincial, Francis Xavier.
4. Italy (Rome not included), December 5, 1551. Provincial: Paschase Broët.
5. Sicily, March 1553. Provincial: Jerónimo Domènech.
6. Brazil, July 9, 1553. Provincial: Manuel de Nóbrega.

On January 7, 1554, the Province of Spain was divided into three:

7. Aragón. Provincial: Francisco Estrada.
8. Bética: Provincial: Miguel de Torres.
9. Castile. Provincial: Antonio de Araoz.
10. France, 1555. Provincial: Paschase Broët.
11. Lower Germany, 1556. Provincial: Bernhard Olivier.
12. Upper Germany, June 7, 1556. Provincial: Peter Canisius.

3. Vision of the Future

We may well imagine that on the night before he died, Ignatius, seeing that his end was imminent cast a glance over the past and present of the Society, with also a projection into its future. That memorable promise which Jesus had made to him in the vision of La Storta, "I shall be propitious to you," or "I shall be with you," had until then been abundantly fulfilled, sometimes in the midst of great difficulties.

In regard to the future of the Society, he had sometimes said that "those who were to come would be better and good for something greater; for ourselves, we have just done what we could."[2] We must believe that his foresight was based not so much on human calculations as on his faith in Providence. In a letter to Francis Borgia on one of the most vexing affairs he had to handle, the financing·of the Roman College, he told him: "For the treasure of hopes which we have, everything is little; God who inspires these hopes, will not let them come to naught."[3] We dare to think that St. Ignatius from heaven will see with approving eyes that this brief biography of him comes to its close with this message of hope.

2 *FN*, II, 111; 493, no. 79.
3 *EppIgn*, IX, 66.

A SELECT BIBLIOGRAPHY

Focusing Especially on Works in English

1. BIBLIOGRAPHICAL WORKS

Gilmont, Jean-François, S.J. and Daman, Paul, S.J. *Bibliographie Ignatienne (1948-1957)*. Museum Lessianum, section historique, no. 17. Paris and Louvain: Desclée de Brouwer, 1958.

Iparraguirre, Ignacio, S.J. *Orientaciones bibliográficas sobre san Ignacio de Loyola*. Subsidia ad historiam Societatis Iesu, no. 1. 2nd ed., rev. Rome: Institutum Historicum S.I., 1965.

Ruiz Jurado, Manuel, S J. *Orientaciones bibliográficas sobre san Ignacio de Loyola, Vol. II (1965-1976)*. Subsidia ad historiam Societatis Iesu, no. 8. Rome: Institutum Historicum S.I., 1977.

Polgár, László, S.J. *Bibliographie sur l'histoire de la Compagnie de Jesus, 1901-1980. I. Toute la Compagnie*. Rome: Institutum Historicum S.I., 1981.

   This work contains extensive entries of publications on St. Ignatius, his life, his works, his spirituality, and the like, which have appeared from 1901 to 1980.

2. THE SOURCES. (The abbreviations are those of the Institute of Jesuit Sources)

MHSJ—MONUMENTA HISTORICA SOCIETATIS JESU: the Historical Sources or Records of the Society of Jesus in critically edited texts.

   This scholarly series which now contains 124 volumes, was begun in Madrid in 1894. The project was transferred to Rome in 1929. Most of the manuscripts on which these volumes are based are in the Archives of the Society of Jesus in Rome. The series is being continued by its publisher, the *Institutum Historicum Societatis Iesu*, Via dei Penitenzieri 20, 00193 Rome.

MI—MONUMENTA IGNATIANA: a section of MHSJ which contains the writings of St. Ignatius and of his contemporaries about him.

Series I

EppIgn — S. Ignatii...Epistolae et Instructiones. [Edd. M Lecina, V. Agustí, F. Cervós, D. Restrepo.] 12 vols., Madrid, 1903-1911. The letters and instructions of St. Ignatius.

Series II

*SpEx*MHSJ — *Exercitia Spiritualia S. Ignatii...et eorum Directoria.*
[Ed. A. Codina.] 1 vol. Madrid, 1919. The critical text of the
Spiritual Exercises and of the *Directories* for conducting them.

New Series II. A revision

*SpEx*MHSJ*Te* — Vol I. *Sti. Ignatii de Loyola Exercitia Spiritualia.
Textuum antiquissimorum nova editio. Lexicon textus hispani.* Edd.
J. Calveras et C. de Dalmases. Rome. 1969. A revision of *SpEx*-
MHSJ.

DirSpEx — Vol. II. *Directoria Exercitiorum Spiritualium* (1540-1599).
Ed. I. Iparraguirre. 1 vol. Rome, 1955. This is a more complete
edition of the *Directories* than the earlier one of 1919 in *SpEx*MHSJ.

Series III

*Cons*MHSJ — *Constitutiones et Regulae Societatis Iesu.* 4 vols. The
critically edited texts of the *Constitutions* and *Rules* of the Society
of Jesus, along with copious introductions and notes.

*Cons*MHSJ, I — Vol.I. *Monumenta Constitutionum praevia.* [Ed.
A. Codina.] Rome, 1934. Sources and records previous to the
texts of the *Constitutions*. Historical introductions.

*Cons*MHSJ, II — Vol. II. *Textus hispanus.* [Ed. A. Codina.] Rome,
1936. Critical texts of the four chief and successive texts of the
Spanish original.

*Cons*MHSJ, III — Vol. III. *Textus latinus.* [Ed A. Codina.] Rome,
1938. The critical text of the Latin translation which was approved by the First General Congregation of the Society in 1558.

*Cons*MHSJ, IV — Vol. IV. *Regulae Societatis Jesu.* Ed. D. F. Zapico.
Rome, 1948. Ancient drafts of rules or directives.

Series IV

SdeSI — *Scripta de Sancto Ignatio.* [Edd. L. M. Ortiz, V. Agustí,
M. Lecina, A. Macia, A. Codina, D. Fernández, D. Restrepo.]
2 vols. Madrid, 1904, 1918. Writings about St. Ignatius by his
contemporaries.

Series IV, revised

FN — *Fontes narrativi de S. Ignatio de Loyola et de Societatis Iesu initiis.*
Edd. D. Fernández Zapico, C. de Dalmases, P. Leturia. 4 vols.
Rome, 1943-1960.
Vol. I — 1523-1556
Vol. II — 1557-1574
Vol. III — 1574-1599
Vol. IV — Ribadeneira's *Vita Ignatii Loyolae* (1572)

Narrative sources, that is, writings about Ignatius by his contemporaries. An enlarged edition of the documents contained in *SdeSI*.

FD — *Fontes Documentales*. Ed. C. de Dalmases, S.J. 1977. On his family, country, youth, acquaintances.

3. ST. IGNATIUS' WORKS

Obras completas de San Ignacio de Loyola. Edición manual. Transcripción, introducciones y notas por Ignacio Iparraguirre, S.J. y Cándido de Dalmases, S.J. 4th ed., rev. Biblioteca de Autores Cristianos, no. 86. Madrid: La Editorial Católica, 1982.

This volume contains the Spanish texts of all the works of St. Ignatius, except his letters — of which, however, there is an ample selection pertaining to his spirituality.

Autobiography

St. Ignatius' Own Story as Told to Luis González de Cámara. Translated by William J. Young, S.J. Chicago, 1956; Loyola University Press reprint, 1968.

The Autobiography of St. Ignatius Loyola, wih Related Documents. Edited with Introduction and Notes by John C. Olin. Translated by Joseph F. O'Callaghan. Harper Torchbooks. New York: Harper and Row, 1974.

A Pilgrim's Testament: The Memoirs of St. Ignatius of Loyola, as faithfully transcribed by Luis Gonçalves da Câmara and newly translated into English by Parmananda R. Divarkar. Rome: Gregorian University Press, 1983.

The Constitutions

The Constitutions of the Society of Jesus. Translated, with an Introduction and a Commentary, by George E. Ganss, S.J. St. Louis: The Institute of Jesuit Sources, 1970.

Letters

Letters of St. Ignatius of Loyola. Selected and Translated by William J. Young, S.J. Chicago: Loyola University Press, 1958.

Saint Ignatius Loyola, Letters to Women, by Hugo Rahner. Translated by Kathleen Pond and S.A.H. Weetman. New York: Herder and Herder, 1960.

Spiritual Diary

The Spiritual Journal of St. Ignatius Loyola, February 2, 1544 to February 27, 1545. Translated by William J. Young, S.J. *Woodstock Letters*, 87 (1958), 195-267. Reprinted, Jersey City, 1971, and Rome: Centrum Ignatianum Spiritualitatis, 1980.

Commentaries on the Letters and Spiritual Diary of St. Ignatius Loyola, Plus the Autograph text of the Spiritual Diary, by Simon Decloux, S J. Rome: Centrum Ignatianum Spiritualitatis, 1980.

Spiritual Exercises. Important among many translations are:

> *The Spiritual Exercises of St. Ignatius of Loyola.* Translated from the Autograph by Elder Mullan, S.J. New York, 1914. Reprinted St. Louis, 1978.
>
> *The Spiritual Exercises of St. Ignatius.* A New Translation Based on Studies in the Language of the Autograph, by Louis J. Puhl, S.J. Westminster, Md., 1951. Reprinted Chicago: Loyola Univ. Press, 1968.

4. SELECT LIVES

Rose, Stewart. *St. Ignatius and the Early Jesuits.* New York and London, 1891.

Thompson, Francis. *St. Ignatius Loyola.* Ed. J. H. Pollen, S.J. London, 1909. Reprinted London: Burns and Oates, Universe Books, 1962. Both the above books are literary lives. A noteworthy feature is the pen sketches by H. W. Brewer, H. C. Brewer, and others, who sought to reproduce the places prominent in Ignatius' life as they appeared to his own eyes.

Brodrick, James, S.J. *Saint Ignatius of Loyola. The Pilgrim Years.* London, 1956.

Dudon, Paul S.J. *St. Ignatius of Loyola.* Translated by W.J. Young, S.J. Milwaukee, 1949.

Purcell, Mary. *The First Jesuit, Saint Ignatius Loyola.* Dublin and Westminster, Md., 1956, 2d ed., rev. Chicago: Loyola Univ. Press, 1981.

5. PARTICULAR ASPECTS

De Guibert, Joseph, S.J. *The Jesuits: Their Spiritual Doctrine and Practice. A Historical Study.* Translated by W. J. Young, S.J. Chicago, 1964. Reprinted St. Louis: Institute of Jesuit Sources, 1972.

> In this classic work, chapter 1, The Personal Interior Life of Ignatius, is a profound study of his conversion, spiritual growth, and mysticism.

Leturia, Pedro de, S.J. *Estudios ignacianos. I. Estudios biográficos. II. Estudios espirituales.* Ed. I. Iparraguirre, S.J. Bibliotheca Instituti Historici S.J., nos. 10, 11. Rome: Institutum Historicum S.J., 1957.

———— *El gentilhombre Iñigo López de Loyola en su patria y en su siglo.* 2 ed. Barcelona, 1949. English translation by A. J. Owen, S.J. Syracuse, 1949. Reprinted Chicago: Loyola Univ. Press, 1965.

Matt, Leonard von and Rahner, Hugo, S.J. *St. Ignatius of Loyola. A Pictorial Biography.* London and New York, 1956.

Rahner, Karl, S.J. *Ignatius of Loyola.* With a Historical Introduction by Paul Imhof, S.J. Colour Photographs by H. N. Loose. Translated by Rosaleend Ockenden. London and Cleveland: Collins, 1979.

Rahner, Hugo, S.J. *The Spirituality of St. Ignatius Loyola. An Account of Its Historical Development.* Trans. F. J. Smith, S.J. Westminster, Md., 1953. Reprint, Chicago: Loyola Univ. Press, 1968.

———— *Ignatius the Theologian.* Trans. M. Barry. London and New York, 1968.

———— *Ignatius the Man and the Priest.* Rome: Centrum Ignatianum Spiritualitatis, 1977.

Ravier, André, S.J. *Les Chroniques: Saint Ignace de Loyola.* Paris: Nouvelle Librairie de France, 1973.

———— *Ignace fonde la Compagnie.* Paris: Bellarmin-Desclée de Brouwer, 1974.

Books and articles about particular aspects of St. Ignatius are very numerous. Consult the bibliographical works listed above by Iparraguirre, Ruiz Jurado, and Polgár — under headings such as God, the glory and service of; Discernment; Christ; the Holy Spirit; the Trinity; Mary; Prayer; Mysticism; Spirituality; Apostolate; and the like.

The numbers refer to pages

¹ This index was compiled by the translator, Jerome Aixalá.

316

on care of orphans, 185
Ignatius and Luther, 190
and Rodrigues, 209, 210
and Paris University, 216
on Jerusalem pilgrimage, 217
Poland, Bobadilla's mission, 202
Ponce de Morentain, governor of Navarre, 5
Poor, the, and Ignatius, of a well-to-do
family, 20-22
his clothing, 52-53, 55-56, 97, 101
lodging, 56, 95, 99, 129, 148
food, 57, 59, 111
his detachment from money, 72-73
begging, 73, 75, 109
almsgiving, 53, 82, 109
sharing the lot of, 77
his travel, 81, 82, 107, 138-139
ill treated, 83, 95, 104, 111
organizes relief for them, at Azpeitia,
132-133; in Rome, 158, 164, 179-185
Pope
seen as Christ's vicar, 121, 190-191
his permission for the pilgrimage, 55, 71,
76
cortege of Adrian VI, 48, 54
and the Society, vow of Montmartre, 120-
121, 168
fourth vow, 121, 171, 176, 217
"the foundation of the whole Society,"
121
his figure in the plan of the group, 121
their offer of themselves to, 162-163
seek his approval of the Society, 168
in the formula of profession, 176
approbation of the Formula of the Institute, 169, 232
of the Society, 169-170, 172, 298
of book of the *Exercises*, 124-125
four popes and Ignatius, 283-287
graces granted by the, 299
dying Ignatius seeks blessing, 287, 294-
295
Portugal, occupies Toro, besieges Burgos, 9
most promising beginnings of Society, 208
great support of King John III, 208
first Jesuit province, 208
missionary fervor and excesses, 209
and Ethiopian mission, 227
alliance of Ethiopia with, 227

springboard to the missions, 229-230
patriarch and bishops elected, 229-231
See also John III
Portuondo, Rodrigo, fellow page at Arévalo,
35
recognizes Iñigo in Genoa and helps him,
83-84
Possessions, renounced, 234; *see also*
Poverty
Potentiana de Loyola, Iñigo's niece, her
testimony, 127, 129
Poverty, of Ignatius, at Montserrat, 53;
Manresa, 55-56
penniless pilgrim, 72-73, 77, 81
at Alcalá, no money for new gowns, 101
begging in Paris, 109
lodging in Azpeitia hospice, 129
works of beneficence, 132-133
in Vivarolo retreat, 147
in *SpEx* and *Cons*, Christ's example, 68-69,
234-235
"give to the poor", 169, 234-235
bulwark of religion, 245
offers Masses for the type of, 271
practice, to live in strict poverty, 120
of the founding members, 235
no fixed stipends, apostolic purpose, 245,
246
its preservation, 245
difference of residences and colleges, 271
Prague college, 193, 197
Prat, Guillaume de, benefactor, 214-215,
216
Prayer, of Ignatius, vigils at Aránzazu, 49;
and Montserrat, 52-53
learns it from Jean Chanon, 53
daily at Manresa, 56, 58-59; in
Barcelona, 72-73
teaches it at Alcalá, 98; in the Holy
Land, 78-80; in a Salamanca chapel,
103; on road to Rouen, 111
in shipwreck, 138
and companions, at Montmartre, 120-121
on way from Paris to Venice, 143
before receiving Holy Orders, 146
in Vivarolo, 147; on way to Bassano, 148;
to La Storta, 152
for deliberations of 1539, 165, 166, 168
for papal approbation, 171